The Special Education Handbook

D0144044

'What a terrific resource: comprehensive and current, this handbook is a vital acquisition for all involved in special education programs. Dr Farrell writes clearly and with a practical flair... highly recommended.'

Michael Arthur-Kelly PhD, Associate Professor and Director,
Special Education Centre, University of Newcastle, Australia.

This acclaimed, best selling and comprehensive guide, now in a fully updated fourth edition, is an essential reference book for anyone involved with special education.

All entries have been reviewed to reflect current practice and the book is enriched with extra resources, including references to useful Internet sites. Focusing on current educational frameworks in the United Kingdom and the United States of America, the author has gathered into one A–Z volume a wide range of information essential to good practice in mainstream and special schools. A thematic index helps the reader plot a course through topics of interest. The broad themes and areas covered are:

- Basic terms, ideas and values
- Venues relating to special education, and school organisation
- Roles and responsibilities
- Individual differences among learners with disabilities and disorders
- Curriculum and assessment, resources and technology
- Pedagogy and classroom organisation
- Therapy and care.

Presented in a handy quick reference format *The Special Education Handbook* also provides a coherent account of the complexities of special education, combining a wealth of practical guidance with the latest research findings.

This clear and concise handbook is indispensable for all those involved in special education, including teachers, teaching assistants, parents, administrators and others.

Michael Farrell is a private consultant in special education working with parents and children, schools, local authorities, voluntary organisations, universities and government ministries.

The Special Education Handbook

An A–Z guide

HARVARD UNIVERSITY
GRADUATE SCHOOL OF EDUCATION
MONROE C. GUTMAN LIBRARY

Fourth edition

Michael Farrell

With a foreword by Lord Rix

Routledge
Taylor & Francis Group

LONDON AND NEW YORK

Ref
LC
3986
.G7
F37
2009

#X127737

HARVARD UNIVERSITY
GRADUATE SCHOOL OF EDUCATION
MONROE C. GUTMAN LIBRARY

First published 2009
by Routledge
2 Park Square, Milton Park, Abingdon, Oxon OX14 4RN

Simultaneously published in the USA and Canada
by Routledge
270 Madison Avenue, New York, NY 10016

Routledge is an imprint of the Taylor & Francis Group,
an informa business

© 2009 Michael Farrell

Typeset in Sabon and Gill Sans
by Swales & Willis Ltd, Exeter, Devon
Printed and bound in Great Britain by CPI Antony Rowe,
Chippenham, Wiltshire

All rights reserved. No part of this book may be reprinted or
reproduced or utilised in any form or by any electronic,
mechanical, or other means, now known or hereafter
invented, including photocopying and recording, or in any
information storage or retrieval system, without permission in
writing from the publishers.

British Library Cataloguing in Publication Data
A catalogue record for this book is available
from the British Library

Library of Congress Cataloging in Publication Data
Farrel, Michael, 1948–
The special education handbook : an A to Z guide / Michael Farrell.—4th ed.
p.cm
Includes index.
1. Special education—Great Britain—Handbooks, manuals, etc. I. Title.
LC3986.G7F37 2009
371.90941—dc22
2008054269

ISBN10: 0–415–49019–7 (hbk)
ISBN10: 0–415–49020–0 (pbk)

ISBN13: 978–0–415–49019–1 (hbk)
ISBN13: 978–0–415–49020–7 (pbk)

September 3, 2009

Contents

About the author

Michael Farrell was educated in the United Kingdom. After training as a teacher at Bishop Grosseteste College, Lincoln, and obtaining an honours degree from Nottingham University, he gained a Masters Degree in Education and Psychology from the Institute of Education, London University. Subsequently, he carried out research for a Master of Philosophy degree at the Institute of Psychiatry, Maudsley Hospital, London and for a Doctor of Philosophy degree under the auspices of the Medical Research Council Cognitive Development Unit and London University.

Professionally, Michael Farrell worked as a head teacher, a lecturer at London University and as a local authority inspector. He managed a national psychometric project for City University, London and directed a national project developing course structures and training materials for initial teacher training for the United Kingdom Government Department of Education.

His present work as a special education consultant includes policy development and training with local authorities, work with voluntary organisations and universities, support to schools in the private and maintained sectors, and advice to government ministries.

Among his books, which are translated into European and Asian languages, are:

Standards and Special Educational Needs (Continuum, 2001)
Understanding Special Educational Needs: A Guide for Student Teachers (Routledge, 2003)
Special Educational Needs: A Resource for Practitioners (Sage, 2004)

Inclusion at the Crossroads: Special Education—Concepts and Values (David Fulton, 2004)

Key Issues in Special Education: Raising Standards of Pupils' Attainment and Achievement (Routledge, 2005)

The Effective Teacher's Guide to Dyslexia and Other Specific Learning Difficulties (Routledge, 2005)

The Effective Teacher's Guide to Moderate, Severe and Profound Learning Difficulties (Routledge, 2005)

The Effective Teacher's Guide to Autism and Communication Difficulties (Routledge, 2005)

The Effective Teacher's Guide to Sensory Impairment and Physical Disability (Routledge, 2005)

The Effective Teacher's Guide to Behavioural, Emotional and Social Difficulties (Routledge, 2005)

Celebrating the Special School (David Fulton, 2006)

The Special School's Handbook: Key Issues for All (Routledge/nasen, 2007)

Educating Special Children: An Introduction to Provision for Pupils with Disabilities and Disorders (Routledge, 2008)

Foundations of Special Education: An Introduction (Wiley, 2009).

Foreword

I am delighted to have been asked to write a foreword to a book that will have such an impact on the support for children with a disability. *The Special Education Handbook* will provide teachers, parents, professionals and many others with a comprehensive guide to the various types of special educational needs and the resources available to help children overcome them. It will no doubt become widely read.

The book covers a broad variety of topics ranging from basic terms, ideas and values to pedagogy and therapy. The thematic index will also help the reader to work systematically through the book, while the A–Z format allows quick reference too. For the reader who wishes to probe further, the book also contains references, further reading suggestions and internet addresses (after most entries) which serve as an entree to more information.

In the United Kingdom, for example, there are 1,400,000 pupils with special educational needs. In fact, in my own field of learning disability there are 210,000 school-aged children alone. What is important is that these children are all welcomed into their educational setting and receive the high-quality education to which they are entitled.

I have been a long-time campaigner for schools to ensure that all children benefit from committed and well-trained staff. I think the material in this book will go a long way to plugging the gap between the information given by national Government and the expectations of pupils and their families about the knowledge that governors and teachers have on disability issues.

Dr Farrell deserves congratulations for the production of this excellent book which I know will be heavily thumbed by families and professionals alike.

Lord Rix
President of the Royal Mencap Society

Preface

I am delighted to be writing the preface to the fourth edition of *The Special Education Handbook*. The generous reviews that earlier editions received and the numerous kind letters and emails sent to me by professionals, parents, students and others indicate that the book is meeting a real need. A growing readership in other English-speaking parts of the world and the publication of the Japanese translation in 2001 are just two indicators of the keen interest the book has attracted abroad.

The first edition appeared in 1997, the second in 2000 and the third in 2003. This fourth edition has been extensively revised and updated to keep up with current developments, yet without becoming unwieldy. Entries that tied previous editions to one national context have been omitted or much reduced making the book span practice in the United States of America and in England and making it more international. The underlying structure of the book that so many readers reported they found helpful has been kept, and this is explained in the introduction and is reflected in the thematic index.

Suggestions

I have tried to cover areas and topics in this Handbook that potential readers would find most helpful. I would be pleased to hear from any readers with suggestions for amendments and additions so that future editions will continue to be as informative as possible.

Michael Farrell
dr.m.j.farrell@btopenworld.com
www.drmjfarrell.co.uk

Acknowledgements

First edition

I am most grateful to the following people who read parts of the book and made valuable comments and suggestions.

Alan Dyson, Department of Education, University of Newcastle upon Tyne; Maria Evans, Head of Audit, Monitoring and Learning Support Services, Surrey Local Education Authority; Dr Ann Hackney, Westminster College, Oxford; Geof Sewell, Special Educational Needs Coordinator, Bishopsgarth School, Cleveland; Martin Sharpe, Special Educational Needs Policy Division, Department for Education and Skills (DfES); and Christopher Stevens, Subject Professional Officer for Special Educational Needs, School Curriculum and Assessment Authority.

Helpful advice on coverage of topics was kindly given by Professor Peter Mittler, then Dean and Director of the School of Education, University of Manchester; and Joan Boucher, President of the National Association of Special Educational Needs 1996–97.

The following people generously read the A–Z text and made helpful comments: Professor Mel Ainscow, Professor of Special Education, and his colleagues at the School of Education, University of Manchester; Pat Locke, Head teacher, Christchurch Church of England Infant School, New Malden; Maria Landy, Education Consultant and Past President of the National Association for Special Educational Needs 1995–96; Clive Webster, Principal Education Psychologist; and John Dewhurst, Education Inspector, London Borough of Hillingdon.

Cedric Dowe, Robert Green and Martin Sharpe of the Special Educational Needs Policy Division, DfES kindly read the section on legislation and made many invaluable comments. Arabella Wood, Library and Information Resource Centre, DfES, was most helpful in providing information and documents. The various drafts and final version were word processed with great efficiency by Sue Foster to whom I am indebted. My daughter Anne gave valuable help in contacting organisations and in indexing.

Second edition

I am grateful to the following people for advice and information in connection with the second edition of the Handbook:

Heather Fry, Award Scheme Development and Accreditation Network; Caroline Geraghty, Marketing Coordinator, RSA Examining Board; Nicki Little, Midland Examining Group; C. J. Mitchell, Deputy Secretary General, The Associated Examining Board; Mel Pierce, City and Guilds of London Institute; and Brian Rogers, Welsh Joint Education Committee.

I also acknowledge the advice received from Mike Bubb, Architects and Building Branch, Department for Education and Skills.

Third edition

I am grateful to the representatives of many of the organisations mentioned in the text for their help in updating details relating to their particular organisations.

While I am most grateful to the above-named colleagues who have assisted with this and previous editions, their assistance does not imply that their views are the same as those given in the text. The view expressed in this Handbook are my own; as, of course, are any of the book's shortcomings.

Fourth edition

This edition is much more Anglo-American that its predecessors and I would like to warmly thank Dr Laurie Sperry, University of Colorado for advising me on a sample of entries with references to procedures in the United States of America. As always Alison Foyle and all the team at Routledge have been helpful and supportive.

Michael Farrell

Introduction

Readers of this Handbook

This Handbook is intended to be helpful for:

- Teachers and classroom aides in mainstream and special schools and elsewhere
- Students and newly qualified teachers
- Senior managers and school administrators
- Parents and carers
- Professionals in the social services and health services
- Voluntary workers
- Anyone wishing to gain an overview of special education.

The Handbook draws particularly on approaches to special education in England and in the United States of America. However, the book is intended for readers internationally.

The underlying structure of the Handbook

Special education embraces a wide and complex area of knowledge and skills. Underpinning the approach and choice of entries in this Handbook are several broad areas or themes. While the entries have an A–Z format there is an underlying structure that is reflected in the classified list/thematic index. Many readers of earlier editions of the book have said that a few minutes spent familiarising themselves with the classified index helps in negotiating the book effectively. There are seven broad areas – some of which are subdivided – as follows:

1   Basic terms, ideas and values

    a   Special education issues/terms
    b   Disciplines associated with special education

2 Venues relating to special education, and school organisation
3 Roles and responsibilities
4 Individual differences among learners with disabilities/disorders
5 Curriculum and assessment; resources and technology

    a Curriculum and assessment
    b Resources and technology

6 Pedagogy and classroom organisation
7 Therapy and care.

The rationale for the Handbook's underlying structure

The rationale for the structure underlying this Handbook is reflected in each broad heading.

1 *Basic terms, ideas and values* Becoming familiar with the basic terms, ideas and values of special education, their significance and their interrelationships, is essential to understanding special education itself. Also, special education involves concepts associated with various disciplines – psychology and sociology, for example – and it is important to be aware of such concepts in understanding special education.

2 *Venues relating to special education, and school organisation* The range and variety of venues relating to special education provision is indicated along with aspects of school organisation, an important part of overall provision for special children.

3 *Roles and responsibilities* The implicit or explicit agreements between those working in special education underlie these entries. The variety of people contributing to effective provision is reflected. Procedures are included to illustrate the approaches to special education. Many roles are described under entries on the discipline they represent. For example, if you look up 'Audiology' in the classified index you will see that you are guided to the entry, 'Audiology/audiologist'. Similarly, 'Behaviour therapist' is covered under, 'Behaviour therapy/behaviour therapist'.

4 *Individual differences among learners with disabilities/disorders* If children with disabilities/disorders are not to be seen as an amorphous mass, individual differences among them and the implications of these differences are important. However, to avoid making the Handbook too long, these entries cover the educational implications of broad topics such as 'reading disorder' and 'hearing impairment', rather than extensive lists of particular conditions and syndromes which can be found in many reference books, including medical dictionaries. Where particular conditions are included this is generally because of the frequency with which the condition occurs (e.g. epilepsy), or the particular attention a condition has attracted in recent years (e.g. Fragile X syndrome).

5   *Curriculum and assessment; resources and technology*   The curriculum offered to pupils with disabilities/disorders reflects the content and structure of that offered to all pupils as far as this is possible. Certain aspects of the curriculum play a particularly significant role for some special children and these are focused upon. Related to the curriculum are the kinds of assessment by which teachers and others try to determine attainment and progress. Entries on specific psychometric and other tests are not given, as the most recent information on such tests can be easily obtained from organisations marketing them. Resources include such topics as journals and other publications, as well as various items of equipment. Technology includes the use of computers in educating special children.

6   *Pedagogy and classroom organisation*   Central to education is the way in which its content is learned by the pupil and taught by the teacher. The way the classroom is organised can also help special children.

7   *Therapy and care*   In special education, approaches grouped broadly as therapies also make a major contribution.

The Handbook entries are in A–Z order. A classified list/thematic index of A–Z entries guides the reader through the Handbook reflecting the seven main areas as outlined above.

Uses of the Handbook

The Handbook can be used for flexible but systematic reading, using the classified list of entries. Any systematic reading would most profitably begin with the entries grouped under 'Basic terms, ideas and values'. However, the order in which you consult subsequent sections will be according to your own preferences and previous experience. Cross-referencing helps you to move across broad areas in the course of reading as desired. As well as using the Handbook for systematic reading, it can equally be used as a handy reference book. References, suggestions for further reading, and examples of relevant internet addresses are given, as appropriate, at the end of an entry.

A

Access

The notion of access in some usages relates to a social model of disability. In some versions of this model, a distinction is made between 'impairment' as a physical entity and 'disability' as the barriers placed on those with impairments by society through physical arrangements or negative attitudes. In this perspective, improving access is associated with seeking to remove barriers (See Shakespeare, 2006, for an outline of social approaches pp. 9–28 and criticisms of them, pp. 29–53).

The expression, 'enabling access' in relation to special education may refer to improving a pupil's participation in the curriculum and in learning. This might involve the school looking at the accessibility of each curriculum subject or area, reviewing teaching strategies and assessment procedures, refreshing working partnerships between parents and professionals and developing advocacy. The converse of enabling access may be seen as insufficiently challenging 'barriers' to learning and participation.

Access to areas of the school and to the community is assisted for children and young people with visual impairment by various means. These include training in mobility and orientation, the use of Braille or tactile maps of the school building perhaps placed in the foyer and tactile indicators of impending different floor levels or parts of the building. Sometimes the term access refers to physical access to a building and areas within the building for special children including those with physical and motor disabilities. Legislation and guidance has been put in place in many developed countries to improve such access. Those involved in designing and adapting schools and other premises are encouraged to make them as accessible as practicable to people with physical and motor impairments.

(See also, *Barriers, Bio-psycho-social model, Disability, Impairment*)

Reference

Shakespeare, T. (2006) *Disability Rights and Wrongs,* Oxford and New York, Routledge.

Further reading

Carpenter B., Ashdown, R. and Bovair, K. (Eds) (2001) *Enabling Access: Effective Teaching and Learning for Pupils with Learning Difficulties*, London, David Fulton Publishers.

Accreditation/examinations

Accreditation refers to the formal acknowledgement of achievements in the form of a qualification, which is widely, sometimes nationally and internationally, recognised. Passing examinations are one form of acquiring accreditation. Continuously assessed coursework may also be associated with a final qualification summarising the pupil's achievements. Qualifications and the courses of study leading to them may be characterised as predominantly academic, such as mathematics, or as predominantly vocational, such as hairdressing or tourism. Sometimes courses and qualifications embrace both areas.

Many pupils with a disability or disorder, of course, take the same accreditation as all pupils. Also, certain programmes are particularly relevant to some learners with disabilities/disorders. For example, in England, the Award Scheme Development and Accreditation Network (ASDAN) have developed a number of programmes. Their Transition Challenge (14–16 years) and Towards Independence (post-16 years) programmes provide an opportunity to develop and accredit personal, independence and learning skills. They are designed for learners with cognitive impairments. In determining whether the qualifications achieved by a special child have been challenging enough for them, reference needs to be made to the pupils' previous attainment.

(See also, *Progress*)

Address

Award Scheme Development and Accreditation Network (ASDAN)
www.asdan.co.uk
ASDAN offers a wide range of awards for young people of all abilities.

Adaptive behaviour

Adaptive behaviour refers to skills in social and personal competence. These include motor skills (fine and gross) and social interaction and communication. Personal living skills are important such as eating, dressing, using the toilet, and other aspects of personal care. Community living skills are included, for example, using money, demonstrating an understanding of time, and finding one's way around the local community using public transport.

It is recognised that there are limitations in using assessments of intelligence as the main criteria from which to determine decisions about suitable provision and other decisions about an individual with disabilities/disorders. At the same time there is a continuing interest in adaptive behaviour particularly in relation to individuals with cognitive impairments. One way of assessing adaptive behaviour is through norm referenced assessment scales. An example is the *Scales of Independent Behaviour* (Bruininks *et al.*, 1996), which assesses adaptive behaviour and 'maladaptive' behaviour (www.nfer-nelson.co.uk).

Reference

Bruininks, R. B., Woodcock, R. W., Weatherman, R. F. and Hill, B. K. (1996) *Scales of Independent Behaviour – Revised (SIB-R)*, Windsor, NFER-Nelson.

Further reading

Schalock, R. L. (Ed.) (1999) *Adaptive Behaviour and its Measurement Implications for the Field of Mental Retardation*, Washington, DC, American Association on Mental Retardation.

Address

The American Association on Intellectual and Developmental Disabilities
www.aaidd.org
An association for professionals who support people with intellectual and developmental disabilities.

Adaptive equipment

Adaptive equipment helps individuals with physical disabilities with normal positioning and movement. Examples are tricycles with trunk support and a low centre of gravity. A walking trainer supports the weight of a person and helps maintain the appropriate posture and balance to enable the person to be taught to take reciprocal steps. Trays attached to these walking trainers can enable communication using communication devices while allowing mobility. Equipment may combine a lifting action, allowing the position to be changed, and walking support allowing the individual's weight to be borne by the trunk and forearms. Standing support equipment including mobile versions allows those who cannot bear their full weight to be held upright through supporting straps. Padded 'supine boards' can be positioned at any angle from horizontal to vertical and give adjustable weight bearing and support for the head, trunk, pelvis, knees and feet.

Special chairs allow a functional sitting position suitable for using the toilet, eating and writing. Chair frames allow activities such as self-feeding, while other adjustable chairs with tables and trays allow a wide range of activities. Other specialised chairs include bath, shower and toileting chairs (giving head and trunk support while using the toilet).

Where individuals require specialist communication aids, advances in technology are providing new opportunities.

(See also, *Augmentative and alternative communication*, and *Computer technology*)

Further reading

Bigge, J. L., Best, S. J. and Heller, K. W. (2001) (4th edition) *Teaching Individuals with Physical, Health or Multiple Disabilities*, Upper Saddle River, NJ, Merrill-Prentice Hall.

Administration/administrator

Administration in special education involves the support required to ensure that processes such as identification, assessment and provision relating to children and young people with disabilities/disorders run smoothly and happen in a timely way. For example, in England the 'special needs officer' plays an important role. She is a caseworker, a named officer, who writes statements of special educational needs, and represents the local authority at meetings to review the statement. Caseworker duties may include liaising with a multidisciplinary panel that makes decisions about the statement of special educational needs and related issues. Named officer responsibilities involve providing information for parents. The statement writing role may involve the special needs officer writing the statements directly or arranging that this be done by a freelance person paid by the local authority. As a representative of the local authority at meetings, the special needs officer will work with psychologists, teachers, parents, and others (Farrell, 2003).

(See also, *Statement of special educational needs, Referral and evaluation*)

Reference

Farrell, M. (2003) 'The role of the special needs officer' *Special Educational Needs Briefing*, Kingston Upon Thames, UK, Croner.

Further reading

Farrell, M. (2003) *Understanding Special Educational Needs: A Guide for Student Teachers*, London and New York, Routledge, chapter 12.

Advocacy/advocate

Advocacy aims to secure rights and facilities for an individual with disabilities/disorders that are appropriate to the individual's perceived needs. A nominated person speaks and acts on behalf of the represented person who is unable to plead effectively for himself. Advocacy may be expressive (expressing the individual's concerns of preferences) or instrumental (helping ensure that appropriate services are provided). It may involve giving emotional as well as practical support.

The advocate may be a selected and trained lay volunteer who is independent of the prospective or existing service providers. Alternatively, the advocate may be a professional who has particular insight into the workings of local special education provision. Lawyers and other appropriately trained people provide legal advocacy, aiming to help clients exercise or defend their legal rights. This may require casework, careful checking of legislation and regulations, and representing the client in front of an administrative tribunal or a court. Self-advocacy involves special pupils making their own case, for example, through a school's council or other representative body. Related to this are efforts by teachers and others to encourage self-awareness and self-assessment in pupils. Examples include pupils making choices, expressing preferences, and reflecting on their own and peers' performance.

Organisations representing and supporting individuals with disabilities/disorders and their families may have advocacy as one of their aims and services.

(See also, *Pupil 'voice'*)

Further reading

Oliver, C. M. and Dalrymple, J. (2008) *Developing Advocacy for Children and Young People: Current Issues in Research, Policy and Practice*, London, Jessica Kingsley.

Weinfeld, R. and Davis, M. (2008) *Special Needs Advocacy Resource Book: What You Can do Now to Advocate for Your Exceptional Child's Education*, Waco, TX, Prufrock Press.

Address

The STARFISH Advocacy Association
www.starfishadvocacy.org
Aims to ensure the well-being of children with neurological disabilities.

Age

The earlier the age of intervention, such as Portage work or educational help, for children with severe disabilities/disorders, the better tends to be the child's progress. Early intervention does not guarantee later progress but it can give maximum opportunity for the child to make good progress. Also early intervention sometimes applies to older children and young people. For example, where a child has anxiety disorder or depressive disorder, early intervention implies timely intervention irrespective of the child's chronological age.

The physical and psychological changes associated with adolescence can pose difficulties for young people with disabilities/disorder as it can for all young people. For some young people with moderate to severe cognitive impairment/severe learning difficulties for example, frustrations can arise when independence is difficult to achieve. For those experiencing emotional and behavioural difficulties, the physical, sexual, emotional and social changes of adolescence can exacerbate their difficulties. For anyone with coordination difficulties, the growth spurt of adolescence and the temporary clumsiness that accompanies it can make coordination even more difficult.

Age also raises issues of age appropriateness, which is particularly relevant to the provision and resources made available to individuals with cognitive impairment. An individual's level of literacy or language development may be low compared with others of the same chronological age. However, this does not make it appropriate to use resources designed for young children with such older students. On the contrary, it is important to use materials suited to the chronological age of the learner, adapted to their attainment level. This relates also to suitable teaching and learning strategies.

(See also, *Portage*)

Further reading

Drew, C. J. and Hardman, M. L. (2006) (9th edition) *Intellectual Disabilities Across the Lifespan*, Upper Saddle River, NJ, Prentice Hall.

Aids to hearing

Aids to hearing may be considered in terms of conventional hearing aids, cochlear implants, radio aids, and induction loop systems.

A conventional hearing aid has three main components: a microphone to receive sound, an amplifier, and a receiver to transmit signals from the amplifier to the ear. It is usually self-contained and worn either on the body or behind the ear and is powered by a battery. Hearing impairment often affects certain frequencies more than others. However, hearing aids do not compensate for this, but simply amplify sounds from all frequencies. Hearing aids work best within two metres of the speaker.

A cochlear implant involves surgery to place an electronic device into the inner ear to increase sound perception. Some people become deaf as adults after having previously developed speech and language normally as children. These individuals appear to benefit from cochlear implants. The use of the technique with prelingually deaf children is more controversial. Some researchers have concluded that there is no evidence for children who have received implants of significantly improved speech or educational attainment (Cullington, 2002).

Radio aids comprise a microphone and transmitter worn by the speaker, and a radio receiver worn by the listener. The speaker's words are picked up by the microphone, converted into a radio signal and broadcast to the receiver, which is tuned to the appropriate frequency. A clear signal is picked up over a range of one hundred metres irrespective of any background noise. This system has assisted some children with severe hearing impairment being educated in ordinary schools rather than special schools.

An induction loop system may be used in schools to assist children with hearing impairment and teachers to communicate. The teacher wears a microphone that emits signals, which are amplified and pass through a wire loop that goes around the classroom. However, the system has limitations. It does not enhance communication between pupils. The system may be picked up in other rooms, and there may be silent spots in the classroom.

Reference

Cullington, H. E. (2002) *Cochlear Implants: Objective Measures*, London, Whurr.

Further reading

Tate-Maltby, M. (2002) (2nd edition) *Principles of Hearing Aid Technology*, London, Whurr.

Addresses

American Society for Deaf Children, USA
   www.deafchildren.org
   A national, independent non-profit organisation founded in 1967 as a parent help network, which also acts as an advocate to improve educational programs and services.

Breakthrough Trust (Deaf-Hearing Integration), UK
   www.breakthrough-dhi.org.uk
   Provides advice, aids and services for those with hearing loss, seeking to integrate deaf and hearing people.

Anger management training

A technique used with individuals with disruptive behaviour disorders; anger management training appears to be effective with mild conduct problems in pre-adolescents (see the review by Quinn *et al.*, 1999). Conduct disturbance may relate to deficits in information processing in that a child with conduct disturbance may be considered to have a distorted appraisal of social events. Such a view suggests that the child is likely to benefit from interventions that modify these distortions, leading to a better ability to regulate emotional responses.

One school-based strategy, 'Coping Power' (Lochman and Wells, 1996) involved 33 structured sessions delivered on school days to primary school children with conduct problems. The children reviewed examples of social interactions discussing social cues and motives. Problem solving tasks are used. Specific skills are practised that help manage the arousal of anger. Anger control strategies are also taught, such as self-talk in which the child learns a script to use when angry to help him put the situation into perspective and calm down.

References

Lochman, J. E. and Wells, K. C. (1996) 'A social-cognitive intervention with aggressive children: Prevention effects and contextual implementation issues' in Peters, R. E. and McMahon, R. J. (Eds) *Preventing Childhood Disorders, Substance Abuse and Delinquency*, Thousand Oaks, CA, Sage, 111–143.

Quinn, M. M., Kavale, K. A., Mathur, S. R., Rutherford, R. B. and Forness, S. R. (1999) 'A meta-analysis of social skill interventions for students with emotional and behavioural disorders', *Journal of Emotional and Behavioural Disorders* 7, 54–64.

Further reading

Larson, J. and Lochman, J. (2005) *Helping School Children Cope with Anger: A Cognitive-Behavioural Intervention*, New York, Guilford Press.

Anxiety disorders

Anxiety disorders include generalised anxiety disorder, obsessive-compulsive disorder, specific and social phobias, separation anxiety, and selective mutism (American Psychiatric Association, 2000). For one or more diagnosable anxiety disorders, prevalence is about 8 to 12 per cent of children and adolescents aged 4 to 20 years (Bernstein and Borchardt, 1991). About a third of children who experience anxiety disorder also experience major depression.

Generalised anxiety disorder involves excessive anxiety and worry on most days for at least six months concerning several events or activities (American Psychiatric Association, 2000, p. 472 and criteria A). The worry is difficult to control and includes additional symptoms such as problems with concentration, fatigue or restlessness. Provision includes cognitive-behavioural therapy (see separate entry). For children with relatively mild anxiety disorder 'focal psychodynamic therapy' has been effective (Muratori *et al.*, 2002). This involves 11 sessions, the first 5 with the whole family, 5 with the child only and a final session with the whole family again. In the family sessions, the therapist looks at the dynamic formulation of the child's conflicts rooted in family relationships. In the child only sessions, the therapist helps the child make connections between his feelings and unconscious conflicts about his relationship with his parents.

Obsessive-compulsive disorder involves recurrent obsessions and compulsions occupying more than an hour a day or that brings about significant impairment or distress (American Psychiatric Association, 2000, p. 456). Obsessions are persistent, ideas, thoughts, desires or images causing significant distress or worry. They might involve the individual needing to have items in a certain order, thoughts about being contaminated through touching others, or impulses to harm others. Compulsions are repetitive behaviours such as hand washing or mental acts – for example, counting to oneself – that are intended to reduce anxiety or distress. Turning to provision, the selective serotonin reuptake inhibitor fluvoxamine has been shown to be effective in reducing symptoms for children aged 8 to 17 years. Cognitive-behaviour therapy is also used. In this context, it involves exposing the individual to the situation or event that appears to be causing the disorder and helping him to prevent the obsessive-compulsive responses.

A specific phobia such as claustrophobia is a persistent and unreasonable fear of a situation, object or activity leading towards its avoidance. It can be distressing and can disrupt social relationships. Although adults may recognise that their fear is irrational, children may not. A social phobia is a marked, persistent unreasonable fear of social situations where the child may be embarrassed (American Psychiatric Association, 2000, p. 450). School refusal may relate to school phobia or to separation anxiety where the child fears being separated from home. Phobias may respond to behavioural interventions. Circumscribed phobia may respond to desensitisation. This involves presenting to the child images of what is feared or gradually desensitising them to the real situations. Modelling is used where the child sees another person whom he admires not showing fear of the situation in question while the child himself is exposed to the situation. Cognitive-behavioural therapy is used which includes gradual exposure techniques for circumscribed phobias such as school phobia.

Separation anxiety disorder is excessive anxiety concerning separation from home or separation from someone to whom the child is attached (American Psychiatric Association, 2000, p. 121). Approaches drawing on group cognitive-behavioural therapy are used for some children and adolescents (Toren et al., 2000).

Selective mutism involves a persistent failure to speak in a particular social situation where it is expected despite the individual speaking in other situations (American Psychiatric Association, 2000, pp. 125–127, paraphrased). It may respond to family-based behavioural treatment. For example, if the child is mute at school, he and a family member may have a planned conversation in the school classroom when others are in the playground. Gradually, people in whose presence the child does not normally speak join the child and family member. As the child is able to continue the conversation with the family member in the presence of other pupils, they or the teacher might join in the conversation. Eventually, the pupil is able to engage in conversations with peers and the child can request the family member to leave.

References

American Psychiatric Association (2000) *Diagnostic and Statistical Manual of Mental Disorders Fourth Edition Text Revision (DSM-IV-TR)*, Arlington, VA, APA.

Bernstein, G. A. and Borchardt, C. M. (1991) 'Anxiety disorders of childhood and adolescence: A critical review', *Journal of the American Academy of Child and Adolescent Psychiatry* 30, 519–532.

Muratori, F., Picchi, I., Castella, C. Tancredi, R., Milone, A., Patarnello, M. G. (2002) 'Efficacy of brief psychodynamic psychotherapy for children with emotional disorders', *Psychotherapy and Psychosomatics* 71, 11, 28–38.

Toren, P., Wolmer, I., Rosenthal, B., Eldar, S., Koren, S., Lask, M., Weizman, R. and Laor, N. (2000) 'Case series: Brief parent-child group therapy for childhood anxiety disorders using a manual based cognitive-behavioural technique', *Journal of the American Academy for Child and Adolescent Psychiatry* 39, 10, 1309–1312.

Further reading

Appleton, P. (Ed.) (2008) *Children's Anxiety: A Contextual Approach*, London and New York, Routledge.

Eisen, A. R. and Schaefer, C. E. (2007) *Separation Anxiety in Children and Adolescents: An Individualised Approach to Assessment and Treatment*, New York, Guilford Press.

Storch, E. A., Geffken, R. A. and Murphy, T. K. (Eds) (2007) *Handbook of Child and Adolescent Obsessive-Compulsive Disorder*, London, Routledge.

Address

Anxiety Disorders Association of America (ADAA)
www.adaa.org
Aims to inform the public, health care professionals and the media about anxiety disorders.

(See also, *Cognitive-behavioural therapy/Cognitive-behavioural therapist*)

Applied behaviour analysis

Applied behaviour analysis is a behavioural approach in which it is important to observe, carefully define and measure behaviour. The behaviour the educator seeks to change (the target behaviour) has to be precisely defined. This helps ensure consistency in the initial baseline observations and subsequent observations after interventions have been tried. Such consistency allows the teacher to determine whether the target behaviour is increasing or decreasing.

Unwanted target behaviour might be a pupil persistently moving around the class without permission and touching other pupils. Desired target behaviour might be the pupil sitting quietly in his own seat. An ABC record may be made of the antecedents (A) to the target behaviour, the behaviour itself (B) and its consequences (C) (Arthur-Kelly *et al.*, 2007, chapter 8).

The teacher or psychologist makes a baseline measure of the behaviour they or others want to change. This forms a basis on which to judge the effectiveness of interventions. The baseline might include measures of the frequency and duration of the behaviour (Alberto and Troutman, 2005). The educator then identifies reinforcers likely to be effective in modifying the behaviour. These may be positive (e.g. praise, a token, food, a favourite activity) or negative (e.g. detention). Reinforcement must be immediate, contingent on the pupil's behaviour, and motivating (Arthur-Kelly *et al.*, 2007, chapter 8). The teacher devises a schedule of reinforcement. This might involve reinforcing the behaviour every time it occurs initially then gradually reducing the frequency of reinforcements as the behaviour is modified. Built into the programme will be ways of eventually replacing the more artificial reinforcers with naturally occurring ones like praise. Through the pairing of these naturally occurring reinforcers and the artificial reinforcers, the behaviour is more likely to be sustained by the natural reinforcer once the artificial one is no longer used.

Strategies for increasing desirable behaviour include:

- Shaping (rewarding successive approximations of the desired behaviour)
- Token economies (where tokens are given as immediate reinforcement that can be later traded for rewards), and
- Contracts (written agreements about the desired behaviours usually agreed by the school, parents and the child).

Strategies to reduce unwanted behaviour include:

- Reinforcing behaviour that is incompatible with the unwanted behaviour (rewarding sitting down if the aim is to reduce out of seat behaviour)
- Extinction, for example ignoring the unwanted behaviour
- Response cost (e.g. losing points in a token economy system), and
- Time out (removing the opportunity of the reinforcement of unwanted behaviour)

(Arthur-Kelly *et al.*, 2007, chapter 8).

Relatedly, functional analysis and functional assessment involve establishing the goal for the student of any unwanted behaviour and seeking to enable him to reach the same goal without exhibiting the behaviour. If the student misbehaves to get attention from the teacher, then the teacher will look for ways of giving the student the attention that do not involve unwanted behaviour. It is often necessary to make a careful analysis of the context in which the behaviour occurs, as well as examining possible triggers for the unwanted behaviour. The educator makes adjustments to the context and management of the possible triggers to see if they are having a positive effect on behaviour. This method has been used with students with very challenging behaviour (Sigafoos, Arthur and O'Reilly, 2003). Applied behaviour analysis more broadly has been used with pupils with different disability/disorder including phobias, selective mutism, and conduct disorder.

References

Alberto, P. A. and Troutman, A. C. (2005) (7th edition) *Applied Behavioural Analysis for Teachers*, Columbus, OH, Merrill/Prentice Hall.

Arthur-Kelly, M., Lyons, G., Butterfield, N. and Gordon, C. (2007) (2nd edition) *Classroom Management: Creating Positive Learning Environments*, Melbourne, Australia, Thompson Learning.

Sigafoos, J., Arthur, M. and O'Reilly, M. (2003) *Challenging Behaviour and Developmental Disability*, London, Whurr.

Further reading

Cooper, J. O., Heron, T. E. and Heward, W. L. (2007) (2nd edition) *Applied Behaviour Analysis*, Upper Saddle River, NJ, Merrill.

Pierce, W. D. and Cheney, C. D. (2008) (4th edition) *Behaviour Analysis and Learning*, New York, Psychology Press.

Addresses

Association for Behavior Analysis International
www.abainternational.org
A professional association based in Portage, Michigan, aiming to enhance behaviour analysis through research, education and practice.

European Association for Behaviour Analysis
www.europeanaba.org
Aims to promote behaviour analysis and provide a forum for the study and discussion of matters relevant to behaviour analysis.

Art therapy/art therapist

While teachers, social workers, psychologists and others may sometimes request and encourage artwork from children, the work of an art therapist is qualitatively different from such approaches (Rubin, 2007). Art therapy is provided in a safe environment in a school, hospital, centre or other suitable venue. It may involve the use of a variety of materials such as paint or clay. Clients, who may be children or adults, use the materials to try to communicate feelings and thoughts in the supportive presence of the therapist. Clients may experience mental illness, cognitive impairment, communication difficulties, autism or other difficulties. The therapy involves the therapist encouraging the client (or clients in the case of group art therapy) to respond to what is being created. This may include suppressed feelings being brought out and acknowledged.

An art therapist is usually understood to be a qualified and registered member of the national association for art therapy in the country in which she practices. Approaches may require the art therapist to have knowledge of psychodynamic theory and practice enabling them to work with client's unconscious and conscious material associated with the artwork produced within the therapeutic relationship. An art therapist may be employed by the health services, schools, centres of adult education, social/welfare services, or the prison services.

Reference

Rubin, J. A. (2007) (2nd edition) *Art Therapy: An Introduction*, London and New York, Routledge.

Further reading

Case, C. and Dalley, T. (2007) *Art Therapy with Children: From Infancy to Adolescence*, London, Routledge.
Rubin, J. (2006) *Child Art Therapy*, Melbourne, Australia, Open Leaves Books.

Addresses

American Art Therapy Association
   www.arttherapy.org
   Provides standards of professional competence and develops and promotes knowledge of art therapy.

The British Association of Art Therapists
   www.baat.co.uk
   Provides information to members and to the public on all aspects of art therapy and oversees standards of training and professional practice.

Asperger's syndrome

There is debate about whether Asperger's syndrome is best regarded as a condition that is separate from autism or as part of a continuum of autistic spectrum disorder in which the individual has higher ability. Although the child with Asperger's syndrome acquires speech that is complex and grammatical, it is not used for communicating in the normal way. The child tends not to make usual eye contact. His speech tends to be used oddly and, beyond an age when it is unusual, topics of conversation are often fixed on the child's own interests rather than taking account of the listener. The tone of the child's speech may be monotonous.

Because features of the syndrome are less obvious than those of autism, Asperger's syndrome may not be identified as early. Educational implications include that teachers and others should make every effort to understand the syndrome and that work is challenging but takes requisite account of the often subtle difficulties the pupil experiences. Other approaches are adapted from those used for children with autism.

Further reading

Myles, B., Cook, K., Miller, N., Rinner, L. and Robbins, L. (2000) *Asperger's Syndrome and Sensory Issues: Practical Solutions for Making Sense of the World,* Shawnee Mission, KS, Autism Asperger's Publishing Company.

Addresses

The National Autistic Society, UK
   www.nass.org.uk
   Provides help, support and services to individuals with autism and their families.

US Autism and Asperger's Association (USAAA)
   www.usautism.org
   A non-profit organisation for autism and Asperger's syndrome education and support.

Attention deficit hyperactivity disorder

The *Diagnostic and Statistical Manual of Mental Disorders* (American Psychiatric Association, 2000, pp. 85–93) defines attention deficit hyperactivity disorder with regard to criteria for inattention, hyperactivity and impulsivity. Further criteria include that, 'some impairment from the symptoms is present in two or more settings' such as at school and home and that 'Some hyperactive-impulsive or inattentive symptoms were present before age 7 years' (p. 92). A child can meet the criteria through different combinations of inattention, hyperactivity and impulsiveness. This influences whether the difficulty is seen as predominantly inattention, or hyperactivity or impulsivity with hyperactivity. There is debate about the extent of attention deficit hyperactivity disorder, whether it is an identifiable condition and about the extent to which medication is used.

Prevalence of attention deficit hyperactivity disorder in the United States of America is estimated to be around 7 per cent of children aged 6 to 11 years old (Pastor and Reuben, 2002, p. 3). A variety of causal factors are associated with attention deficit hyperactivity disorder: genetic, physiological, psychological and environmental (Farrell, 2008, pp. 186–187).

The curriculum and related school organisation for pupils with attention deficit hyperactivity disorder may have to take account of long periods of missed schooling during which the child may have fallen behind. The focus may therefore be more than is typical on access subjects of literacy, numeracy, and information and communications technology. Personal and social education may have a bigger place in the timetable to allow such programmes as behaviour management training. Regarding pedagogy, structure, short coherent work sessions, clear teacher direction, and behaviourally informed schedules of reinforcement are used. Active, experiential learning which is concrete and relevant helps concentration.

Remedial teaching is used to help the child catch up on missed learning. Social skills may be explicitly taught including giving attention. Where medication such as the psychostimulant methylphenidate (Ritalin) is used, it appears optimally effective in combination with behaviour management techniques. School and classroom organisation play an important role. Clear structure with regular breaks and a classroom layout that avoids distractions but is not bleak are helpful. Training programmes for parents of children with attention deficit hyperactivity disorder have been developed.

References

American Psychiatric Association (2000) *Diagnostic and Statistical Manual of Mental Disorders Fourth Edition Text Revision (DSM-IV-TR)*, Arlington, VA, APA.

Farrell, M. (2008) 'Attention deficit hyperactivity disorder' in *Educating Special Children: An Introduction to Provision for Pupils with Disabilities and Disorders*, New York and London, Routledge.

Pastor, P. N. and Reuben, C. A. (2002) 'Attention deficit hyperactivity disorder and learning disability: United States, 1997–98', *National Center for Health Statistics. Vital Health Statistics* 10, 208.

Further reading

Weyandt, L. L. (2007) (2nd edition) *An ADHD Primer*, New York, Taylor and Francis.

Addresses

ADHD Association
   www.adhd.co.nz

A New Zealand-based organisation aiming to support members and all those involved with the care, upbringing, management and education of individuals with ADHD.

Children and Adults with Attention deficit hyperactivity disorder (CHADD)
www.chadd.org
A non-profit organisation in the USA for individuals with ADHD and their families, offering support to individuals, parents, professionals and others.

Audiology/audiologist

Audiology has been defined as the science of hearing, especially diagnostic testing, and 'the study of impaired hearing that cannot be improved by medication or surgical therapy' (Anderson, 2007, p. 180). An important aspect of audiology is audiometry, the measurement of hearing. This is achieved through the use of various instruments and procedures including the following. A pure tone audiometer produces sounds of a known pitch and loudness to establish hearing thresholds. It prints the information graphically as an audiogram. A speech audiometer measures hearing for speech. In impedance audiometry, the audiologist measures the amount of sound reflected by the eardrum when a sound wave stimulates it. This yields information about the effectiveness of the middle ear and possible conductive hearing loss. In brainstem electric response audiometry, or electric response audiometry, minute voltages produced in the nerves of the hearing system are measured as they respond to sound (Moser, 2008).

An audiologist is qualified in the study and evaluation of hearing and hearing impairment. Usually based in a hospital, the audiologist performs audiometric examinations. She gives information for diagnosing hearing impairment and prescribing and monitoring the use of hearing aids. An audiologist can help the teacher develop suitable classroom procedures for children with hearing loss.

References

Anderson, D. M. (Chief lexicographer) (2007) (31st edition) *Dorland's Illustrated Medical Dictionary*, Philadelphia, PA, Elsevier/Saunders.
Moser, P. J. (2008) *Electronics and Instruments for Audiologists*, New York and London, Routledge.

Further reading

Tate-Maltby, M. and Knight, P. (2000) *Audiology: An Introduction for Teachers and Other Professionals*, London, David Fulton Publishers.

Addresses

American Academy of Audiology
  www.audiology.org
  An organisation in the USA whose membership is open to audiologists.

British Academy of Audiology
  www.baaudiology.org
  The body for the audiology profession in the UK.

Augmentative and alternative communication

Augmentative and alternative communication (AAC) is a means of enhancing communication using single or combined approaches. This is determined according to a pupil's skills and preferences. As long ago as the 1980s, the skills necessary for developing competence in communication have been identified (Light, 1989). These are:

- Linguistic skills including learning the meaning of pictures and symbols and combining symbols to make sentences
- Learning the technical skills (such as the way symbols are set out) needed to operate the communication system
- Developing the knowledge and skills in social rules of interaction
- Developing skills to communicate effectively beyond the limits of competence in AAC (Ibid., paraphrased).

Approaches in AAC include the use of signing, speech synthesisers, objects of reference and symbols. Signing might employ a system found particularly useful with individuals experiencing cognitive impairments such as Makaton. Speech synthesisers may be used where the pupil's own spoken language is not possible or unintelligible. An object of reference is used to indicate an event or activity that may not be happening in the present. It may involve remembering something that has happened or something that is planned to occur later. An object of reference is used to enable a pupil to indicate a choice or decision. It is symbolic of the object or event. Objects of reference can be used to indicate a proposed activity, signal a proposed change of activity, help the pupil anticipate a task, or enable him to make a choice/decide an activity. Visual symbols are often used in connection with computer technology. Symbols are used to support emerging literacy. They can be employed in a way that relates to language sequencing skills as pupils select and place the symbols in order, and for reading and writing.

An approach used to supplement alternative and augmentative communication is talking mats developed at the University of Stirling, Scotland. An ordinary textured mat is used to which various card symbols can be attached. Three sets of symbols covering 'issues', 'emotions' and 'influences' are employed. Using these, the pupil can indicate in various ways including eye pointing if he has a physical impairment. The innovative and flexible use of these symbols enables quite extensive communication. A smiling face and a frowning face can be attached to different halves of the mat and beneath them can be sorted things and experiences the student likes and dislikes. A task such as using a computer can be represented. The pupil can indicate what they finds helpful and unhelpful in learning computing by indicating symbols grouped according to these criteria.

Reference

Light, J. (1989) 'Towards a definition of communicative competence for individuals using augmentative and alternative communication systems', *Augmentative and Alternative Communication* 5, 134–137.

Further reading

Cockerill, H. and Carrollfew, L. (2007) *Communicating without Speech: Practical Augmentative and Alternative Communication for Children*, New York, Blackwell Publishing.

Address

American Speech-Language-Hearing Association
www.asha.org
A professional, scientific and credentialising association for members and affiliates who are audiologists; speech-language pathologists; and speech, language and hearing scientists.

Autism

Leo Kanner an American child psychiatrist first identified autism as a separate condition in the 1940s. Criteria for diagnosing autism relate to impairment in all modes of communication and their timing, impairment of social relationships, evidence of rigidity and inflexibility of thought processes, and onset before 30 months. There is widespread acceptance that autism is a lifelong condition caused by organic brain damage. Three times as many boys as girls are affected. Asperger's syndrome is regarded by some as a distinctive condition. Others view it as the higher ability aspect of the continuum of autism.

The curriculum for pupils with autism is designed to be suitable for the child's cognitive level but appropriate for the child's chronological age and interests. It may emphasise communication, social skills and play as well as academic skills training. Pedagogy must ensure that the content of the curriculum is presented in a way that is tolerable to the child. The focus is often on developing skills including those of social interaction with sensitivity. At times the child may perceive the process as confusing and threatening.

Among approaches is 'structured teaching' (www.teacch.com) which includes organising the classroom to reduce visual and auditory distractions to help the child focus on his learning. The four components of structured teaching are: physical structures, daily schedules, work systems, and visual structure and information. Another approach is discrete trial teaching. This structured and therapist-led intervention involves breaking behaviour into small parts. One sub-skill is taught before the pupil moves on to another and required behaviours are shaped until they are securely learned using behavioural methods. In many approaches the way the classroom is organised is important. The aim is to make the environment meaningful and safe without being too rigid and to ensure that the levels of stimulation are not too great as to hinder learning. Parent support and training is helpful to ensure consistency between home and school.

Further reading

Farrell, M. (2008) 'Autism' in *Educating Special Children: An Introduction to Provision for Pupils with Disabilities and Disorders*, New York and London, Routledge.
Gabriels, R. and Hill, D. E. (2007) *Growing Up with Autism: Working with School Age Children and Adolescents*, New York, Guilford Press.
Siegel, B. (2008) *Getting the Best for Your Child with Autism: An Expert's Guide to Treatment*, New York, Guilford Press.

Addresses

The National Autistic Society, UK
www.nass.org.uk
Provides help, support and services to individuals with autism and their families.

US Autism and Asperger's Association (USAAA)
www.usautism.org
A non-profit organisation for autism and Asperger's syndrome education and support.

Autonomy and independence

Developing autonomy and independence, while important for all children and young people, is very important for pupils with disability/disorders. The aim for educators and others is to help ensure that the difficulties brought about by the disability/disorder are tackled and other skills and knowledge the pupil has are brought to bear to move towards the greatest independence. A balance requiring tact and sensitivity from adults is struck between providing necessary support and encouraging autonomy.

For pupils with moderate to severe cognitive impairment, security and routine are important aids to learning. However, opportunities for choice and decision-making are also important. Within routines such as snack times, and in lessons, choices can be built into provision. The pupil can be encouraged to select the type of drink and food they like from several choices. In music, they can choose the instrument they will use. In science, they can select whether to examine the effects of exposure to the air for fruit or vegetables. Choices might initially be from two items or activities and this can be widened as the pupil comes to understand the nature of choice. Children with cognitive impairment tend to have difficulties using strategies for remembering and monitoring their performance (Henry and Maclean, 2002). These may need to be explicitly taught and supported, perhaps using visual cues.

For learners with visual impairment, independence is encouraged through such means as orientation training, perhaps helping the individual to use local transport facilities safely and with confidence. Opportunities to develop skills in personal and social development and leisure are given high priority. In sports, running can be aided by using a guide wire system, a sighted guide or a caller. Cycling can be done in tandem, or with stationary cycles. A pole with a padded end may be used to alert a lap swimmer that the end of the pool is approaching (Lieberman, 2002).

Relatedly, self-management may be approached and encouraged by involving the child in implementing strategies to help changes in behaviour. Once a target behaviour is identified, self-management strategies may be applied to its antecedents and consequences. This technique has been used with individuals with mild or moderate to severe cognitive impairment. The individual may use self-observation, evaluation, recording, and reinforcement. Applying self-management techniques to antecedents of target behaviour allows the learner to make choices and use self instruction (such as self-talk or printed instructions). Self-management involves the child or young person:

- recognising the problem
- recasting the problem in terms of behaviour that requires changing
- finding naturally occurring events (contingencies) which will support change or alternatively creating contingencies
- arranging the contingencies so change will occur.

Where a child can achieve only partial participation in changing behaviour, teaching and support may be provided to enable change. Self-management is important in learning new skills, for learning to manage time effectively, for addressing problems and for achieving goals. All these are aspects of moving towards autonomy.

References

Henry, L. C. and Maclean, M. (2002) 'Working memory performance in children with and without intellectual disabilities', *American Journal of Mental Retardation* 107, 6, 421–432.

Lieberman, L. J. (2002) 'Fitness for individuals who are visually impaired or deaf-blind', *RE View (Rehabilitation and Education for Blindness and Visual Impairment)* 34, 1, 13.

B

Barriers

Different aspects of provision can be presented in terms of the extent to which they might get in the way of a pupil with disability/disorder making better progress or participating more fully.

Taking the example of a pupil with orthopaedic impairment, aspects of the curriculum can be re-examined to see if it is possible to remove or reduce constraints. The curriculum can help ensure the best involvement and support of the pupil in activities such as technology or science where special equipment may be necessary. In physical education, the teacher may seek advice from the physical therapist and occupational therapist and may work with the physical therapist to devise programmes to engage the pupil. Any special programmes to develop skills or encourage movement can be planned into the pupil's school day to ensure that the pupil still experiences a balanced range of subjects.

Effective pedagogy can also be presented as removing barriers that would exist if such pedagogy were not used. Evidence-based practice that behavioural approaches encourage the academic progress and personal development of pupils with autism is an example.

An educator's choice and use of resources can remove potential barriers to a pupil's participation. For a pupil with orthopaedic impairment, furniture will take account of pupil's stature and need for good posture and support. Participation can be helped if the teacher ensures the pupil is properly positioned perhaps using pads and cushions or specially adapted seat inserts (Bigge, Best and Heller, 2001, pp. 199, 201–204). Where classroom organisation constrains access to facilities or opportunities for independence and self-care, adapting it can be seen as removing barriers. For a child who is deafblind, tactile clues to the different parts of the classroom can be helpful.

Regarding therapy and care, the support of services other than education is generally required in order for the student to function successfully and maintain better life quality (Snell and Brown, 2000). Close multi-professional working can contribute to the pupil's well-being as well as reducing barriers and extending opportunities. Attitudinal barriers may be created if adults do not have high enough expectations of pupil's educational progress and personal and social development and these can be challenged and modified.

(See also, *Access*)

References

Bigge, J. L., Best, S. J. and Heller, K. W. (2001) (4th edition) *Teaching Individuals with Physical, Health or Multiple Disabilities*, Upper Saddle River, NJ, Merrill-Prentice Hall.

Snell, M. and Brown, F. (2000) (5th edition) *Instruction of Students with Severe Disabilities*, Upper Saddle River, NJ, Merill.

Behaviour chain interruption strategy

The behaviour chain interruption strategy can encourage communication, for example with pupils experiencing moderate to severe cognitive impairment. It is used in already established contexts and routines. The teacher interrupts a stream of the pupil's well-established behaviour so that the pupil has to adopt new types of communication (Carter and Grunsell, 2001). The pupil may be preparing to lay the table for lunch. Previously the teacher has always set the cups at one end of the table and the pupil's task has been to put one of the cups at the top of each place setting. This has become a well-established procedure. A behaviour interruption strategy might involve starting laying the table with the cups still in the cupboard so the pupil has to request them, perhaps initially being guided towards them. The motivation for communication is the momentum of the routine task and the expectation that it will be completed.

The teacher has to exercise professional judgement and skill so the behaviour interruption strategy acts as an incentive to the child's communication, not as a frustration. This suggests that: the strategy is not over used; the required communication is within the child's capacity; the approach is used to trigger, not to teach, the communication; and the child is rewarded for communicating, for example by being praised.

Reference

Carter, M. and Grunsell, J. (2001) 'The behaviour chain interruption strategy: a review of research and discussion of future directions', *Journal for the Association of the Severely Handicapped* 26, 1, 37–49.

Behaviour therapy/behaviour therapist

Behaviour therapy is a type of psychotherapy used in treating various disorders including anxiety disorders and depressive disorders. Behaviour therapy is not inevitably viewed as a unified approach and many behavioural strategies are used in treating psychological problems (Antony and Roemer, 2003,

p. 186). A behavioural perspective defines personality with reference to individual behaviours assumed to arise mainly from an individual's 'learning history' (Ibid. p. 182). Behavioural approaches such as operant conditioning regard behavioural reactions and emotional reactions as the result of reinforcement history and environmental contingencies. By contrast, a cognitive-constructivist model sees behaviour as, 'goal directed, purposive, active, and adaptive' (Reinecke and Freeman, 2003, p. 226). In practice, it is very common for therapists to draw on both cognitive therapy and behavioural therapy approaches. Behaviour analysis has similarities with but is not identical to behaviour therapy.

A behaviour therapist may be qualified in one of several disciplines and behaviour therapy is carried out by a number of mental health professionals. These include a psychologist, psychiatrist, clinical social worker, or a qualified counsellor.

References

Antony, M. M. and Roemer, L. (2003) 'Behaviour Therapy' in Gurman, A. S. and Messer, S. B. (Eds) *Essential Psychotherapies: Theory and Practice*, New York, Guilford Press.

Reinecke, M. A. and Freeman, A. (2003) 'Cognitive Therapy' in Gurman, A. S. and Messer, S. B. (Eds) *Essential Psychotherapies: Theory and Practice*, New York, Guilford Press.

Further reading

American Psychiatric Association (2000) *Diagnostic and Statistical Manual of Mental Disorders Fourth Edition Text Revision*, Arlington, VA, APA.

Addresses

Association for Behaviour Analysis International™
  www.abainternational.org
  A professional organisation based in the USA, for those interested in the philosophy, science, application and teaching of behaviour analysis.

National Association of Cognitive-Behavioural Therapists
  www.nacbt.org
  A professional association for supporting, promoting, teaching and developing cognitive-behavioural therapy and those who practise it.

Biofeedback

Biofeedback is a technique used to measure an individual's physiological states and responses including blood pressure, sweat secretion and heart rate as they occur. This enables the individual to become aware of these responses and potentially control them. For example, with some pupils with attention deficit hyperactivity disorder an instrument may be used that is sensitive to muscle tension, associated with hyperactivity. The instrument emits a signal such as a sound tone when muscles are over tense. This gives the child the opportunity to respond by using previously learned relaxation techniques to reduce the muscle tension. In a broader sense biofeedback devices enable a child to monitor his own behaviour and, using cognitive-behavioural principles, gain greater control over it.

Further reading

Schwartz, M. S. and Andrasik, F. (Eds) (2005) (3rd edition) *Biofeedback: A practitioner's Guide*, New York, Guilford Press.

Address

Association for Applied Psychophysiology and Biofeedback
    www.aapb.org
    A non-profit association promoting understanding of biofeedback and encouraging the further development of practice.

Bio-psycho-social model

A bio-psycho-social model refers to a model of disability/disorder that draws on biological, psychological and social perspectives. Such a model can avoid limitations of a view that focuses excessively on biological features, sometime caricatured as a 'medical model'. It can also sidestep the weakness of models that overemphasise social influences, a so-called 'social model'. The bio-psycho-social model does not necessarily avoid explaining the relative influence of the three aspects however.

The *International Classification of Functioning, Disability and Health (ICF)* (World Health Organisation, 2002) seeks to recognise biological, psychological and social factors relevant to functioning. A version for children and young people, the *International Classification of Functioning, Disability and Health for Children and Youth* or ICF-CY (World Health Organisation, 2007) uses the same model and assumptions.

Frith (1997, p. 13) outlines a biological, psychological and behavioural model of reading disorder. It is proposed that there is a genetically determined abnormality of the peri-Sylvian region of the brain (the region around the Sylvian fissure). The genetically determined abnormality of the peri-Sylvian region is related to a core cognitive deficit of phonological processing. This deficit is further related to behavioural manifestations of poor performance in reading, naming, verbal memory, and phonological awareness.

(See also, *International classification of functioning, Disability and health*)

References

Frith, U. (1997) 'Brain, mind and behaviour in dyslexia' in Hulme, C. and Snowling, M. (Eds) *Dyslexia: Biology, Cognition and Intervention*, London, Whurr Publishers, pp. 1–19.

World Health Organisation (2002) *International Classification of Functioning, Disability and Health: Towards a Common Language for Functioning, Disability and Health*, Switzerland, Geneva, WHO.

World Health Organisation (2007) *International Classification of Functioning, Disability and Health: Children and Youth Version*, Switzerland, Geneva, WHO.

Birth difficulties

Disabilities/disorders may arise as a result of birth difficulties before, during and after birth and are considered respectively as prenatal, perinatal and post-natal difficulties.

Prenatal factors

Prenatal factors related to disability/disorder include infections, chemicals and malnutrition. Infections that can affect the foetus include congenital cytomegalovirus (CMV) infection. If a woman during pregnancy is infected, the foetus may also become infected. CMV infection is the most common congenital (present at birth) infection in the United States of America (www.cdc.gov/cmv/). Around 1 in 750 children are born with or develop permanent disabilities as a result of CMV infection.

Chemicals, including alcohol, can adversely affect the foetus. Foetal alcohol syndrome is a significant cause of cognitive impairment and is associated with mothers drinking alcohol during pregnancy. There is debate about the degree to which the timing, amount or frequency of consumption of alcohol causes a difference in the degree of damage done to the foetus. Pregnant women are advised to avoid alcohol consumption altogether during pregnancy. Alcohol can stunt foetal growth and lead to lower birth weight. It can lead to cognitive impairment and other disabilities. Attempts to reduce the incidence of foetal alcohol syndrome include educating potential parents and raising the general levels of public awareness.

Malnutrition is a difficult phenomenon to assess in relation to disability and disorder. Its relation with severe to moderate cognitive impairment and to mild cognitive impairment is unclear. The child of a poorly nourished mother may also be ill nourished in early life, making it difficult to disentangle the influence of maternal malnutrition and neonatal malnutrition. The foetus of a malnourished mother may be at greater risk from such noxious influences as alcohol, drugs and infections, which can influence intellectual functioning. As well as broadly defined malnutrition, a lack of specific dietary ingredients is influential. For example, iodine deficiency is linked to cognitive impairments.

Perinatal factors

Anomalies may occur in the process of birth and soon after, causing conditions that can lead to disability and disorder. The perinatal period is from birth to four weeks.

Asphyxia (not having enough air) can lead to permanent damage (Candy Davies and Ross, 2001, pp. 25–26). Cerebral palsy can be caused by asphyxia. So-called mechanical injury and asphyxia are often closely associated and sometimes grouped together as 'birth injuries'. It is unclear what proportion of births is affected by asphyxia or injury or both because research shows varied results. Such discrepancies probably reflect different views of the causes of disabilities/disorders. Furthermore, it is difficult to distinguish the effects of asphyxia in children because of the many confounding variables associated with it. Hypoxia is the deprivation of or reduction of the normal supply of oxygen just before, during, or just after birth. Interruption of the supply of oxygen to the baby's brain can cause problems, for example, it may lead to cerebral palsy.

Postnatal factors

Postnatal influences on disability and disorder include infection, malnutrition, poisoning and cerebral trauma.

Meningitis (Candy, Davies and Ross, 2001, pp. 280–283) is an example of inflammation of the meninges (membranes covering the brain and spinal column). It is usually due to infection by various microorganisms, most often viruses or bacteria. While viral meningitis is comparatively mild, bacterial meningitis can be life threatening without prompt treatment. Encephalitis, inflammation of the brain, is also usually caused by a viral infection. In some cases the child is left with brain damage resulting in cognitive impairment, behavioural difficulties and epilepsy.

Malnutrition is difficult to link directly to disorders and disabilities because it tends to be associated with other adverse circumstances, including socio-economic and psychological factors that can contribute.

An example of poisoning is the ingestion of noxious chemicals such as lead, mercury or copper. Persistently raised lead blood levels can cause cognitive impairment. Research into the issue is complicated by the fact that people living in areas where there is higher than typical lead exposure, for example those living near lead works, may be socially disadvantaged. A reduction in lead poisoning can be achieved by reducing industrial pollution and by using lead free fuel.

Cerebral trauma can cause cognitive impairment and other problems such as behaviour difficulties. Traumatic brain injury may have an accidental cause such as a traffic accident or may be intentional, for example physical abuse of a child.

Reference

Candy, D., Davies, G. and Ross, E. (2001) *Clinical Paediatrics and Child Health*, London and New York, Elsevier/Saunders.

Further reading

Lissauer, T. and Clayden, G. (2007) (3rd edition) *Illustrated Textbook of Paediatrics*, London, Elsevier Mosby.

Address

Centers for Disease Control and Prevention, Atlanta, Georgia, USA.
www.cdc.gov/cmv/

Boarding special school

A boarding special school may offer suitable provision for a range of pupils. It may offer provision for children with rare disabilities where local provision is unavailable or not feasible. In such instances the expertise that is necessary for the child to thrive and progress and develop well may be concentrated in a few schools. Some disabilities may require fuller education and care than can be provided in a day school. These include provision for pupils with severe medical conditions. Pupils may experience damaging home circumstances so that boarding provision is considered an alternative, although foster care in a group home or by individual foster parents may be an alternative. Some pupils with severe disorders of conduct or experiencing severe anxiety disorder or depressive disorder may benefit from a residential special school offering round the clock support and care as well as education closely allied with this.

Residential provision can have certain disadvantages. It separates pupils from their local community from which they often have to return. Residential schools may take great care to plan transition back to the local community, sometimes arranging with local schools to support such a transfer. They also may work with parents, perhaps arranging days and weekends when parents can stay in accommodation provided by the school. Nevertheless where residential schools are a long distance from the pupil's home, such arrangements are not easy to sustain. Boarding arrangements can be flexible and some schools provide all year boarding, termly boarding, weekly boarding and occasional respite.

Numerous examples of well-established residential special schools can be cited, for example, case studies of several residential special schools in England are available (Farrell, 2006, 2008).

References

Farrell, M. (2006) *Celebrating the Special School*, London, David Fulton Publishers.
Farrell, M. (2008) *The Special School's Handbook: Key Issues for All*, London, Routledge/nasen.

Address

The National Association of Independent Schools and Non Maintained Special Schools. (NASS)

www.nasschools.org.uk

A member organisation working with and for special schools, including boarding special schools, in the voluntary and private sectors in the UK.

Braille and Moon

Reading and writing in Braille

Braille is a well-known system of tactile reading and writing using a 'cell' of six raised dots, combinations of which make up letters, punctuation and contracted words. In British Braille, there are two grades. Grade 1 consists of alphabet and punctuation signs, and grade 2 comprises contractions of words such as 'RCV' for 'receive'. Early teaching of Braille reading and writing is usually based on contracted Braille from the start. While an average print reader reads at about a rate of 250 words per minute, an average Braille reader reads about 100 words per minute, around two or three times slower (Aldrich and Parkin, 1989). Because there is no peripheral touch equivalent to peripheral vision a Braille reader cannot scan ahead in the same way as a sighted reader of print. Computer programes are available to translate print files into Braille files, which are then downloaded to Braille embossers. There are reading schemes to develop Braille skills for pupils transferring from print to Braille, for example because of deteriorating sight.

Electronic Braille typewriters use a six-key format for input, each key corresponding to a dot in the Braille cell. Output may be through a synthetic speech device or a renewable tactile display on the machine. Text may be stored in the machine's memory to be transferred later to a standard printer or Braille embosser. Software can translate Braille text downloaded to a conventional printer into print. It is debated whether or not to teach older students to use dedicated Braille writing devices as the main medium for recording information. The alternative is to teach children who are educationally blind to touch type using the conventional QWERTY keyboard in elementary/primary school to develop word processing skills early. In high school/secondary school, students may use conventional computers with adaptive software and synthesised speech as their main way of writing and storing information.

Reading and writing in Moon

Moon is a tactile medium based on a simplified raised line adaptation of the Roman print alphabet. It may be used for pupils with visual impairment and additional difficulties who are unable to learn Braille. Moon is slow to read but does provide basic access to literacy.

Moon characters may be written by hand on special plastic material ('german film'). Moon fonts have also been developed for computers. In this way, Moon text is typed onto the computer screen then downloaded through a conventional printer onto paper. The Moon is then copied onto 'swell' paper and raised by being passed though a stereo-copying machine.

Reference

Aldrich, F. K. and Parkin, A. J. (1989) 'Listening at speed', *British Journal of Visual Impairment* 7, 1, 16–18.

Further reading

Sardegna, J., Shelley, S., Shelley, A. and Steidl, S. M. (2002) (2nd Edition) *The Encyclopaedia of Blindness and Vision Impairment*, New York, Facts on File.

Addresses

National Federation for the Blind
   www.nfb.org
A membership organisation of blind people in the USA. The site includes a programme to teach sighted children about Braille.

Royal National Institute for the Blind
   www.rnib.org.uk

A UK-based organisation. Its website includes pages giving descriptions and a history of Braille and Moon.

Brain basics

In discussing various disabilities/disorders, reference may be made to brain areas and functions. This entry concerns the main structures and functions with the exception of the cerebrum, which is discussed in the entry, 'Cerebral hemispheres and lobes'.

Brain stem

The brain stem is a stalk of nerve tissue linking the cerebrum and the cerebellum with the spinal cord. Operating largely automatically beneath the level of consciousness, it regulates functions such as breathing and body temperature. Main components of the brain stem are the: medulla oblongata, pons and midbrain (Traurig, 2003, p. 237). The brain stem also contains fields of neurons and nerve fibres termed the brain stem reticular formation.

The medulla oblongata contains groups of nerves involved with the automatic regulation of heartbeat, with breathing and with other functions. It contains the nuclei of the ninth, tenth, eleventh and twelfth cranial nerves. By these it receives and relays sensations of taste from the tongue and sends signals to muscles implicated in movements of the neck and tongue and those involved in the articulation of speech. The pons contains nerves connecting to the cerebellum, which is located behind it. Containing the nuclei to the fifth, sixth, seventh and eight cranial nerves, the pons relays sensory information from the ear, face and teeth and also has other functions. The midbrain connects the pons and cerebellum with the forebrain (that is, the central structures and the cerebrum) (Standring, 2005, p. 342). The midbrain contains the nuclei of the third and fourth cranial nerves controlling eye movements. It also contains cell groups, for example, the substantia nigra and the red nuclei involved in the smooth coordination of movements of the limbs (Kandel, Schwartz and Jessell, 2000, pp. 317–336). Throughout the brain stem is a collection of nerve cell groups, the reticular formation, controlling the sleep-wake cycle and thought to be involved in signalling to the higher brain centres novel or important sensory information that may need a conscious response. Damage to the reticular formation may lead to paralysis and coma.

Cerebellum

The cerebellum (diminutive of the Latin 'cerebrum', or 'little brain') is located under the occipital lobes. It connects to the rest of the brain by tracts or bundles of nerve fibres, which enter the brainstem. It has two hemispheres and a medial part. The cerebellum receives sensory information from the balance structures of the middle ear, muscles and joints and other sources and integrates planning information concerning the position of the body and limbs (proprioceptive), balance (vestibular) and movement. It is concerned with maintaining body posture and balance and with coordinating gross and fine motor activity. It appears to be involved in timing, memory and learning and in coordinating cognitive functions (Rapoport, van Reekum and Mayberg, 2000). Injury to the cerebellum may, among other effects, cause clumsiness, difficulties with balance, and impaired planning and timing of activities (Drubach, 2000). The cerebellum has an important role in controlling and coordinating articulation (Obler and Gjerlow, 1999).

Diencephalon

The diencephalon ('di' = 'across'; 'enkephalos' meaning 'brain'), the posterior part of the forebrain, includes the thalamus, hypothalamus, subthalamus and epithalamus (Standring, 2005, pp. 369–385). The *thalamus* (from the Greek 'thalamos', meaning 'bed') is positioned near the centre of the brain and transmits sensory information passing towards the cerebellum. The *hypothalamus* is implicated in the regulation of body temperature, thirst and appetite and affects other behaviours including sexual behaviour and aggression. It has connections with the pituitary gland, which produces hormones affecting other glands, and therefore influences growth, sexual development and other aspects of physiology. The *subthalamus* is a region of nuclear groups and fibre tracts (Ibid. p. 383). Part of the *epithalamus* (the pineal gland) secretes the hormone melatonin and has been associated with cycles of sleeping and waking and other rhythms.

Basal ganglia

The basal ganglia refers to several subcortical nuclear masses implicating the corpus striatum (caudate nucleus, putamen and globus pallidus) and associated structures in the midbrain and the diencephalon (Standring, 2005, p. 419). The striatum has efferent connections with the globus pallidus and the substantia nigra. The basal ganglia and its associated structures are involved in the control of movement and in motivation. Disorders of the basal ganglia are typified by effects on posture, muscle tone and movement (Ibid. p. 421).

(See also, *Cerebral hemispheres and lobes*)

References

Drubach, D. (2000) *The Brain Explained*, Upper Saddle River, NJ, Prentice Hall Health.

Kandel, E., Schwartz, J. H. and Jessel, T. M. (2000) *Principles of Neural Science*, New York, McGraw-Hill.

Obler, L. K. and Gjerlow, K. (1999) *Language and the Brain*, Cambridge, Cambridge University Press.

Rapoport, M. D., van Reekum, R. and Mayberg, H. (2000) 'The role of the cerebellum in cognition and behaviour', *Journal of Neuropsychiatry* 12, 193–198.

Standring, S. (2005) (39th edition) *Gray's Anatomy: The Anatomical Basis of Clinical Practice*, London, Elsevier Churchill Livingstone.

Traurig, H. H. (2003) 'The brain stem: An overview' in Conn, P. M. (Ed.) (2003) (2nd edition) *Neuroscience in Medicine*, Totowa, NJ, Humana Press.

Further reading

Kandel, E., Schwartz, J. H. and Jessel, T. M. (2000) *Principles of Neural Science*, New York, McGraw-Hill.

Addresses

Build a Brain
http://www.stanford.edu/group/hopes/basics/braintut/ab9.html

Digital Anatomist Information System
http://sig.biostr.washington.edu/projects/da/

Harvard Medical School – Atlas of the human brain
http://www.med.harvard.edu/AANLIB/

Michigan State University – Human Brain Atlas
http://www.msu.edu/~brains/humanatlas/

University of Utah, Salt Lake City – Atlases of the brain
http://medlib.med.utah/kw/brain_atlas/

Breaks and lesson structure

Particular care with lesson structure and providing optimum breaks from work are part of the provision for pupils with attention deficit hyperactivity disorder. Allowing periods of physical activity in lessons that may be predominantly sedentary may reduce inattention and to help a pupil manage impulsiveness. Some research indicates that pupils with attention deficit hyperactivity disorder can sustain effort and concentration in structured and controlled situations where the activity is stimulating. However, they find it particularly difficult to return to an activity once distracted (Borger and Van der Meer, 2000). This suggests that a beneficial environment would be structured and controlled (e.g. having predictable schedules); have stimulating learning tasks; and offer minimal distractions.

Accordingly, a Swedish researcher has made recommendations concerning children with attention deficit hyperactivity disorder/deficits in attention, motor control and attention. They should have breaks at regular intervals and short periods of concentrated work, perhaps of only a few minutes, for children in early school years (Gillberg, 1996).

References

Borger, N. and Van der Meer, J. (2000) 'Visual behaviour of ADHD children during an attention test', *Journal of Child Psychology and Psychiatry* 41, 4, 525–532.

Gillberg, C. (1996) *Ett barn I varje klass. Om DAMP, MBD, ADHD*, Södertälje, Cura.

Buildings and design

For pupils with disabilities/disorders, school buildings and their design are important considerations. A few examples should illustrate. A tactile pathway outside a school can help confidence and orientation for blind children (see the Internet address that follows for an example of this in Tangalle, South West Sri Lanka). For children who are deafblind, their mobility and independence can be helped by the use of physical aids to mobility including tactile maps and clues in rooms and corridors.

For pupils with orthopaedic impairments the school will ensure they have good access to classrooms and other facilities. Separate rooms are provided for personal care procedures and toilets are adapted as necessary. For a child with health impairments, for example a heart condition, there are also considerations where the school has stairs. The school may ensure that the classroom and other facilities are on the lower floor to minimise the necessity of stair climbing. Alternatively, an elevator/lift may be used.

Address

www.usaid.gov/about_usaid/disability/dissrilankamotivation07.pdf

Bullying

Associated with both physical and psychological intimidation, bullying may involve excluding a child from a group, physical violence, or threats of violence. In developing approaches to bullying, schools strive to lay the ground for wide consultation, develop a clear, agreed policy, and ensure that strategies to deal with bullying are implemented and understood by all. Strategies include setting up preventative whole school anti-bullying programmes, intervening when bullying occurs and monitoring so that it is less likely to recur (Sullivan, 2000).

Particular concerns arise with regard to pupils with disabilities/disorders.

Children with emotional and behavioural disorder may bully others, and while such bullying still has to be tackled, the children will need particular help to understand their behaviour and change it. Pupils with cognitive impairment may be more vulnerable to bullying than others because they may not understand the nature of bullying nor the action to take if they are being bullied.

Reference

Sullivan, K. (2000) *The Anti-bullying Handbook*, New York, Oxford University Press.

Further reading

Varnava, G. (2002) *How to Stop Bullying in Your School*, London, David Fulton Publishers.

Young, S. (2002) *Solutions to Bullying*, Stafford, National Association of Special Educational Needs.

Addresses

Bully Police USA
  www.bullypolice.org
  A watchdog organisation in the USA advocating for bullied children and reporting on state anti-bullying laws.

Kidscape
  www.kidscape.org.uk
  A UK-based organisation campaigning for children's safety.

Care

Care refers to protection and nurturing. While it is clearly an aspect of provision for all children and young people, care may have particular implications for pupils with disabilities/disorders. A balance is found that provides the necessary care yet encourages independence and autonomy. For pupils with profound cognitive impairment, the care aspect of provision may include help and support with personal care, feeding, personal hygiene and so on. For children in a residential special school, care is also associated with provision after school when children may stay in group homes on the premises. Members of staff providing for children after school in a residential special school are sometimes called 'care staff'. In this context, one may speak of residential care and education (e.g. Care Commission and Her Majesty's Inspectorate of Education, 2007).

Reference

Care Commission and Her Majesty's Inspectorate of Education (2007) *Residential Care and Education: Improving Practice in Residential Special Schools and Secure Care Accommodation Services in Scotland: A Staff Development Guide to Support the Evaluation of Quality Across Care and Education*, Livingston, Scotland, HMIE.

Address

Scottish Commission for the Regulation of Care
www.carecommission.com
Regulates adult, child and independent care in Scotland. The site includes the guide on residential care mentioned in the preceding reference.

Causal factors

Aetiology concerns, 'the study or theory of the factors that cause disease' and how they find their way to the individual, and more generally, 'the causes or origin of a disease or disorder' (Anderson, 2007, p. 660). In cystic fibrosis, which involves dysfunction of the exocrine glands leading to signs such as chronic pulmonary disease, aetiology concerns a defect in a gene on chromosome 7. For some disabilities/disorders, some causal factors may be known, but others may not. In congenital heart disease, aetiology is often unknown although there are associations including maternal prenatal rubella infection (Kumar and Clark, 2005, pp. 832, and 832–839). In such cases it may be more accurate to speak of causal factors. Sometimes precipitating factors are implicated. For asthma, such factors include inhaling cold air, the effects of atmospheric pollution, and exercise (Ibid. pp. 912–915).

References

Anderson, D. M. (Chief lexicographer) (2007) (31st Edition) *Dorland's Illustrated Medical Dictionary*, Philadelphia, PA, Elsevier/Saunders.
Kumar, P. and Clark, M. (Eds) (2005) (6th Edition) *Clinical Medicine*, New York/London, Elsevier Saunders.

Further reading

Kumar, P. and Clark, M. (Eds) (2005) As above.

Cerebral hemispheres and lobes

In discussing various disabilities/disorders, reference may be made to brain areas and functions. This entry concerns the cerebrum and a related entry *Brain basics* concerns other important brain areas and functions.

The cerebrum (Latin 'cerebrum' = 'brain') comprises the cerebral hemispheres, associated with thinking, communicating, and carrying out skilled, coordinated tasks. The surfaces of both right and left cerebral hemispheres have raised areas (sulci) and fissures (gyri). The hemispheres are divided by a deep longitudinal fissure, but connected by the corpus callosum.

The outer (grey matter) portion of the hemisphere is the cortex where the cell bodies of neurons are located. Beneath the grey matter is the white matter comprising axons (projections from the neurons). Through these axons, which are covered with an insulating myelin sheath, impulses travel to other parts of the brain and to the body, communicating with other nerve cells or muscles.

Within the hemispheres are nerve cell clusters, the basal ganglia, which are connected to the brainstem and to the cerebellum and are involved in relaying and modifying motor output from the cerebral cortex, coordinating movements to the skeletal muscles. They are also involved with executive and sensory functions (Middleton and Strick, 2000).

Generally, the dominant hemisphere is the left hemisphere for nearly all right-handed people and most left-handed people too. The dominant hemisphere controls speech and language, verbal memory, reading and writing, calculations and (usually) the dominant hand. The non-dominant hemisphere is more involved with visual functions and rhythm. It processes information such as memory and perception of shape, pattern, texture, three-dimensional spatial relationships, construction (including drawing and copying), and understanding and expressing emotion.

The left side of the brain controls movements and interprets sensation for the right side of the body and the right side of the brain acts similarly for the left side of the body. The left hemisphere is dominant for most people. For most left-handed people, the left hemisphere is likely to control speech and language function although motor control of the left hand will be in the right hemisphere. Most cognitive acts involve the coordination of both hemispheres.

Each cerebral hemisphere can be divided into four lobes, named after overlying bones, each lobe being associated with a certain type of cognitive functioning. They are the frontal, temporal, parietal and occipital lobes. Further structures are the limbic lobe (part of the 'limbic system') and the insula, sometimes called the insular lobe. This entry considers the frontal lobes, temporal lobes, parietal lobes, occipital lobes, limbic lobe and insula.

The frontal lobe is the brain's output centre, involved with coordinated fine movement: the motor aspect of speech; executive function; motivation, social skills, and aspects of personality. Part of the inferior frontal gyrus is referred to as Broca's area after the neuro-anatomist who identified the area with speech. The temporal, parietal and occipital lobes are input centres.

The temporal lobe receives and processes auditory information (hearing, understanding and remembering what is heard) and is implicated for memory, receptive language and musical awareness. Behind Heschl's gyri is a flat area known as the planum temporale, which has been studied in relation to reading disorder. An area known as Wernicke's area, located in the superior temporal gyrus, was named after the German neurologist Karl Wernicke. It was identified for some time as relating to speech comprehension although there has been uncertainty about the extent of the area (Bogen and Bogen, 1976). The left hemisphere temporal lobe is involved in long-term verbal memory while in the right hemisphere it is the seat of long-term non-verbal memory.

The parietal lobe is important for attention and for interpreting sensory information, being the destination for sensors in skin and joints conveying information about touch and position. The angular gyrus, a convolution of the inferior parietal lobule, has an important role in arithmetic and in word reading. The inferior parietal lobe is implicated in writing.

The occipital lobe is involved in processing and interpreting visual stimuli, being the receiving area for nerve cell activity in the retinas of the eyes.

The limbic lobe (French 'limbique' from Latin 'limbus' = 'edge') is situated along the corpus callosum. It includes the cingulate gyrus and the hippocampal formation (including the hippocampus). The cingulate gyrus is involved with executive control and attention (e.g. Gehring and Knight, 2000). The hippocampus is implicated in memory encoding and consolidation.

The term limbic system has come to be used to refer to the limbic lobe and associated subcortical nuclei including the hypothalamus, amygdala and septum (Standring, 2005, p. 404). The amygdala is involved in the recall and recognition of emotional stimuli (Adolphs *et al.*, 1995). It is important in evaluating the significance of events in the environment including stimulus and reward associations (Standring, 2005, p. 411). The limbic system is characterised as influencing emotions such as fear and anger, aspects of memory and the processing of sensations of smell.

The insula is covered by parts of the temporal, parietal and frontal lobes and is isolated (hence the name) from other areas by a circular sulcus. It has been described as, 'an integrative multimodal association area' for information coming from different senses (Mildner, 2008, p. 21).

(See also, *Brain basics*)

References

Adolphs, R., Tranel, D., Damasio, H. and Damasio, A. R. (1995) 'Fear and the human amygdala', *Journal of Neuroscience* 15, 5879–5891.

Bogen, J. E. and Bogen, G. M. (1976) 'Wernicke's region – where is it?', *Annals of the New York Academy of Sciences* 280, 834–843.

Gehring, W. J. and Knight, R. T. (2000) 'Prefrontal-cingulate interactions in action monitoring', *Nature Neuroscience* 3, 516–520.

Middleton, F. A. and Strick, P. L. (2000) 'Basal ganglia output and cognition: Evidence from anatomical behavioural and clinical studies', *Brain and Cognition* 42, 183–200.

Mildner, V. (2008) *The Cognitive Neuroscience of Communication*, New York, Lawrence Erlbaum Associates.

Standring, S. (2005) (39th edition) *Gray's Anatomy: The Anatomical Basis of Clinical Practice*, London, Elsevier Churchill Livingstone.

Further reading

Kandel, E. R., Schwartz, J. H. and Jessell, T. M. (2000) (4th edition) *Principles of Neural Science*, New York, McGraw-Hill.

Addresses

Build a Brain
    http://www.stanford.edu/group/hopes/basics/braintut/ab9.html

Digital Anatomist Information System
  http://sig.biostr.washington.edu/projects/da/

Harvard Medical School – Atlas of the human brain:
  http://www.med.harvard.edu/AANLIB/

Michigan State University – Human Brain Atlas:
  http://www.msu.edu/~brains/humanatlas/

University of Utah, Salt Lake City – Atlases of the brain:
  http://medlib.med.utah/kw/brain_atlas/

Cerebral palsy

Cerebral palsy is the most common cause of permanent physical disability in children. It has been defined as, 'a disorder of movement and posture that is due to non-progressive abnormality of the immature brain' (Kurtz, 1992, p. 441). Brought about by lesions to the brain in early life, cerebral palsy may involve impairment of vision, hearing, speech and cognition. About 60 per cent of individuals with cerebral palsy also have some degree of cognitive impairment (Turnbull *et al.*, 2002). Around a third of people with cerebral palsy experience epileptic seizures. The combination and variety of brain lesions influence the different types of cerebral palsy. Various effects are grouped according to the impairments of movement associated with them: spastic, athetoid, and ataxic. Cerebral palsy can involve a mixture of spasticity, athetosis and ataxia.

Spastic movements are experienced by about a third of individuals with cerebral palsy owing to the failure of muscles to relax. These are caused by damage to the motor cortex. One arm and one leg on the same side of the body may be affected (hemiplegia); all limbs may be affected (quadriplegia); all limbs may be affected but with the legs being more affected (diplegia); or the legs only may be affected (paraplegia). More rarely the arms may be more affected than the legs, or three limbs or one limb may be affected.

Slow writhing movements of the limbs that cannot be controlled typify athetoid cerebral palsy caused by damage to the basal ganglia.

Ataxia is associated with poor concentration and movement and disturbed balance. It is caused by damage to the cerebellum.

Among the educational implications of cerebral palsy is that a multidisciplinary assessment is undertaken to ensure that all aspects are taken into account when preparing an Individual Education Programme/Plan (IEP). The IEPs are particularly important because of the individual and varied nature of the condition. Attention is paid to motor and medical aspects such as coordination and motor control because these influence general educational development. For motor impairments, aids may include head pointers, individualised wheelchairs, electronic devices, and a variety of adaptive equipment. Most children require a structured programme of occupational therapy and physical therapy. Special language programmes are used where there is language impairment.

References

Kurtz, L. A. (1992) 'Cerebral palsy' in Batshaw, M. L. and Perret, Y. M. (Eds) (3rd edition) *Children with Disabilities: A Medical Primer*, Baltimore, Brookes, 441–469.
Turnbull, R., Turnbull, A., Shank, M., Smith, S. and Leal, D. (2002) (3rd edition) *Exceptional Lives: Special Education in Today's Schools*, Upper Saddle River NJ, Merrill-Prentice Hall.

Further reading

Best, S. J. and Bigge, J. L. (2001) 'Multiple disabilities' in Bigge, J. L., Best, S. J. and Heller, K. W. (2001) (4th edition) *Teaching Individuals with Physical, Health or Multiple Disabilities*, Upper Saddle River, NJ, Merrill-Prentice Hall, 92–117.
Parkes, J., Donnelly, M., and Hill, N. (2001) *Focusing on Cerebral Palsy*, London, Scope.

Addresses

Scope
   www.scope.org.uk
   A UK-based organisation providing a range of services for people with cerebral palsy and their families.

United Cerebral Palsy
   www.ucp.org
   A US-based organisation committed to change and progress for people with disabilities.

Challenging behaviour

The nature of challenging behaviour

Parents, professionals and others cannot always agree on what constitutes challenging behaviour. This is partly owing to different standards of what is acceptable relating to social class, culture, the chronological and developmental ages of children, and the influence of different settings. However, challenging behaviour may be described as that which is socially unacceptable and significantly blocks learning. The intensity, duration or frequency of the behaviour puts at risk the safety of other people or the child himself. It is likely to limit the pupil's access to community facilities or temporarily prohibit it altogether.

Challenging behaviour includes aggression, self-injury, stereotyped behaviour and problematic sexual behaviour (Baroff, 1999, pp. 370–395). Examples are: self injury or injury to others; damage to surroundings; severe lack of compliance; repeated absconding; stereotyped speech or movement; faecal smearing; habitually eating substances such as paper or dirt; inappropriate sexual behaviour such as public masturbation; persistent screaming; repeated vomiting; and extreme hyperactivity.

Related factors

There are particular difficulties managing challenging behaviour where a child also has profound cognitive impairment, where the child has difficulties communicating, and where other difficulties hinder the child from realising some behaviours are harmful or undesirable. Challenging behaviour is sometimes linked to particular conditions such as Lesch-Nyhan syndrome, which is associated with self-injurious behaviour, spitting, vomiting, and often violence to others (Goldstein and Reynolds, 1999). The side effects of drugs, pain, stress, anxiety and depression can also contribute to challenging behaviour. Further reasons are being unable to convey basic needs; the effects of phobias; intolerance of perceived overstimulation or a low boredom threshold.

The child may exhibit challenging behaviour as a way of communicating. This underscores the importance of schools developing individual communication programmes with a speech-language pathologist/speech therapist. Challenging behaviour may constitute a request for items such as food or a toy. It may be a protest or refusal to comply with a request, or a wish to escape from a situation. The behaviour may indicate dissatisfaction; a comment or declaration such as a greeting or compliance with a request; or boredom, pain or tiredness. Analysing the possible communicative function of challenging behaviour can lead to effective interventions.

Assessments and interventions

Functional behavioural assessment is a problem-solving process for tackling pupils' problem behaviour. It aims to identify the purpose of the behaviour and find ways to intervene to address it. Factors are considered which influence the behaviour: social, affective, cognitive and environmental. Behavioural interventions are informed by the apparent reasons for the behaviour so that its purpose and function for the child can be better understood.

Interventions may relate to functional analysis. However, their long-term effectiveness may be compromised if the elimination of unwanted behaviour is not supported by naturally occurring events reinforcing the new behaviour. A way of ensuring natural contingencies are applied is to teach new functional behaviours. In order to be effective, these must result in reinforcing consequences similar to those available following the unwanted behaviour and the new behaviour must be reinforced by the same consequences that reinforced the unwanted behaviour.

Schools try to create optimal learning environments for children with challenging behaviour. They try to work out intervention programmes taking into account medical care and the child's developmental level. Specific programmes are individually planned, systematically implemented and rigorously assessed, then modified or changed if ineffective.

Successful intervention depends on expanding the limited response repertoires of individuals with cognitive impairment. Some interventions are designed to teach new communicative behaviours to replace unwanted behaviour. A child wanting food may be taught to use a non-verbal sign rather than be disruptive. Other interventions are developed to teach alternative functionally related behaviour to replace unwanted behaviour. The pupil might be taught to listen to peaceful music on a headset to suppress an overstimulating environment, instead of screaming. Yet other interventions involve changing the events leading up to the inappropriate behaviour. Where unwanted behaviour suggests a wish to escape from a demanding activity, simplifying the tasks and using errorless learning might reduce it. Children with challenging behaviour may need from time to time, additional staff or equipment, or a modified timetable.

References

Baroff, G. S. with Olley, J. G. (1999) (3rd edition) *Mental Retardation: Nature, Causes and Management*, Philadelphia, PA, Brunner/Mazel.
Goldstein, S. and Reynolds, C. R. (Eds) (1999) *Handbook of Neurodevelopmental and Genetic Disorders in Children*, New York, Guilford Press.

Further reading

Emerson, E. (2002) *Challenging Behaviour: Analysis and Intervention in People with Severe Intellectual Disabilities*, New York, USA and Cambridge, UK, Cambridge University Press.

Addresses

American Institute for Research (AIR) Center for Effective Collaboration and Practice
   www.air.org/cecp
   This site provides a description of functional behavioural assessment.

Child and adolescent mental health

Child and adolescent mental health can affect the way individuals think, feel and behave. It influences self-perception, life chances and relationships with others. Community systems of care operate through the child's family, school and local community. Mental health difficulties may be associated with youth crime and drug abuse. They may be reactions to trauma. Mental health disorders include depressive disorders (Goodyer, 2001), disorders of conduct (Bloomquist and Snell, 2005), and anxiety disorders (Rachman, 2004).

Provision for child and adolescent mental health may be organised in different ways but an important principle is enabling multi-professional working. For example in England, the Child and Adolescent Mental Health Services are part of the National Health Service local trusts. Children are normally referred through their family doctor ('general practitioner'). Child and Adolescent Mental Health Services staff may include a clinical psychologist, social/welfare worker, occupational therapist, psychiatrist, a community nurse, a community mental health worker, a community psychiatric nurse and arts therapists.

In the United States of America, national organisations such as Mental Health America aim to educate the public about ways to preserve and strengthen mental health and foster innovation in policy, services, research and practice. They press for access to effective care and end discrimination; and support individuals and families living with mental health and substance abuse problems. The Substance Abuse and Mental Health Services Administration (SAMSHA) National Health Information Center provides information about mental health. At state level also, support is provided. For example, the South Carolina Department of Mental Health gives priority to adults, children and families affected by serious mental illness or emotional disorders. It seeks to involve supports from many sources including health services and community services (www.state.sc.us).

References

Bloomquist, M. and Snell, M. (2005) *Helping Children with Aggression and Conduct Problems*, New York, Guilford Press.

Goodyer, I. M. (Ed.) (2001) (2nd edition) *The Depressed Child and Adolescent*, Cambridge, Cambridge University Press.

Rachman, S. (2004) (2nd edition) *Anxiety*, London and New York, Taylor and Francis.

Further reading

Atkinson, M. and Hornby, G. (2002) *Mental Health Handbook for Schools*, London, Routledge Falmer.

Addresses

Child and Adolescent Mental Health
www.camh.org.uk
Provides an information resource, discussion forum and bulletin for child and adolescent mental health for professionals, young people and parents.

Mental Health America
www.nmha.org
The organisation's aims include supporting individuals and families living with mental health and substance abuse problems.

Substance Abuse and Mental Health Services Administration (SAMSHA) National Health Information Center
www.mentalhealth.samsha.gov/child/childhealth.asp
An organisation based in the USA providing information about mental health.

Child development

Child development is one of the foundational disciplines of special education and of education more generally. Maturation has been defined in relation to development as follows. 'The term *maturation* implies both *growth*, a measurement of physical characteristics over time, and *development*, the acquisition of metabolic functions, synaptic circuits, reflexes, secretory and other cellular functions, sensory awareness, motor skills, language and intellect' (Sarnat and Flores-Sarnat, 2006, p. 13, italics in original). In this context, development is a process of growth by which a child matures in various ways: physical, motor, sensory, cognitive, emotional and social.

Child development information contributes to a framework of expected progress of children's development. Indicators of progress are often expressed as 'milestones', which a child developing typically is expected to reach within a certain age range. Milestones for gross and fine motor development (Bayley, 1993) may indicate an average age for the development of a skill and the age range within which the skill usually develops. In the Bailey framework, the average age at which a child builds a tower of two cubes is 11 months and 3 weeks. In the age range of 10 to 19 months, 90 per cent of children develop this skill. When a child does not achieve expected milestones within the typical age range, this suggests 'developmental delay' in which the course of development is the same as for other children but slower. Where there is 'developmental difference', development does not occur in the usual sequence.

Children may be assumed to be subject to broadly similar types of stimulation. However, it is accepted that a child in an impoverished home environment is unlikely to progress as well as one in a more privileged setting. The difficulties of estimating the relative contributions of the environment and apparent cognitive and other abilities are recognised. They are apparent in debates about assessing mild cognitive impairment (Greenspan, 2006). It is difficult to ascertain the extent to which mild cognitive impairment might relate to environmental impoverishment or 'within child' factors, given the two interact. Yet such judgements may affect educational provision. It may be judged that the main factor is an impoverished home environment. In this case, the aim of the child's education may be seen as providing a stimulating environment to compensate and enable the child to develop well. Alternatively, it may be considered that the child has 'cognitive impairment' requiring specific interventions. The school may place a strong emphasis on developing concrete operations (using concrete examples in mental operations) and extending these toward logical thought that is less dependent on concrete exemplars (Farrell, 2008, chapter 4).

The strands of child development are not separate and different strands of development interrelate. For example, cognitive development is influenced by motor development. A child is less able to move and explore his surroundings because of motor impairment and this can constrain his exploring and relating motor information and sensory information. For a child with motor disabilities, there are implications not only for motor development but also for perceptual, cognitive, social and emotional development, and for communication.

More generally, it is accepted that there are variations in the rates at which different children progress. But a period is reached where slower progress than is typically expected or lack of progress may indicate difficulties. Slower than usual development may be temporary and when the child later develops typically it is seen retrospectively there was no cause for concern. But slower than expected development may also indicate problems which if unresolved can exacerbate later difficulties.

(See also, *Developmental delay*)

References

Bayley, N. (1993) (2nd edition) *Bayley Scales of Infant Development*, New York, The Psychological Corporation.

Farrell, M. (2008) *Educating Special Children: An Introduction to Provision for Pupils with Disabilities and Disorders*, New York and London, Routledge.

Greenspan, S. (2006) 'Functional concepts in mental retardation: Finding the natural essence of an artificial category', *Exceptionality* 14, 4, 205–224.

Sarnat, H. B. and Flores-Sarnat, L. (2006) 'Human nervous system development and malformations' in Wyllie, E., Gupta, A. and Lachhwani, D. K. (Eds) (4th edition) *The Treatment of Epilepsy: Principles and Practice*, Philadelphia, PA, Lippincott Williams and Wilkins, 13–36.

Further reading

Pressley, M. and McCormick, C. B. (2007) *Child and Adolescent Development for Educators*, New York, Guilford Press.

Sandall, S, Hemmeter, M., Smith, B. and McLean, M. (2005) *DEC Recommended Practices: A Comprehensive Guide for Practical Application in Early Intervention/ Early Childhood Special Education*, Missoula, MT, Division for Early Childhood (DEC) of the Council for Exceptional Children (CEC).

Address

Division for Early Childhood
www.dec-spec.org
A division of the Council for Exceptional Children in the USA.

Child and adolescent psychiatry/child and adolescent psychiatrist

Psychiatry is a branch of medicine dealing with 'the study, treatment and prevention of mental disorders' (Anderson, 2007). It follows that child and adolescent psychiatry is a branch of psychiatry applied to children and young people. It includes investigating various factors relating to disorders such as genetic, biological, psychological, and environmental. It also encompasses the treatment of disorders including through medication and psychotherapy. Criticisms have been made of child and adolescent psychiatry on the grounds that it may not give sufficient account of cultural differences among children, for example that it may impose essentially Western perspectives on the treatment of children and adolescents from other cultures (Timimi and Maitra, 2006).

A psychiatrist is a physician specialising in psychiatry and a child and adolescent psychiatrist specialises in work with individuals in this age range and their families. A child and adolescent psychiatrist may be based in a specialised inpatient unit, a hospital outpatient clinic or centre and works closely with other professionals in providing treatment and support. Initially, the psychiatrist will carry out a diagnostic assessment then develop a treatment plan, discussing the elements with the child and his parents/carers. Treatment may involve individual or family psychotherapy, medication, or consultation with others.

(See also, *Child and adolescent mental health*)

References

Anderson, D. M. (Chief lexicographer) (2007) (31st edition) *Dorland's Illustrated Medical Dictionary*, Philadelphia, PA, Elsevier/Saunders.

Timimi, S. and Maitra, B. (Eds) (2006) *Critical Voices in Child and Adolescent Mental Health*, London, Free Association Books.

Further reading

Barker, P. (2004) *Basic Child Psychiatry*, London and New York, Blackwell.
Rutter, M. and Taylor, E. (2005) *Child and Adolescent Psychiatry*, London and New York, Blackwell Science.

Addresses

American Academy of Child and Adolescent Psychiatry
   www.aacap.org
   A national professional medical association aiming to treat, and improve the quality of life for children and youth and their families affected by mental, developmental and behavioural disorders.

International Association of Child and Adolescent Psychiatry and Allied Professions
   www.iacapap.org
   Promotes the study, treatment, care and prevention of mental and emotional disorders and deficiencies in children, adolescents and their families.

Royal College of Psychiatrists
   www.rcpsych.ac.uk
   The professional and educational body for psychiatrists in the United Kingdom and the Republic of Ireland.

Classification of disabilities/disorders

Classification systems for disabilities/disorders are used in many countries. Typologies of any kind are based on certain assumptions such as common features within the classification and the usefulness of the classification (Farrell, 2008). In the United States of America, pupils considered to need special education covered by federal law have a defined 'disability' and are also deemed to need special education because the disability has an adverse educational impact. Categories of disability under federal law as amended in 1997 (20 United States Code 1402, 1997) reflected in 'designated disability codes' are:

01   Mentally Retarded (mild, moderate, severe, profound)
02   Hard-of-hearing
03   Deaf
04   Speech and Language Impaired

05 Visually Handicapped
06 Emotionally Disturbed
07 Orthopaedically Impaired
08 Other Health Impaired
09 Specific Learning Disability
10 Multi-handicapped
11 Child in Need of Assessment
12 Deaf/Blind
13 Traumatic Brain Injury
14 Autism.

As well as these categories, an amendment to the Individuals with Disabilities Education Act 1997 allows states and local school districts to use a different categorisation for pupils aged three through nine years. These children may be defined as having a disability if they have a developmental delay in one or more of certain developmental areas. These are physical, cognitive, communication, social or adaptive development.

In England, a similar classification (Department for Education and Skills, 2005, *passim*) comprises:

• Learning difficulty (moderate, severe, profound)
• Hearing impairment
• Speech, language and communication needs
• Visual impairment
• Behavioural, emotional and social difficulty
• Physical disability
• Specific learning difficulties (e.g. dyslexia, dyscalculia, dyspraxia)
• Multi-sensory impairment
• Autistic spectrum disorder.

In the American system, 'mental retardation' is similar to the English classification of 'learning difficulties'.

To be useful, classifications require certain properties. A classification requires validity. To say that an individual is a member of a group classification should convey something meaningful about the group and the individual. For example, to say an individual has profound cognitive impairment should convey some general information about the individual's level of global cognitive functioning. Classifications must have a satisfactory degree of reliability. That is, if a classification of say autism is used to identify a child supposed to have the condition, then others using the criterion associated with the classification should come to the same assessment. Also the classification should distinguish other children who do not have autism.

Classification systems ideally should be underpinned by a consistent rationale. In considering the classifications of the disabilities represented by the disability codes listed above, it can be seen that the classification system is not completely consistent. Some disabilities listed refer to broad areas of development such as cognition, speech and language, physical development or emotional development. Others refer to impairments in sensory abilities such as visual, hearing impairment and deafblindness. However, 'autism' concerns a syndrome, which is typified by impairments in social development, communication, and behavioural and cognitive flexibility. 'Traumatic brain injury' refers to an injury after which certain consequences may follow for behaviour, cognition, communication, and personal and social development. Part of the reason for this is pragmatic. For example, the concern of parents and others that there was sufficient focus on children with traumatic brain injury may have contributed to it being made a category in the United States of America and not in some other countries, such as the United Kingdom.

There is debate about the usefulness and the necessity of classifications according to disabilities/disorders. On the positive side, in the United States of America, the aim of the Individuals with Disabilities Education Improvement Act of 2004 is to establish students entitled to additional educational services, interventions and resources to meet individual needs. Contributing to a common understanding of what constitutes a child with a disability or disorder, such categorisation can help ensure parity in allocating resources and instructional services. Classification can offer a structure for the organisation of supports and services and how children are allocated to them (Burke and Reudel, 2008, p. 69, paraphrased). Labels sometimes associated with classifications such as autism can be a positive recognition that help the parent's understanding of their child (Farrell, 2008, p. 36).

Among potential negative associations of classification is that it can be associated with negative connotations and lower expectations of pupils and with alienation from other children. It can be taken to describe the whole child rather than an aspect of his abilities or development. Where classification systems are used, it is therefore important that potential negative effects are addressed.

(See also, *Diagnostic and statistical manual of mental disorders* and *international classification of functioning, disability and health for children and youth*)

References

Burke, P. J. and Reudel, K. (2008) 'Disability classification, categorisation in education' in Florian, L. and McLaughlin, M. J. (Eds) *Disability Classification in Education*, Thousand Oaks, CA, Corwin Press.

Department for Education and Skills (2005) (2nd edition) *Data Collection by Special Educational Need*, London, DfES.

Farrell, M. (2008) *Educating Special Children: An Introduction to Provision for Pupils with Disabilities and Disorders*, New York and London, Routledge.

Further reading

Florian, L. and McLaughlin, M. J. (Eds) (2008) *Disability Classification in Education*, Thousand Oaks, CA, Corwin Press.

Classroom organisation and layout

Classroom organisation and the way the classroom is set out can optimise the learning environment for pupils with different types of disability and disorder. For a pupil with profound cognitive impairment the teachers may create a 'responsive environment' (Ware, 2003) to help the child's social, intellectual and communicative development. This involves creating an environment in which pupils 'get responses to their actions, get the opportunity to give responses to the actions of others, and have the opportunity to take the lead in interaction' (Ibid. p. 1). 'Room management' is a way of organising staff roles when working with groups of pupils to maximise pupils' participation. Adults take on the role of individual helper, group activity manager, or mover (Lacey, 1991). The individual helper tends to be involved in intensive work with one pupil at a time. The duration of the activity may be several minutes or longer depending on factors such as the pupil and the task. The group activity manager ensures other pupils are occupied, perhaps experiencing a game or activity not focused intensively on skill building. The mover ensures the group runs smoothly. This can involve preparing materials, dealing with visitors, or tidying away. The adult roles may be rotated about every hour.

To consider a few other examples more briefly, when a pupil has hearing impairment, the classroom is organised to optimise listening to and seeing other speakers. For a child with visual impairment, the aim is to reduce background noise. For a child who is deafblind, it is important to optimise any hearing and visual sensitivity the child may have. For autism, class-room physical structure adds meaning and context to environment as in 'Structured Teaching' and is organised to reduce difficulties, for example through the use of a daily schedule. Finally for a child with traumatic brain injury, to encourage the child's attention, the classroom layout should minimise distractions. The child may be taught for a time in small groups.

References

Lacey, P. (1991) 'Managing the classroom environment' in Tilstone, C. (Ed.) *Teaching Pupils with Severe Learning Difficulties*, London, David Fulton Publishers.

Ware, J. (2003) *Creating a Responsive Environment for People with Profound and Multiple Learning Difficulties*, London, David Fulton Publishers.

Cognitive-behavioural therapy/cognitive-behavioural therapist

A cognitive-behavioural approach draws on both behavioural and cognitive perspectives and therapies. The merging of cognitive therapy and behavioural therapy is now common. It is proposed that behaviour is influenced by attitudes and assumptions and by the process of thinking and reasoning. Cognitive-behavioural approaches are said to represent, '... hybrids of behavioural strategies and cognitive processes, with the goal of achieving behavioural change' (Dobson and Dozoiz, 2001, pp. 11–12). Cognitive-behavioural interventions involve: monitoring cognitions; seeking connections between thoughts, feelings and behaviour; and seeking to replace negative cognitions with positive ones. Examples that might further indicate some of the rationale of cognitive-behavioural therapies include: cognitive therapy, rational-emotive behavioural therapy, and problem-solving dialogues and training.

Cognitive therapy (Beck *et al.*, 1979) concerns the cognitive processes of perceiving, thinking and reasoning and their effect on behaviour and emotions. An individual constructs his own experiences and beliefs. Psychosocial problems arise as exaggerations of normal responses. The therapist encourages the child to reappraise beliefs logically and empirically. This includes looking for alternative explanations for events, different ways of acting and responding, and different ways of behaving.

Rationale-emotive behavioural therapy focuses on rational and irrational beliefs (Ellis *et al.*, 1997). Psychosocial disturbances are seen largely as self-created and arising from beliefs, interpretations and evaluations of events in an individual's life. A child or young person's beliefs, held about himself, others and his environment can influence thought, emotions and behaviour. Correcting or modifying irrational thinking encourages adaptive behaviour. This is because disturbances are brought about mainly by current beliefs rather than past events and memories. Change is achieved as the child works on his irrational beliefs through dialogue with the therapist. The beliefs are identified, discussed, challenged and tested.

Interventions using problem-solving dialogues and training assume the child lacks the necessary problem-solving skills for effective social functioning. Such approaches use structured programmes having cognitive and behavioural elements. Problem-solving skills training (D'Zurilla, 1986) involves being aware of the problem; defining and formulating it; putting forward alternative solutions; deciding the approach, and testing the solution. Children are trained to identify problems, prevent their initial impulses, produce several alternatives, consider possible consequences, plan their solutions and evaluate them.

Teachers can support a cognitive-behavioural approach, in liaison with the psychotherapist. In their day-to-day work with the pupil, teachers might encourage more positive interpretations of events where a child tends to view them very negatively. 'Self-talk', a type of internal monologue, sometime used as part of therapy, might be reinforced in the school setting to aid the child's learning and development, for example by helping manage anxiety.

References

Beck, A. T., Rich, A. J., Shaw, B. F. and Emery, G. (1979) *Cognitive Theory of Depression*, New York, Wiley.

Dobson, K. S. and Dozoiz, D. J. A. (2001) 'Historical and philosophical bases of cognitive-behavioural therapies' in Dobson, K. S. (Ed.) (2nd edition) *Handbook of Cognitive-Behavioural Therapies*, New York, Guilford Press.

D'Zurilla, T. J. (1986) *Problem Solving Therapy*, New York, Springer Publishing.

Ellis, A., Gordon, J. Neenan, M. and Palmer, S. (1997) *Stress Counselling: A Rational Emotive Behaviour Approach*, London, Cassell.

Further reading

Christner, R. W., Stewart, J. and Freeman, A. (2007) *Handbook of Cognitive-Behaviour Group Therapy with Children and Adolescents*, New York and London, Routledge.

Dobson, K. S. (Ed.) (2003) (2nd edition) *Handbook of Cognitive-Behavioural Therapies*, New York, Guilford Press.

Addresses

British Association for Behavioural and Cognitive Psychotherapies
   www.babcp.com
   A multidisciplinary organisation for cognitive-behavioural therapy in the UK.

National Association of Cognitive-Behavioural Therapists, West Virginia, USA
   www.nacbt.org
   Supports, promotes, teaches and develops cognitive-behavioural therapy and those who practise it.

The Australian Association for Cognitive-Behavioural Therapy – Western Australia
   www.aacbtwa.org.au
   A multidisciplinary professional organisation promoting scientific study and ethical practice in understanding and changing cognitions and behaviours in applied settings.

Communication difficulties – comprehension

Comprehension has been characterised as, 'a process whereby information is successfully transformed from one kind of *representation* to another' (Bishop, 1997, p. 2, italics added). It involves a process by which sounds are recognised and translated into meaningful representations. Difficulties with comprehension may have various sources, making careful assessment essential. A child may find it difficult to maintain attention because of visual or hearing impairment. He may have difficulty discriminating sounds and therefore may not receive sufficient information to be able to comprehend an utterance. If auditory processing is slower than typical, the child may be trying to understand one part of an utterance and missing what the speaker is currently saying.

To aid comprehension where a pupil tends to pay better attention to visual stimuli, these may be linked to auditory ones to help attract and maintain attention. More broadly, the teacher may support sequences and instructions by providing visual clues such as a series of pictures. She can also name a child when giving instructions and can question the pupil to check attention.

The pupil may need to be taught prerequisites of listening such as: sitting still, looking at the speaker and watching gestures. The teacher and classroom aide can model good listening behaviour perhaps using role play activities. Useful tasks have been devised for introducing and practising listening (e.g. Thompson, 2003, pp. 30–33, 59–61). To take just one example, to help the pupil identify sounds, a recording might be used of various city, rural and domestic sounds for the pupil to match the sound to a picture. The child might be asked to listen to various speech sounds and guess the speaker's gender, age and other features.

One programme seeking to help language processing and comprehension is the Fast ForWord® training programme (Tallal, 2000, p. 143). More generally, the teacher can take practical steps to help a child having difficulties storing and retrieving the necessary information understand adult-like grammatical utterances. The teacher might use more single phrase utterances. Where longer utterances are used, the teacher can try to make sure the sequence supports understanding. For example, instructions can be given in the order in which the pupils are asked to carry them out.

The teacher may allow a pupil having difficulties with comprehension extra time to respond to a question. If done skilfully in whole class teaching, this need not slow the pace of the lesson for others. In small group work and individual work it is easier. Pre-lesson tutoring may be used to prepare the pupil for what is to come, to further reduce processing demands. This might include learning special vocabulary for curriculum subjects so that attention can be better focused on comprehension of the content of the lesson.

Some pupils may use signing boards to encourage kinaesthetic and visual memory to supplement comprehension. Communication boards and computer technology can assist comprehension. Also, reading and writing can help in providing visual information to supplement auditory information.

References

Bishop, D. V. M. (1997) *Uncommon Understanding: Development and Disorders of Understanding in Children*, Hove, Psychology Press.
Tallal, P. (2000) 'Experimental studies of language learning impairments: From research to remediation' in Bishop, D. V. M. and Leonard, L. B. (Eds) *Speech and Language Impairments in Children: Causes, Characteristics, Intervention and Outcome*, Philadelphia, PA and Hove UK, Psychology Press.
Thompson, G. (2003) *Supporting Children with Communication Disorders: A Handbook for Teachers and Teaching Assistants*, London, David Fulton Publishers.

Further reading

Cain, K. and Oakhill, J. (2008) *Children's Comprehension Problems in Oral and Written Language: A Cognitive Perspective*, New York and London, Guilford Press.

Addresses

American Speech-Language Hearing Association
   www.asha.org
   The professional, scientific and credentialing association for audiologists, speech-language pathologists, and speech, language, and hearing scientists in the USA.

The Royal College of Speech and Language Therapists
   www.rcslt.org
   The professional body for speech and language therapists in the UK, maintaining high standards of ethical conduct, clinical practice and education of therapists.

Communication difficulties – grammar

Grammar concerns the rules for putting words together to make sentences both in writing and in spoken utterances. It embraces syntax (the rules for making words into sentences) and morphology (grammatical changes to particular words). To develop age appropriate grammar a child needs a good vocabulary, so a child lacking this requires help developing it. Where assessment has confirmed there are problems with developing grammar various interventions can help.

One approach is elicited imitation. This may begin with an adult showing the child a non-verbal stimulus such as a picture. The adult then says an utterance connected to the picture and asks the child to repeat it. Next, the child attempts to repeat the utterance and the adult rewards a correct response. If the child is incorrect, the adult repeats the correct utterance and asks the child to try again. Gradually the adult utterance and the reward are phased out and the child is able to respond correctly to the picture and question only. Modifications can be made to ensure that utterances are meaningful even if the task is greatly broken down. For example the adult would not begin with simply asking the child to say the word 'is' in response to a picture and build up to 'The car is red'. They would begin with 'car' then 'the car' then 'the car red' then 'the car is red' (Fey and Proctor-Williams, 2000, pp. 180–183).

Modelling, an aspect of social learning theory (Bandura, 1977), can also be brought into use. In modelling, learning takes place as the child observes and imitates another person more accomplished at a particular skill or task. In the present context, the adult might produce about 10 to 20 sentences expressing the target grammatical form. The sentences might be descriptions of pictures or responses to questions. The child listens quietly to the whole sequence. This avoids any response interfering with the child's concentration on the forms being modelled. Then the adult asks the child to respond to the same or a different set of stimuli in the way the adult has demonstrated. This might be trying to describe a picture.

Another intervention is sentence recasting. This involves an adult responding to a child's utterance by modifying it. In responding, the educator keeps the meaning, context, referents and main lexical items of the child's utterance. However, she modifies one or more of the sentence constituents (for example the verb) or changes the sentence modality (perhaps from declarative to interrogative). The recasting often corrects errors in the child's utterance. But using a conversational and natural approach, the adult does not try to get the child to correct his original utterance. A child with language difficulties is likely to require more frequent recasting than other children in order to progress. Speech pathologists may teach parents and teachers the procedure, which may be more successful if focused on specific grammatical targets.

References

Bandura, A. (1977) *Social Learning Theory*, Englewood Cliffs, NJ, Prentice-Hall.
Fey, M. E. and Proctor-Williams, K. (2000) 'Recasting, elicited imitation and modelling in grammar intervention for children with specific language impairment' in Bishop, D. V. M. and Leonard, L. B. (Eds) *Speech and Language Impairments in Children: Causes, Characteristics, Intervention and Outcome*, New York, Psychology Press.

Further reading

Bishop, D. V. M. and Leonard, L.B. (Eds) (2000) *Speech and Language Impairments in Children: Causes, Characteristics, Intervention and Outcome*, New York, Psychology Press.
Farrell, M. (2008) *Educating Special Children: An Introduction to Provision for Pupils with Disabilities and Disorders*, New York and London, Routledge, chapter 15: Communication disorders: grammar and comprehension.

Addresses

American Speech-Language Hearing Association

The Royal College of Speech and Language Therapists
 (Details as in entry for *Communication difficulties – comprehension*.)

Communication difficulties – pragmatics

Pragmatics concerns the use of language. Difficulties may include problems with basic skills and knowledge; grammatical sense in the use of language; social and linguistic sense; and conversational skills.

Basic skills and knowledge

Among prerequisites to using language effectively is turn taking. The child needs the ability and motivation to interact (e.g. with another person initiating an interaction) or to take part in an activity such as singing a song. Sharing attention is important. Among helpful interventions are interactive activities such as 'peek-a-boo' and rhymes and songs with repeated sounds and movements. Communication facilitation techniques may be used in which the teacher is very responsive to the child's communicative attempts, attending particularly to the child's interests and preferred activities. These techniques can be used at a pre-linguistic level (attention sharing); the linguistic stage (repeating what the pupil says); and the complex language stage (making a statement likely to lead the child to say something). Relatedly, 'contingent responding' involves sensitively and alertly responding to what the child says or indicates (Anderson-Wood and Smith, 1997, p. 85).

Grammatical sense in language use

Grammatical cohesion is an important aspect of language use. It includes linking utterances to one another to avoid unnecessary repetition, and drawing on shared assumptions and understanding. Among ways this is achieved are reference and conjunctions. In reference, grammatical short forms might be used to carry over meaning from earlier utterances as when recurring words or phrases are replaced by a pronoun. Conjunctions join utterances to avoid repetition. Instead of saying 'I went to the shops. I went to the bank. I went to the cinema', we say, 'I went to the shops, the bank and the cinema'. To help a child with difficulties involving grammatical sense in language use, the speech therapist and the teacher may provide models of grammatical cohesion devices and help the child practise them, perhaps using role play.

Social and linguistic sense

Several important features enable utterances to make social and linguistic sense. A speaker's intention might involve asking a question or making a criticism. The context of an utterance needs to be mutually understood so the speaker and listener have to understand with whom they are communicating. Speakers and listeners need to understand and be able to respond suitably to various conventions such as polite, indirect requests. Without such skills and understanding, the pupil may respond inappropriately to utterances, finding it hard to maintain meaningful exchanges. Useful interventions include the educator teaching the child possible signals of the speaker's intentions and examples of implication and inference. Role play can provide opportunities to use similar signals and these can be encouraged when they appear in day-to-day communication. The programmes on the social use of language (e.g. Rinaldi, 2001) can be used as a teaching framework to develop language skills in real life settings. It can help the child develop basic social communication skills and better awareness of himself and others.

Conversational skills

Conversational skills are subtle and complex. A child may have difficulty with conversational topics because he does not understand signals indicating that his conversation partner is introducing a topic. The child can be taught to recognise common opening gambits such as the use of open-ended questions ('What did you think of the game yesterday?') and respond accordingly. This may involve asking a question ('Do you mean the tennis?') or commenting from his experience ('It was good but not as good as the badminton'). The child may not recognise when a partner is trying to round off a conversation. If so, he can be taught to listen to possible signals that someone would like to change the topic. A child having difficulties with turn taking can be taught to recognise and respond to signals that his partner wants a turn (a pause or question). Role play can help along with encouragement when such devices appear in everyday conversation. If the pupil has problems using and interpreting non-verbal communication the teacher can assist, taking account of its culturally variable nature. The teacher or others may model suitable non-verbal communication, help the child practise it through role play and encourage suitable approximations as the child demonstrates them in day-to-day communication.

References

Anderson-Wood, L. and Smith, B. R. (1997) *Working with Pragmatics: A Practical Guide to Promoting Communicative Competence*, Bicester, Winslow Press.

Rinaldi, W. (2001) *Social Use of Language Programme*, Windsor, NFER-Nelson.

Further reading

Farrell, M. (2008) *Educating Special Children: An Introduction to Provision for Pupils with Disabilities and Disorders*, New York and London, Routledge, chapter 16: Communication Disorders: Semantics and Pragmatics.

Firth, C. and Venkatesh, K. (2001) *Semantic-Pragmatic Language Disorder*, Brackley, UK, Speechmark.

Goldstein, H., Kaczmarek, L. A. and English, K. M. (2001) *Promoting Social Communication: Children with Developmental Disabilities from Birth to Adolescence* Baltimore, MD, Brookes.

MacKay, G. and Anderson, C. (Eds.) (2000) *Teaching Children with Pragmatic Difficulties of Communication: Classroom Approaches*, London, David Fulton Publishers.

Addresses

American Speech-Language Hearing Association

The Royal College of Speech and Language Therapists
(Details as in entry for *Communication difficulties – comprehension*)

Communication difficulties – semantics

An important feature when considering semantics (meaning) in language is the lexeme. This is a unit of meaning that can be conveyed in one or several words ('begin', 'start', 'take the plunge'). For a lexeme to be meaningful the speaker has to have some knowledge of the concept involved (e.g. 'toy'). Other cognitive factors have to support understanding of meaning. The child's memory needs to link object and word (e.g. 'box'). This enables the child when the object is next seen to call on the word. Also when the child next uses the word it will be with some memory of the associated concept and object. The verbal context in which the child uses a word also indicates he has understood its meaning. As long ago as the 1980s Aitchison (1987) suggested that in acquiring meaning, children have three basic, related tasks: labelling, packaging and network building. These (and other aspects of semantics concerning grammar) are also discussed in more recent sources (Farrell, 2008). The approaches suggested below would be modified according to the child's age and interests.

Labelling

Labelling involves the child discovering that sound sequences can be used as names for things. A child having difficulties with labelling may have problems with the processes involved. For example he may not be able to make sense of and store auditory information as effectively as can children of the same age. A child may have word finding problems and may therefore make excessive use of certain devices. These include using expressions lacking meaning but which sustain the utterance ('ehm') or using stereotyped phrases ('sort of').

Children having labelling difficulties may benefit from individual tutoring to help them develop the required skills and understanding. This may include making links between the spoken word and the object, action or other phenomena. The educator may also help the child develop more secure concepts through extending his experience, for example providing structured experience of spoons of different shapes and sizes. Another aspect is explicit teaching to direct the child's attention to an object or event being labelled. Explicit teaching coupled with extensive structured experiences may be used to encourage the child to recognise that objects have permanent existence.

If the child has difficulty storing the auditory information needed to make the links for labelling, using gestures or sign language may help. This allows auditory information to be linked with the tactile, kinaesthetic and visual features and memory. However, the child still has to be able to recognise the symbolic nature of signs and gestures. For a child with poor auditory memory, graphic symbols may help with labelling, because they provide visual clues and draw on visual memory. A child may have a sense of symbolising through play and the use of pictures. Nevertheless, he may still find it difficult to learn words because of problems making sense of and storing information. Here, picture matching, printed labels and sign language may be of help (Martin and Reilly, 1995).

Packaging

Packaging involves the child establishing which things can be packaged together under one label. Conceptual meaning may be 'underextended' where a child can correctly label his pet as 'cat' but does not understand the word and its meaning in relation to other cats. Concepts are 'overextended' if the word is used with too widely, as when the word 'cat' refers to all small animals. This may relate to lack of knowledge. For example, the child may know and correctly use the word 'duck' but also uses it for other birds, whose correct names he does not know.

Where a child has under extended concepts, the adult can provide one-to-one sessions to show the pupil other examples. If a child uses 'cat' only for his own pet, he can be encouraged to talk about photographs, of his own pet and later of other cats. The educator can draw attention to similar features extending the use of the word to other cats. She might begin with cats similar in appearance to the child's own (e.g. small, long tail) then gradually move on to less similar cats.

Where a pupil has overextended conceptual meaning, he can be taught to distinguish small animals that are not cats. Several photographs of cats and of say rabbits might be used. The teacher asks the pupil to look for ways in which the two creatures differ (tail, ears, what they are eating). Clear, unambiguous pictures can be used initially and other sets of photographs or video clips can be introduced once discrimination begins to develop.

Networking

In the network-building task, children must show how words relate to each other. Through networking, the lexeme acquires meaning from its relationship with other words. This is because it is a synonym, antonym or is in the same category (as 'dictionary' and 'encyclopaedia' are both in the category 'book'). A child may have difficulties with networking relating to synonyms because he has the idea that one word can only mean one thing. Antonyms can be problematic for any child because they can be relative. A hamster can be 'small' beside a 'big' dog, but 'big' in comparison with a 'small' spider. Some children have difficulties with subordinate and superordinate words, in keeping boundaries of different semantic fields. They may include fruits in a list of vegetables and vice versa.

The adult can help with difficulties relating to synonyms or antonyms by teaching them explicitly, particularly as they arise in curriculum subjects. Similarly, the teacher can explicitly teach and check understanding of subordinate and superordinate words and serial connections.

References

Aitchison, (1987) *Words in the Mind: An Introduction to the Mental Lexicon*, Oxford, Basil Blackwell.

Farrell, M. (2008) *Educating Special Children: An Introduction to Provision for Pupils with Disabilities and Disorders*, New York and London, Routledge, chapter 16: Communication disorders: semantics and pragmatics.

Martin, D. and Reilly, O. (1995) 'Global language delay: analysis of a severe central auditory processing deficit' in Perkins, M. and Howard, S. (Eds) *Case Studies in Clinical Linguistics*, London, Whurr.

Further reading

Firth, C. and Venkatesh, K. (2001) *Semantic-Pragmatic Language Disorder*, Brackley, UK Speechmark.

Schwartz, R. G. (2008) *Handbook of Child Language Disorders*, New York and London, Guilford Press.

Addresses

American Speech-Language Hearing Association

The Royal College of Speech and Language Therapists
  (Details as in entry for *Communication difficulties – comprehension*)

Community-based vocational instruction

Careers advice for students with disabilities/disorders follows similar principles to advice for all students: attempting to match the strengths and weaknesses of the student to suitable work. Particular sensitivity is required in advising and supporting students with life limiting conditions. A school may arrange work experience enabling a student to sample several jobs as part of its support in helping the student to decide which career to follow. For example, for older students with cognitive impairment, vocational instruction including community-based vocational instruction can have an important role. Community-based vocational instruction forms part of transition from school to post-school settings and can have a positive impact on the development of adaptive behaviour of students.

In a study with 34 high school students with 'moderate to profound mental retardation' students made statistically significant gains in a measure of independent behaviour (McDonnell *et al.*, 1993). The research indicated several enabling factors. To get the most benefit from the provision, the coordination of all parties involved is crucial. This includes potential employers, the school, the rehabilitation counsellor, those making transport arrangements, volunteers, and those involved in other support services. Training schedules are used to help students develop the necessary skills for employability and employment. Educators may make a task analysis of the main activities such as cleaning procedures or packing skills the student will have to carry out. Such training helps students develop choices about what they would like to do. It also enables employers to see what a student with profound cognitive impairment, perhaps with co-worker support, is able to do.

Education supports suitable for students with cognitive impairment and aged 18 to 21 have been outlined (Wehmeyer *et al.*, 2002). They include providing an age appropriate setting allowing social contact and encouraging participation in the community.

Colleges may offer opportunities in community-based vocational instruction. For example, Catawba College, North Carolina (www.catawba.edu) offers students from a local high school's 'Basic Education Students in Transition' programme the opportunity to help the Office of Waste Disposal and Recycling with recycling projects one morning a week. The aim is to enable students with disabilities to sample various jobs in the community, evaluate themselves with regard to work habits and job interests and gain skills that will help them become employed in the community.

References

McDonnell, J., Hardman, M. L., Hightower, J., Keifer-O'Donnell and Drew, C. (1993) 'Impact of community based instruction on the development of adaptive behaviour of secondary level students with mental retardation', *American Journal on Mental Retardation* 97, 5, 575–584.

Wehmeyer, M. L., Sands, D. J., Knowlton, E. and Kozleski, E. B. (2002) *Teaching Students with Mental Retardation: Providing Access to the General Curriculum*, Baltimore, MD, Brookes.

Computer technology

Except where computer skills are being explicitly taught, it is important to remember that computer technology is a learning tool, not an end in itself. The teacher will keep a check on the extent to which computer technology genuinely enhances learning and participation for particular pupils.

Computer technology has a very wide range of applications for pupils with disabilities/disorders, as a few examples should indicate. A pupil with a health impairment being educated in hospital may be reluctant to move from the ward to the classroom following an operation. Videoconferencing facilities can therefore enable him to communicate with staff and pupils and have some experience of the classroom environment. Hospital schools have developed 'virtual classrooms' to increase the opportunities for a pupil to interact with other pupils and allow collaborative work. Internet projects in hospital can help pupils maintain contact with what is happening elsewhere and obtain materials to support their coursework (Department for Education and Skills, 2001, p. 37).

For pupils with orthopaedic impairment, computerised architectural simulations of a school building have been used for pupils in wheelchairs. These can help the pupil 'experience' the layout of a school and plan and practice routes through the building before trying them out in reality. Pupils having physical difficulties with writing may use predictive software to reduce the time spent on the mechanics of word processing. For homework or other independent work, speech to text software may be used.

Regarding reading disorder, computer software that supports reading is employed. For a pupil who is unable to independently read his textbooks, text to speech software can help. This enables him to listen to information 'read' by the computer. Other aids include ReadPlease (www.readplease.com), Kurzweil 3000 (www.kurzweiledu.com) and Read and Write Gold (www.texthelp.com). Materials such as printed lessons and computer activities associated with particular programmes may be used. Printed or computer displayed symbols may be employed. The pupil may experience organisational difficulties. These may be concurrent with reading disorder or may be related to problems with memory. Technological reminders can help, such as web-based reminder services or e-mail messages.

For pupils with disorder of written expression computer software can help with essay structure. Where graphical symbols are used the relevant resources are required. The teacher can vary the extent essay writing is structured and the degree of prompting according to the individual pupil. Should a pupil experience mathematics disorder, computational difficulties can be compensated for by using web-based support such as WebMath (www. webmath.com) (see also Edyburn, 2002, pp. 23–25).

Where a child has very severe communication difficulties of which speech difficulties are an aspect, dedicated communication devices may be used. Communication systems may consist of a computer with input options, communication software, and a speech synthesiser. The system may speak programmed messages when the pupil activates locations marked by symbols. Symbols may also be used as a form of communication using electronic or non-electronic devices. Among commercially available symbols sets are Widget Literacy symbols (www.widget.com) and Blissymbols (www. blissymbolics.us).

References

Department for Education and Skills (2001) *Access to Education for Children and Young People with Medical Needs*, London, DfES.

Edyburn, D. L. (2002) 'Remediation vs. compensation: A critical decision point in assistive technology consideration' (Essay) www.connsensebulletin.com/edyburnv4n3.html.

Further reading

Farrell, M. (2009) *Foundations of Special Education*, New York and London, Wiley, 'Technological' chapter.

Hardy, C. (2000) *Information and Communications Technology for All*, London, David Fulton Publishers.

Addresses

British Educational Communications Technology Agency
   www.becta.org.uk
   Aims to develop and promote the use of information and communications technology in education and training, and produces publications including ones relating to special education.

Centre for Technology in Education
   www.cte.jhu.edu
   The Centre for Technology in Education at Johns Hopkins University aims to improve the quality of life of children and young people especially those

with special needs, through teaching, research and leadership in the use of technology.

Concrete learning and mild cognitive impairment

Providing and extending concrete learning is emphasised with pupils having mild cognitive impairment.

Piaget and Inhelder (1966/1969) sought to identify typical ways in which children respond that are associated with qualitatively different sequential stages of cognitive development. Piaget's ideas have been criticised and further developed but may still productively inform some approaches to teaching. Piaget's stages were considered to occur at approximate ages: the sensory motor stage (0–2 years); the pre-operational stage (2–7 years); the concrete operational stage (7–11 years); and the formal operational stage (11–12 years onwards). In the concrete operational stage, complex and systematic mental problem-solving using mental representations can take place in relation to concrete and actual events. In the formal operations stage, concrete operations are restructured and subordinated to new structures. This enables the child to reason hypothetically (Ibid. p. 152). The child becomes able to use the form of logical systems to create and test hypotheses about real or imagined events. For example, using a balance scale, a child will be able to work out the rule relating weight and distance from the centre of the fulcrum.

The teacher may assess that a pupil with mild cognitive impairment is working at the concrete operational level at an age when most children have developed formal operations. Extra experience of working at the concrete operations stage (concrete learning) and structured opportunities to build on this to begin to develop formal operation thinking can aid progress.

For example, a child working in a way typified by concrete operations may know that Peter is taller than Mary and Mary is taller than John. If asked who is smallest, he might work out the answer by mentally picturing Peter, then Mary, then John. He would then recognise that John was the smallest child. The teacher would provide the pupil with many examples of this kind of problem in which the pupil mentally visualises the problem to reach the solution. The pupil is encouraged to recognise that in the examples, whatever the heights of the pupils, so long as the first is taller than the second, and the second is taller than the third, the first will always be the tallest. This begins to reach into logical thinking and abstraction rather than concrete thinking. The examples are then extended further to reinforce the principle. Other examples are used to develop similar formal operations thinking, for example concerning weight, area, the order of events and so on. The distinctiveness of the pedagogy involved is in the need for learning to be structured in this way at an age when most other pupils will work in a formal operations way and in the great amount of structure and practice needed for progress to be made.

Reference

Piaget, J. and Inhelder, B. (1966/1969) *The Psychology of the Child* (translated from the French by Helen Weaver) London, Routledge and Kegan Paul.

Further reading

Morra, S., Gobbo, C., Marini, Z. and Sheese, R. (2007) *Cognitive Development: Neo-Piagetian Perspectives*, New York/Hove, Psychology Press.

Address

Jean Piaget Society
  www.piaget.org
  An international, interdisciplinary society of scholars, teachers, and researchers interested in looking at the nature of the developmental construction of human knowledge.

Conduct disorder

Conduct disorder can include aggression, destroying property, stealing, housebreaking, truanting and other infringements of other people's rights and violations of social rules. Such behaviour forms a repetitive and persistent pattern. It is commonly associated with other disorders including attention deficit hyperactivity disorder and substance abuse disorders. Conduct disorder involves the violation of the rights of others or the transgression of major age-appropriate social norms (American Psychiatric Association, 2000, p. 98 criterion A). Effective provision differs according to whether children (aged 3 to 10 years old) or adolescents (aged 10 to 17 years old) are involved. Estimates of the prevalence of conduct disorder vary considerably. In the general population, rates range from 1 per cent to 10 per cent. Suggested causes include genetic influences and that such behaviour relates to family learning. A social learning theory suggests that conduct disorder may be learned from family interactions, as a boy may model the aggressive behaviour of his father.

Children

Regarding children, parent training tends to draw on behavioural management principles drawn from social learning theory. These include role play, behavioural rehearsal and homework exercises. The 'Incredible Years Training Series' (Webster-Stratton and Reid, 2003, pp. 224–240) consists of three training curricula for parents; children aged 2 to 8 years, and teachers. It seeks to improve parents' competence, for example by encouraging them to work together, increasing positive parenting, and reducing negative parenting.

In the school-based strategy, 'Coping Power' (Lochman and Wells, 1996) children review examples of social interactions discussing social cues and motives. Particular skills as well as anger control strategies such as self-talk are practised to manage anger arousal. Social skills training and anger management coping skills training can help reduce mild conduct problems in children.

Problem-solving skills training aims to influence interpersonal cognition. It helps develop necessary interpersonal and cognitive problem-solving skills. Typically, this teaches children to recognise and alter how they think about and respond to social situations. This might involve using modelling and role play. In individual sessions the therapist examines ways in which the child usually responds to interpersonal situations. She encourages a structured approach to solving these problems, using tasks related to real life situations. Social behaviours are encouraged by modelling and direct reinforcement. Problem-solving skills training can be effective, particularly in combination with parent training. The more severe the child's dysfunction, the smaller is likely to be the effects of the treatment (Kazdin and Wasser, 2000).

One study (Barkley et al., 2000) compared many behavioural interventions, the effect of parent training and the combined treatments. Among the classroom interventions were a token system, over correction, response cost, time out, group cognitive-behavioural self control training, group anger control training, group social skills training, and support for home-based reinforcement. Although multiple behavioural interventions reduced the aggression of participants, no effects were found for parent training. Such approaches have not been shown to generalise to other settings such as the child's home or to continue beyond the end of the programme.

Adolescents

By the time young people with conduct disorder have reached adolescence, many behaviours relating to conduct disorder involve law breaking. Effective approaches include those drawing several interventions together in a multiple level package.

Functional Family Therapy (Alexander et al., 1988) sees an adolescent's difficult behaviour is serving a function such as regulating distance between family members. Consequently intervention does not just tackle the adolescent's behavioural problems and cognitive dysfunction. It also addresses family interactions aiming to change patterns of interaction and communication to encourage adaptive family functioning.

Many group homes for aggressive and delinquent adolescents in the United States of America use Teaching Family Model principles. Each home is run by a married couple with at least one year's training in the approach (Kirigin,

1996). Treatment includes academic tutoring, a reinforcement system for monitoring school behaviour, social skills training, and a multi-level points system. Though there appear to be benefits while adolescents are on the programme, the effects tended to be lost when they leave.

Equipping Youth to Help One Another brings together anger management, social skills training, moral reasoning training and problem-solving skills training in a group setting (Gibbs *et al.*, 1996). Recidivism rates have been reduced with a small sample of incarcerated male offenders aged 15 to 18 years.

In Gang Resistance Education Training, tackling gang involvement (Esbensen and Osgood, 1999), law enforcement officers taught a nine-week curriculum to middle school students. It included exercises and interactive approaches showing consequences of gang violence. Activities taught goal setting, conflict resolution and standing up to peer pressure. Participating students had lower levels of self-reported delinquency and gang membership than a comparison group.

Medication

Psychostimulants are effective in reducing antisocial behaviour in adolescents who have both attention deficit hyperactivity disorder and attention deficit disorder/conduct disorder. Combinations of psychosocial treatments and stimulant treatments appear to be more effective than either on their own. Drugs including methylphenidate (Ritalin) are used in the treatment of antisocial behaviour. Anticonvulsants have been used with impulsive behaviour but strong side effects have been reported. While traditional neuroleptics seem to reduce aggressiveness, side effects include sedation and interference with learning. Atypical antipsychotic drugs appear to reduce aggressiveness but can lead to weight gain. Summaries of evidence of the effectiveness of these drugs are available (Fonagy *et al.*, 2005, pp. 182–192). Educators need to be aware of the intended effects and the potential side effects of any medication prescribed for pupils, including the possible impact on learning and behaviour.

References

Alexander, J. F., Waldron, H. B., Newberry, A. M. and Liddle, N. (1988) 'Family approaches to treating delinquents' in Nunnally, E. W., Chilman, C. S. and Cox, F. M. (Eds) *Mental Illness, Delinquency, Addictions and Neglect*, Newbury Park, CA, Sage, 128–146.

American Psychiatric Association (2000) *Diagnostic and Statistical Manual of Mental Disorders Fourth Edition Text Revision*, Arlington, VA, APA.

Barkley, R. A., Shelton, T. L., Crosswait, C. C., Moorehouse, M., Fletcher, K., Barrett, S., Jenkins, L. and Metevia, L. (2000) 'Multi-method psychoeducational intervention for preschool children with disruptive behaviour: Preliminary results at post treatment', *Journal of Child Psychology and Psychiatry* 41, 319–332.

Esbensen, F. A. and Osgood, D. W. (1999) 'Gang resistance education and training (GREAT): Results from the national evaluation', *Journal of Research in Crime and Delinquency* 36, 194–225.

Fonagy, P., Target, M., Cottrell, D., Phillips, J. and Kurtz, Z. (2005) *What Works for Whom? A Critical Review of Treatments for Children and Adolescents*, New York, Guilford Press.

Gibbs, J. C., Potter, G. B., Barriga, A. Q. and Liau, A. K. (1996) 'Developing the helping skills and prosocial motivation of aggressive adolescents in peer group programmes', *Aggression and Violent Behaviour* 1, 283–305.

Kazdin, A. E. and Wasser, G. (2000) 'Therapeutic changes in children, parents and families resulting from treatment of children with conduct problems', *Journal of the American Academy of Child and Adolescent Psychiatry* 39, 414–420.

Kirigin, K. A. (1996) Teaching-Family model of group home treatment of children with severe behaviour problems' in Roberts, M. C. (Ed.) *Model Programs in Child and Family Mental Health*, Mahwah, NJ, Erlbaum, 231–247.

Lochman, J. E. and Wells, K. C. (1996) 'A social-cognitive intervention with aggressive children: Prevention effects and contextual implementation issues' in Peters, R. E. and McMahon, R. J. (Eds) *Preventing Childhood Disorders, Substance Abuse and Delinquency*, Thousand Oaks, CA, Sage, 111–143.

Webster-Stratton, C. and Reid, M. J. (2003) 'The Incredible Years Parents, Teachers and Children Training Series' in Kazdin, A. E. and Weisz, J. R. (Eds) *Evidence Based Psychotherapies for Children and Adolescents*, New York, Guilford Press, 224–240.

Conductive education/conductor

Conductive education is a special form of education for individuals with motor disorders such as those associated with cerebral palsy, multiple sclerosis, head injuries, Parkinson's disease and strokes. Andras Peto, founder of the Peto Institute in Budapest, developed it in Hungary. Orthofunction, that is the ability to carry out functional movements independently, is the aim of conductive education.

Conductors are specially trained staff members who provide conductive education. Two or more of these work with a small group of children throughout the day in a residential setting. The conductor teaches the child skills such as walking, feeding and grasping as well as reading and numeracy. Parents are involved from an early stage so they can take over from the conductors when the child leaves the residential setting. A review of studies (Darrah *et al.*, 2003) including less well-designed ones concluded that evidence is inconclusive for or against conductive education.

Reference

Darrah, J., Watkins, B., Chen, L. and Bonin, C. (2003) 'Effects of conductive education intervention for children with a diagnosis of cerebral palsy: an AACPDM evidence report' Rosemont, IL, USA, American Academy for Cerebral Palsy and Developmental Medicine (AACPDM), (AACPDM Evidence Report) 34.

Further reading

Cottam, P. J. and Sutton, A. (1987) *Conductive Education: A System for Overcoming Motor Disorder*, London, Routledge.

Addresses

Foundation for Conductive Education, UK
www.conductive-education.org.uk
The site includes a register of centres for conductive education worldwide.

The Peto Institute, Budapest, Romania
www.petoinstitute.org
The site includes references to other organisations and related links.

Co-occurrence of conditions

Disorder of written expression and mathematics disorder are often associated with reading disorder. It is in fact relatively unusual for either to be present in the absence of reading disorder (American Psychiatric Association, 2000, p. 52). Language deficits and perceptual motor deficits may accompany disorder of written expression (Ibid. p. 55). About half of clinic-referred children with attention deficit hyperactivity disorder also have oppositional defiant disorder or conduct disorder (Ibid. p. 88). Such co-occurrence of various disorders/disabilities is sometimes seen as a limitation on the use of categories.

Considering the co-occurrence of attention deficit hyperactivity disorder, oppositional defiant disorder and conduct disorder, this may reflect an overlapping of the characteristics of the disorders. For example, conduct disorder is sometimes associated with impulsiveness and not thinking through the implications of one's behaviour. It is also possible that some disorders have similar underlying factors and that these predispose a child to several disorders. In some instances, this might suggest that the boundaries of categories are changed. Indeed this has happened with impulsiveness disorder and hyperactivity disorder that are now usually considered under the broader category of attention deficit hyperactivity disorder. Future research in genetics, brain imaging and neuroscience may lead to a reshaping of some of the categories presently used.

Despite the challenges of delineating such disorders, much that is useful to teachers and others can be identified in research and professional practice that refers to categories. This includes practical implications for provision

(Fletcher, Shaywitz and Shaywitz, 1999). Nevertheless, it is important that the validity and reliability of categories can be tested leading to categories being even clearer and more robust. Also important is the relationship between constructs and forms of assessment, and between assessment and interventions (Larkin and Cermac, 2002, p. 90).

References

American Psychiatric Association (2000) *Diagnostic and Statistical Manual of Mental Disorders Fourth Edition Text Revision*, Arlington, VA, APA.
Fletcher, J. M., Shaywitz, S. E. and Shaywitz, B. A. (1999) 'Comorbidity of learning and attention disorders: Separate but equal', *Paediatric Clinics of North America* 46, 885–897.
Larkin, D. and Cermac, S. A. (2002) 'Issues in identification and assessment of developmental coordination disorder' in Cermak, S. A. and Larkin, D. (2002) *Developmental Coordination Disorder*, Albany, New York, Delmar Thompson Learning.

Counselling/counsellor

To the extent that a distinction is clear between psychological health and psychological ill health, counselling may be taken to refer to an interaction between a counsellor and an individual facing problems but who is essentially psychologically healthy. The problems may relate to a difficult situation such as bereavement or a move to a new area. When counselling children, a trusting relationship between the counsellor and child is important. Among the skills used are observation, listening and helping the child convey his story (Geldard and Geldard, 2002).

In the United States of America, a professional counsellor may be trained and licensed as a mental health professional. Titles vary but typically are a 'licensed professional counsellor' or a 'licensed mental health counsellor'. Training involves taking a masters degree in counselling or an equivalent qualification, gaining supervised clinical experience and passing a state licensing examination. A counsellor may use one or several approaches but may take an eclectic stance. Some counsellors specialise in working in a school context.

Reference

Geldard, K. and Geldard, D. (2002) (2nd edition) *Counselling Children: A Practical Introduction*, London, Sage.

Further reading

Egan, G. (2007) (8th edition) *The Skilled Helper: A Problem-Management and Opportunity Development Approach to Helping*, Belmont, CA, Thompson/ Brookes Cole.

Kiselica, M. S., Englar-Carlson, M. and Horne, A. M. (Eds) (2007) *Counselling Troubled Boys: A Guidebook for Professionals*, New York and London, Routledge.

Palmer, S. (2000) (Eds.) *Introduction to Counselling and Psychotherapy: The Essential Guide*, London, Sage.

Addresses

American Counselling Association
www.counselling.org
A not for profit professional and educational organisation based in the USA and concerned with the growth and enhancement of the counselling profession.

The British Association for Counselling and Psychotherapy
www.bacp.co.uk
Based in England, the Association is a professional body for counselling and psychotherapy.

Criteria for disabilities/disorders

The World Health Organisation *International Statistical Classification of Diseases and Related Health Problems 10th Revision* (www.who.int/classifications/apps/icd/icd10online/) often summarised as ICD-10 and revised in 2007 is used to classify diseases and health problems. Complementing this, the World Health Organisation *International Classification of Functioning, Disability and Health* (ICF) is a framework for measuring health and disability. Revised in 2001, it presents disability as a 'universal human experience' (www.who.int/classifications/icf/en/). The classification takes account of social aspects of disability as well as biological dysfunction. The ICF is structured around: body functions and structure; activities and participation; and additional information on severity and environmental factors. 'Activities' refers to an individual's tasks and actions. 'Participation' concerns a person's involvement in his life situation. The domains are classified from the perspectives of the body, the individual and society. The *International Classification of Functioning, Disability and Health: Children and Youth Version* or ICF-CY (World Health Organisation, 2007) covers ages birth to through 18 years. It is multidimensional, focusing on activities and participation, and allows change to be monitored through the life span.

The *Diagnostic and Statistical Manual for Mental Disorders (DSM-IV-TR)* (American Psychiatric Association, 2000) is a handbook for mental health professionals and others. It sets out categories of mental disorders and other conditions and criteria by which they are diagnosed. A draft of a new revision (*DSM-V*) is published in 2009 for comments with a new edition scheduled for 2012. The two systems, ICF and DSM, have developed along-side one another.

(See also, *International classification of functioning, disability and health for children and youth* and *diagnostic and statistical manual of mental disorders*)

References

American Psychiatric Association (2000) *Diagnostic and Statistical Manual of Mental Disorders Fourth Edition Text Revision*, Arlington, VA, APA.
World Health Organisation (2007) *International Statistical Classification of Diseases and Related Health Problems 10th Revision*, Geneva, WHO.
World Health Organisation (2001) *International Classification of Functioning, Disability and Health*, Geneva, WHO.
World Health Organisation (2007) *International Classification of Functioning, Disability and Health: Children and Youth Version*, Switzerland, Geneva, WHO.

Addresses

American Psychiatric Association
www.psych.org
Based in Virginia, USA, the American Psychiatric Association represents mental health physicians.

World Health Organisation
www.who.int
The directing and coordinating authority for health within the United Nations system.

Curriculum

The curriculum as, 'the formal and informal content and process by which learners gain knowledge and understanding, develop skills, and alter attitudes, appreciations and values under the auspices of that school' (Doll, 1996, p. 15). Another view is that it is the content of what is taught and learned including the aims and objectives of teaching and learning, and the design and structure of what is taught in relation to areas of learning and programmes within those areas (Farrell, 2008, pp. 11–12). In England, where there is a National Curriculum, a national body, the Qualifications and Curriculum Authority, is responsible for maintaining and developing school curricula and related assessments.

The curriculum may be organised by subjects such as mathematics or history or areas such as communication or personal and social education. Some aspects permeate the whole curriculum and include literacy, numeracy and problem-solving skills. These may have different designations in different countries. In the United States of America, they may be termed 'basic skills' and in England 'curriculum strands' or 'key skills'. In the curriculum there may be differences in:

- Content
- Level, and
- Balance.

Areas of learning and programmes might have a different content for pupils with different disabilities/disorders. For a pupil with a health or orthopaedic impairment, aspects of the usual content of programmes for independence might be inapplicable. He might be taught some self-care skills involving different ways of carrying out tasks, perhaps learning different dressing procedures with modified clothing and aids. A pupil with communication disorders might learn alternative ways of communicating. The learning aims of such programmes are often the same as for other children. The pupil is still learning how to communicate, but the specific content differs.

In a curriculum for pupils with disabilities/disorders, the level of the curriculum is considered in relation to what is expected for children attaining typically for their age. For pupils with mild, moderate to severe, and profound cognitive impairment, the general levels of the curriculum subjects and areas will be several years below what is age typical. For pupils with profound cognitive impairment, the curriculum may build on content associated with infant sensory and perceptual development. The level of particular curriculum subjects or areas may be lower reflecting the difficulty the child has had and the slower progress he has made in certain areas. A child with a reading disorder is likely to have made slower progress in reading than other children of the same age. The content of the reading aspects of the curriculum would therefore be lower than is age typical.

The balance of elements (subjects or areas) within overall curriculum structure may differ from what is typical. These may be emphasised so 'communication' or 'reading' has extra time devoted to it and planning ensures these elements are reinforced in other areas of the curriculum. Within particular curriculum subjects and areas there may be a distinctive difference in the balance of the programme. In a physical education programme for pupils with developmental coordination disorder, emphasis may be placed on carefully graded steps to improve coordination and develop pupils' confidence in movement.

Small steps of assessment may be used to recognise progress. This may be progress in phonics and other aspects of reading for a pupil with reading disorder or progress in basic social skills for a pupil with autism.

Turning to particular subject areas of the curriculum, provision for these may be particularly important for pupils with some disabilities/disorders. For example, literacy is a central focus for pupils with reading disorder or disorder of written expression or developmental coordination disorder (where the process of handwriting can be particularly challenging). Numeracy is similarly a focus, for example, for pupils with mathematics disorder. Personal and social development is a further focus for many children with disabilities/disorders including those with cognitive impairment, conduct disorder, and attention deficit hyperactivity disorder. Physical education has particular implications for some pupils with orthopaedic impairment, health impairment, or developmental coordination disorder.

References

Doll, R. C. (1996) (9th edition) *Curriculum Improvement: Decision Making and Process*, Needham Heights, MA, Allyn and Bacon.
Farrell, M. (2008) *Educating Special Children: An Introduction to Provision for Pupils with Disabilities and Disorders*, New York and London, Routledge.

Further reading

McLaughlin, C. and Byers, R. (2001) *Personal and Social Development for All*, London, David Fulton Publishers.
Wright, H. and Sugden, D. (1999) *Physical Education for All: Developing Physical Education in the Curriculum for Pupils with Special Educational Needs*, London, David Fulton Publishers.

Address

Qualifications and Curriculum Authority
www.qca.org.uk
The body develops and maintains school curricula and accredits and monitors school (and other) qualifications.

Dance movement therapy/dance movement therapist

Dance movement therapy has broad application for a wide range of clients from adults with dementia to children with disabilities/disorders (Payne, 2006, *passim*). In dance movement therapy, emotions can be expressed and released. Increased physical skills can improve confidence and self-esteem. Pupils with sensory impairments and orthopaedic impairments may be introduced to movements to improve their body awareness and self-image.

Dance movement therapists may come from various backgrounds such as dance, education, physiotherapy or psychology. Practitioners undergo training in dance movement therapy with supervised clinical practice.

Reference

Payne, H. (Ed.) (2006) *Dance Movement Therapy: Theory and Practice*, New York and London, Routledge.

Further reading

Meekums, B. (2002) *Dance Movement Therapy: A Creative Psychotherapeutic Approach*, Thousand Oaks, CA and London, Sage.

Addresses

American Dance Therapy Association
   www.adta.org
   This association, based in the USA, aims to maintain high standards of professional education and competence in dance/movement therapy.

Association for Dance Movement Therapy UK
   www.admt.org.uk

This UK-based association oversees a professional code of conduct and promotes dance movement therapy in the community.

Dance Movement Association of Australia
www.dtaa.org
The association is the professional body for practitioners in Australia.

Deafblindness

The nature of deafblindness

Deafblindness (multisensory impairment) is defined in different ways. This is associated with a range of possible interventions that may work for pupils within one definition but not another. For example, some aspects of provision associated with deafblindness relate to children who are congenitally deafblind and without other disabilities.

The United Kingdom body, the Qualifications and Curriculum Authority (1999, p. 7) states: 'Pupils who are deafblind have both visual and hearing impairments that are not fully corrected by spectacles or hearing aids. They may not be completely deaf and blind. But the combination of these two disabilities on a pupil's ability to learn is greater than the sum of its parts.' In the United States of America, the *Individuals with Disabilities Act 1997* (section 330.7 (c) (2)) indicates, '"Deaf-blind" means concomitant visual and hearing impairments, the combination of which causes such severe communication and other developmental and educational problems that they cannot be accommodated in special education programmes solely for deaf or blind children.'

A child who is deafblind has interrelated difficulties in finding out information, communicating with others, and in moving around the environment (Aitken *et al.*, 2000, pp. 3–4). Common patterns may be discernable depending on whether hearing impairment, or visual impairment or both are congenital/early onset or have a later onset. The child may or may not have other difficulties or disabilities such as cognitive impairment, physical or motor difficulties.

In the United States of America it is estimated that about 0.01 per cent of the school population is deafblind. Causes of deafblindness include infections, genetic or chromosomal syndromes, and birth trauma.

Provision

The curriculum for pupils who are deafblind will include support such as the use, as necessary, of manual signing or reading through a tactile medium. The curriculum may draw on developmental models, especially models of early communication and takes account of the importance of the environment and communication partners. It is important for the child to have opportunities for free play and self-occupation between adult-led tasks (Pease, 2000, pp. 83–118).

Among approaches to develop communication are co-creative communication and resonance work. These enable the adult to encourage and develop the child's competence and sense of being in control of things. *Co-creative communication* emphasises a 'symmetrical' relationship between the child and the communication partner (Nafstad and Rodbrøe, 1999). *Resonance work* (van Dijk, 1989) tends to be an initial form of encouragement of communication in which an adult reflects back to the child the child's movements or vocalisation to encourage the child's awareness of himself. In other words, the adult resonates the child's actions and vocalisations, continuing when the child continues and stopping when he stops.

Improving the child's mobility begins with the adult developing the child's trust, and building his confidence and motivation to move. For deafblind children with additional difficulties, mobility is more difficult and any aspect of the environment that can help is used. A tactile environment helps a child who is deafblind explore and build up a mental map of each space. Strips of carpet, textured surfaces and handrails can be used to mark out different spaces and levels. It is helpful if routes through a room or building are obstacle free, furniture is kept in the same position, and tactile clues are added to objects such as specific lockers. Tactile pictures can be used as wall clues.

The teacher will provide information to encourage the deafblind pupil to exercise choice, for example deciding on an item of clothing according to texture. Also important are 'structured opportunities' to interact with people, the environment, objects, places and activities (Aitken, 2000, p. 23). Part of this involves building routines to encourage anticipation and help the pupil begin to make sense of a sequence of events.

A very wide range of professionals are likely to be involved with children who are deafblind and their parents. Given that some of the individual professionals with whom the child and parent have contact may move on, the number of people involved is daunting. The school will need to collate information and advice from these many sources to determine what will enable the child to learn and develop best.

References

Aitken, S. (2000) 'Understanding deafblindness' in Aitken, S., Buultjens, M., Clark, C., Eyre, J. T. and Pease, L. (Eds) (See further reading).

Nafstad, A. and Rodbrøe, I. (1999) *Co-creating Communication*, Oslo, Forlaget-Nord Press.

National Institute of Clinical Excellence (2000) *Guidance on the Use of Methylphenidate for ADHD*, London, NICE.

Pease, L. (2000) 'Creating a communicating environment' in Aitken, S., Buultjens, M., Clark, C., Eyre, J. T. and Pease, L. (Eds) (See further reading).

Qualifications and Curriculum Authority (1999) *Shared World – Different Experiences: Designing the Curriculum for Pupils who are Deafblind*, London, QCA.

van Dijk, J. (1989) 'The Sint-Michielsgestel approach to diagnosis and education of multisensory impaired persons' in Best, A. B. (Ed.) *Sensory Impairment with Multi Handicap: Current Philosophies and New Approaches*, A European Conference, Warwick University, 6–11 August 1989: Papers on the Education of the Deafblind, International Association for the Education of the Deafblind.

Further reading

Aitken, S., Buultjens, M., Clark, C., Eyre, J. T. and Pease, L. (Eds) (2000) *Teaching Children who are Deafblind: Contact, Communication and Learning*, London, David Fulton Publishers.

Smith, M. and Levack, N. (1997) *Teaching Students with Visual and Multiple Impairments: A Resource Guide*, Texas, Texas School for the Blind and Visually Impaired (www.tsbvi.edu).

Addresses

Deafblind International, New Delhi, India
www.deafblindinternational.org
A world association promoting services for deafblind people.

Sense
www.sense.org.uk
A voluntary association in the UK providing advice, information and specialist services for people of all ages who are deafblind, their families, carers and professionals working with them.

USA Organisations for Deafblind People
www.deafblind.com/usa
A list of organisations relating to deafblindness.

Dentistry/dentist

A dentist providing dental care to children and young people with disabilities/disorders may need to be aware of particular issues. The treatment of children and adolescents with cognitive impairment, emotional disorders and other disabilities forms part of the study of paediatric dentistry (Koch and Poulson, 2001).

Dental hygiene is particularly important for some individuals with cognitive impairment especially with profound cognitive impairment. The child may not understand the purpose of dental hygiene. When treatment is necessary, he may not understand what is happening or why. Some conditions are associated with teeth abnormalities. For example, in Down syndrome, teeth develop late, may be abnormal in shape and size and may not be in alignment. Teeth grinding may be associated with cognitive impairment and if not controlled, leads to excessive wear on the protective enamel covering the teeth.

Reference

Koch, G. and Poulson, G. (2001) *Paediatric Dentistry: A Clinical Approach*, London and New York, Blackwell.

Depressive disorders

The nature of depressive disorders

A distinction is made between major depressive disorder and dysthymic disorder. In major depressive disorder, the individual experiences one or more major depressive episodes; and the depressed mood is evident for most of the day, almost every day for at least two weeks. The disorder may be mild, moderate or severe (American Psychiatric Association, 2000, p. 369). Dysthymic disorder involves less severe symptoms. The child or adolescent may be irritable rather than depressed and this lasts for a minimum of a year (Ibid. p. 377). In children dysthymic disorder may be associated with other conditions including attention deficit hyperactivity disorder, anxiety disorders, and conduct disorder. Equal numbers of boys and girls are affected and school performance and social interaction are often impaired (Ibid. p. 378). While depressed two or more of other features are present including: poor appetite or over eating, low energy or fatigue, low self-esteem, and poor concentration (Ibid. p. 380).

In children, depression is comparatively rare tending to be expressed through anxiety, frustration or somatic complaints. Adolescents tend to show more biological complaints and thoughts of suicide or actual suicidal behaviour. Prevalence is around 2 per cent for children and 2 to 5 per cent for adolescents for both depression and dysthymia (Lewinsohn and Clarke, 1999). In children, depressive disorders are equally distributed among boys and girls. After the age of 14 years, girls predominate over boys by a ratio of 2 to 1. There may be an hereditary element to depression (American Psychiatric Association, 2000, pp. 373, 379).

Provision

For children with depressive disorder, open communication can be encouraged in personal and social education sessions, discussions, art, drama, dance and play. As well as the school developing a listening ethos, staff may be specifically trained to listen and respond helpfully through counselling. Group work can offer supportive opportunities to share problems and experiences. The role of the facilitator is crucial. The school establishes the consent of parents and pupils (Geldard and Geldard, 2001).

In educating children with depressive disorders (and also for pupils with anxiety disorders), the teacher and the school will be aware of and supportive of any psychotherapy the child may be receiving. A training coordinator may ensure that members of staff have the knowledge and skills to provide well for pupils with depressive disorders. In less formal times such as recess and lunchtimes, staff may require special awareness training. Where teachers or others are specially trained, they may contribute to psychotherapeutic interventions.

Cognitive behavioural therapy (CBT) appears effective for treating adolescents with mild or moderate depression. Where treatment of the usual duration appears ineffective, a longer course of CBT or booster sessions may reduce relapse and improve recovery (Clarke *et al.*, 1999).

In a series of studies comparing CBT and some other approaches, for adolescents CBT showed the greatest improvement particularly for those also experiencing anxiety. Where the mother was clinically depressed, the treatment outcome for the adolescent was worse, suggesting that maternal depression be concurrently treated (Brent *et al.*, 1998).

The 'Primary and secondary control enhancement training for youth depression' programme is used for treating depressed individuals aged 8 to 15 years, drawing on the cognitive-behavioural tradition (Weisz *et. al.*, 2003, pp. 165–183). It distinguishes between primary and secondary control. In 'primary control' coping involves making objective conditions conform to one's wishes. These conditions might be activities in which the individual participates and his acceptance by others. Secondary control concerns efforts to cope by adjusting oneself to fit conditions including adjusting one's beliefs, expectations and interpretations of events.

Interpersonal Psychotherapy Adapted for Adolescents (IPT-A) concentrating on certain interpersonal problems that may underlie the depression appears a promising treatment for adolescent depression (Mufson *et al.*, 1999).

Regarding medication, the most promising appear to be selective serotonin reuptake inhibitors and are associated with fewer side effects than alternative medication.

References

American Psychiatric Association (2000) *Diagnostic and Statistical Manual of Mental Disorders Fourth Edition Text Revision*, Arlington, VA, APA.

Brent, D. A., Kolko, D., Birmaher, B., Baugher, M., Bridge, J., Roth, C. and Holder,

D. (1998) 'Predictors of treatment efficacy in a clinical trial of three psychosocial treatments for adolescent depression', *Journal of the American Academy for Child and Adolescent Psychiatry* 37, 906–914.

Clarke, G. N., Rohde, P., Lewinsohn, P. M., Hops, H. and Seeley, J. R. (1999) 'Cognitive-behavioural treatment of adolescent depression: Efficacy of acute group treatment and booster sessions', *Journal of the American Academy for Child and Adolescent Psychiatry* 38, 272–279.

Geldard, K. and Geldard, D. (2001) *Working with Children in Groups*, Basingstoke, Palgrave.

Lewinsohn, P. M. and Clarke, G. N. (1999) 'Psychosocial treatments for adolescent depression', *Clinical Psychology Review* 19, 329–342.

Mufson, L., Weisman, M. M., Moreau, D. and Garfinkel, R. (1999) 'Efficacy of inter-personal psychotherapy for depressed adolescents', *Archives of General Psychiatry* 56, 573–579.

Weisz, J. R., Southam-Gerow, M. A., Gordis, E. B. and Connor-Smith, J. (2003) 'Primary and secondary control enhancement training for youth depression: Applying the deployment-focused model of treatment development and testing' in Kazdin, A. E. and Weisz, T. R. (Eds) (2003) *Evidence Based Psychotherapies for Children and Adolescents*, New York, Guilford Press, 165–183.

Further reading

Abela, J. R. Z. and Hankin, B. L. (2008) *Handbook of Depression in Children and Adolescents*, New York, Guilford Press.

Developmental coordination disorder

Developmental coordination disorder

There is debate about the definition of developmental coordination disorder and related matters. These include possible subtypes of the condition. Another issue is how developmental coordination disorder should be understood in the context of conditions such as reading disability, specific language disabilities and attention deficit hyperactivity disorder. Developmental coordination disorder is considered a 'marked impairment of motor coordination', which 'significantly interferes with academic achievement or activities of daily living' and is 'not due to a general medical condition' (American Psychiatric Association, 2000, pp. 56–57). It is not associated with any medically evident neurological signs. Where the term 'dyspraxia' (from the Greek, 'difficulty in doing') continues to be used, definitions tend to focus on the planning and organisation of movement. Dyspraxia is sometimes seen as a subtype of developmental coordination disorder (Dixon and Addy, 2004, p. 9).

Characteristics of the motor performance of children with developmental coordination disorder include: slower movement time, and inconsistency in some aspects of motor performance in relation to other skilled movement. The child also relies more on visual information than on proprioceptive information (relating to an understanding of the position of one's limbs and other aspects of body awareness). Children tend to show difficulties with gross and fine motor skills in terms of both speed and accuracy. They have problems with sequencing movements. It is important that teachers and others note the amount of effort and time it takes a child to perform a task, as well as whether or not he can perform it (Cermak and Larkin, 2002).

Estimates of developmental coordination disorder vary considerably from 6 to 22 per cent possibly depending on the methods of assessment and the experience of the assessor. The causes of the disorder are many, involving genetic predisposition, brain structure, prenatal influences and post-natal effects.

Provision

Particular care is taken with the curriculum in areas where motor coordination is central. These include handwriting, physical education, art and geometry; subjects where tools are used; and laboratory work. The assessment of motor development may be finely graded to monitor small steps of progress.

Suitable pedagogy includes task analysis, identifying tasks that are difficult for the child and breaking them into smaller steps so that they may be easier to teach and learn. These are taught in contexts where they are useful. The activity may be adapted and/or equipment used to enable activities to be accomplished.

In acquiring handwriting skills a child with developmental coordination disorder faces difficulty learning the motor plan or programme of the letters owing to problems in motor planning or spatial orientation. Interventions include ensuring the child has a good writing posture (Benbow, 2002, p. 271). To improve his grip on a writing implement, the pupil may use a three-cornered pencil grip or a pen with a rubber finger grip. The pressure of the pencil on paper may be too light or too heavy because of proprioceptive difficulties. To help with this, physical tasks can be used to temporarily boost limb awareness (Addy, 2004).

For a child with developmental coordination disorder, physical activities pose a challenge. In the United States of America, 'adapted physical education' (APE) is an individualised programme provided by specialist APE teachers (Gabbard, LeBlanc and Lowry, 1994). The classroom teacher and the APE teacher jointly develop and teach programmes of physical education as well as leisure and recreation.

The child can become frustrated and demoralised because of the persistent difficulties he faces that may not always be understood by others. At mealtimes, younger pupils with developmental coordination disorder may have difficulty co-ordinating a knife and fork. They may spill liquids and may take a long time to finish eating a meal. In preparing a meal, activities such as using a can opener and spreading butter on bread may be problematic so a wall can-opener and cutlery with thick rubber handles may be used. Some social skills can be taught by rewarding behaviours that approach what is desired. Also, using social learning techniques, the adult can model appropriate behaviour followed by the pupil engaging in role play to practise the skill.

The teacher's organisation of the classroom can help the child by ensuring relatively free movement around the room without unnecessary clutter. The child may sit near to the classroom entry door to avoid a long walk to his seat perhaps bumping into other children and objects. If the classroom is large enough, the teacher can permanently lay out different furniture arrangements for different activities such as group work. The child with developmental coordination disorder thus avoids having to constantly adapt as furniture is moved for different activities. Failing this, the furniture positions can be marked on the classroom so positions are predictable and consistent.

One approach, CO-OP (Polatajko *et al.*, 2001) involves an occupational therapist working closely with the parents and the child. It aims to help children discover the particular cognitive strategies that will improve their ability to carry out everyday tasks. The therapist teaches the child a 'Goal–Plan–Do–Check' strategy to act as a framework for solving motor-based performance problems. The therapist then guides the child to discover strategies to enable the activity to be performed. CO-OP appears promising in promoting skill acquisition and transfer in children with developmental coordination disorder aged 7 to 12 years.

References

Addy, L. M. (2004) *Speed Up! A Kinaesthetic Approach to Handwriting*, Cambridge, LDA.
American Psychiatric Association (2000) *Diagnostic and Statistical Manual of Mental Disorders Fourth Edition Text Revision*, Arlington, VA, APA.
Benbow, M. (2002) 'Hand skills and handwriting' in Cermak, S. A. and Larkin, D. (2002) *Developmental Coordination Disorder*, Albany, NY, Delmar Thompson Learning, 248–279.
Cermak, S. A. and Larkin, D. (2002) *Developmental Coordination Disorder*, Albany, NY, Delmar Thompson Learning.
Dixon, G. and Addy, L. M. (2004) *Making Inclusion Work for Children with Dyspraxia: Practical Strategies for Teachers*, London, Routledge-Falmer.
Gabbard, C., LeBlanc, B. and Lowry, S. (1994) (2nd edition) *Physical Education for Children: Building the Foundation*, Upper Saddle River NJ, Prentice-Hall.
Polatajko, H. J., Mandich, A. D., Miller, L. T. and Macnab, J. J. (2001) 'Cognitive orientation to daily occupational performance (CO-OP): Part II – The evidence', *Physical and Occupational Therapy in Paediatrics* 20, 2/3, 83–106.

Further reading

Sugden, D. and Chambers, M. (2005) *Children with Developmental Coordination Disorder*, London, Wiley.

Addresses

Dyspraxia Foundation, 90
  www.dyspraxiafoundation.org
  Aims to support individuals and families affected by dyspraxia and provide information on this condition.

Dyspraxia USA
  www.dyspraxiausa.org
  Provides information and resources for dyspraxia.

Developmental delay

Children may develop more slowly than is typical for their age in various areas including cognitive and motor development. Where a child appears to be developing very slowly the teacher will discuss her observations with parents and with other colleagues. Where further exploration appears advisable, development can be assessed using developmental schedules and other structured assessments. So long as they are used judiciously, these allow comparisons to be made with statistically normal levels of development at a specified age in areas such as motor, social, language and emotional development.

Schedules are norm referenced, that is they allow comparisons of a particular child's score or level to be compared within a range of scores expected when children are developing typically. Consequently, not all differences below the norm are indications of difficulty, the size of the difference being important. Delay may be indicated in one area such as motor development, and not in others. Or the delay may be general across several areas.

Indicators of progress are often expressed as 'milestones', which a child developing typically is expected to reach within a certain age range. A variety of milestones have been identified (e.g. Berk, 2006) including gross motor development in early and middle childhood (Ibid. p. 175); the development of touch, taste, smell, balance and hearing (Ibid. p. 153); visual development in infancy (Ibid. p. 161); cognitive attainments (Ibid. pp. 230, 242, 246); language development (Ibid. p. 388); and emotional development (Ibid. p. 411).

There is sometimes an assumption that children developing age typically and children with disabilities/disorders progress in the same way. However, some children with disorders and disabilities progress differently as well as more slowly. This is captured, for example, in the notion of language delay and language disorder. Another issue is that delay in one area can affect development in another. Delayed motor development can affect the ability to handle objects and explore the immediate environment, in turn affecting the child's cognitive development.

Reference

Berk, L. E. (2006) (7th edition) *Child Development*, London, Pearson (Pearson International Edition).

Further reading

Lewis, V. (2003) (2nd edition) *Development and Disability*, Malden, MA/Oxford, UK, Blackwell.

Diagnostic and statistical manual of mental disorders

The *Diagnostic and Statistical Manual of Mental Disorders (DSM-IV-TR)* (American Psychiatric Association, 2000) is the fourth edition, text revision of a manual used to categorise various disorders. Clinicians and researchers use it. The manual takes the view that, 'The need for classification of mental disorders has been clear throughout the history of medicine' while recognising there has been little agreement on which disorders should be included or the best way they should be organised (Ibid. p. xxiv). *DSM-IV-TR* is a categorical classification dividing mental disorders into types based on 'criteria sets with defining features' (Ibid. p. xxxi). There is no assumption that each category of mental disorder is a completely distinct entity separated from other mental disorders or from no mental disorder by some absolute divide.

The classification includes 'Disorders usually first diagnosed in infancy, childhood or adolescence'. These include the following, although the examples given are not exhaustive:

- Mental retardation (mild, moderate, severe or profound)
- Learning disorders (reading disorder, mathematics disorder, disorder of written expression); developmental coordination disorder
- Communication disorders (expressive language disorder, mixed receptive-expressive language disorder, phonological disorder, stuttering)
- Pervasive developmental disorders (autistic disorder, Rett's disorder, childhood disintegrative disorder, Asperger's disorder)
- Attention deficit and disruptive behaviour disorders (attention deficit hyperactivity disorder, conduct disorder, oppositional defiant disorder, disruptive behaviour disorder)
- Feeding and eating disorders of infancy and early childhood (pica, rumination disorder)

- Tic disorders (Tourette's disorder, chronic motor or vocal tic disorder, transient tic disorder)
- Elimination disorders (encopresis, enuresis)
- Other disorders (separation anxiety disorder, selective mutism, reactive attachment disorder of infancy and early childhood, stereotypic movement disorder).

There are sections on 'mood disorders' (including depressive disorders); and 'anxiety disorders' (including panic disorder, specific phobia, social phobia, obsessive-compulsive disorder and generalised anxiety disorder). A multi-axial system allows assessment on several axes. Each of these refers to a different domain of information aimed at helping the clinician to plan treatments and predict the outcome. The axes are:

I   Clinical disorders, other conditions that may be the focus of clinical attention
II Personality disorders, mental retardation
III General medical conditions
IV Psychosocial and environmental problems
V   Global assessment of functioning.

(American Psychiatric Association, 2000, p. 27)

It will be seen that many of the disorders listed above are referred to in the present Handbook. In many entries, the criteria used in the *DSM-IV-TR* are mentioned. For example, the entry on attention deficit hyperactivity disorder refers to *DSM-IV-TR* (Ibid. pp. 85–93) and the criteria used to determine the condition.

Criticisms of essentially categorical and non-dimensional categorisations such as *DSM-IV-TR* include that the labels it uses can be stigmatising, especially if the label for the condition is transferred to a label for the child. The categorisation may be unhelpful to multi-professional working because it focuses on condition rather than for example, functioning. On the other hand, categorical labels can also be argued to convey useful information about the causation of a condition, its likely outcomes and course and may have implications for provision including curriculum, pedagogy, resources, classroom organisation and therapy (Farrell, 2008, *passim*).

(See also, *International classification of functioning, disability and health for children and youth*)

References

American Psychiatric Association (2000) *Diagnostic and Statistical Manual of Mental Disorders Fourth Edition Text Revision*, Arlington, VA, APA.

Farrell, M. (2008) *Educating Special Children: An Introduction to Provision for Pupils with Disabilities and Disorders*, New York and London, Routledge.

Address

American Psychiatric Association
  www.psych.org
  Based in Virginia, USA, the American Psychiatric Association represents mental health physicians.

Diet/dietician

A dietician has expertise in food and nutrition and helps promote good health through encouraging and advising about healthy eating. Diet is sometimes associated with disabilities/disorders.

Phenylketonuria is a condition caused by the deficiency of an enzyme, phenylalanine hydroxylase, which can lead to severe cognitive impairment. The individual does not convert phenylalanine into the amino acid tyrosine. Instead, phenylalanine takes alternative metabolic pathways creating toxins that damage the brain. Tests indicate the presence of phenylketonuria and the infant is given a diet low in phenylalanine, often until reaching the teenage years.

For individuals with severe epilepsy that does not respond to anticonvulsant drugs, ketogenic diets have been followed. These involve reducing the intake of protein and carbohydrates and providing 80 per cent of the individual's calorie intake through fats.

The Feingold diet has been tried in an attempt to reduce hyperactivity. Based on the belief that hyperactivity can be caused by food allergy, the diet excludes such ingredients as synthetic colours and flavours.

Further reading

Butriss, J., Wynne, A. and Stanner, S. (2001) *Nutrition: A Handbook for Community Nurses*, London, Whurr.

Addresses

American Dietetic Association
  www.eatright.org
  An organisation for food and nutrition professionals.

British Dietetic Association
  www.bda.uk.com

Professional organisation and trade union for state registered dieticians worldwide.

Difficulty

The term 'difficulty' is used in special education with its usual everyday meaning. In England, classification (Department for Education and Skills, 2005, *passim*) includes, 'learning difficulty (moderate, severe, profound)', 'behavioural, emotional and social difficulty', and 'specific learning difficulties'. Learning difficulty corresponds to 'mental retardation' or 'cognitive impairment' in the United States of America. 'Behavioural, emotional and social difficulties' include anxiety disorders, depressive disorders, and disorders of conduct. Specific learning difficulties include dyslexia/reading disorder, dyscalculia/mathematics disorder, and dyspraxia/developmental coordination disorder.

Reference

Department for Education and Skills (2005) (2nd edition) *Data Collection by Special Educational Need*, London, DfES.

Disability

Disability has different meanings in different contexts and in different countries. In the United States of America, pupils considered to require special education covered by federal law have a defined 'disability' having an adverse educational impact. Categories of disability under federal law are indicated in 'designated disability codes' and include mental retardation, speech and language impaired, autism and others.

In England, a disability is understood under the remit of the Education Act 1996 312(2) and (3) as described in a *Code of Practice* (Department for Education and Skills, 2001). One of the definitions under this Act is of 'learning difficulty' in terms of a 'disability' that either prevents or hinders a child from making use of local educational facilities normally provided. In this context a disability is distinguished from a 'difficulty in learning'.

'Disability' is used in a very broad sense to include disabilities/disorders in the United States of America, the United Kingdom and other countries in a social model of disability. It is argued that a distinction may be made between 'impairment' and 'disability'. An impairment is seen as a physical manifestation and a 'disability' is regarded as the response of society to the impairment. The impairment might be in this scenario a limb paralysis that leads to an individual using a wheelchair. The disability might be the difficulties caused if there was poor wheelchair access to various venues and if others had a negative view of the individual using the wheelchair. Social attitudes are also potentially disabling in this view. The focus therefore is on the removal of 'barriers' and on perceived rights. Various problems have been identified with the social model of disability. For example, if disability were about social arrangements and not physical or cognitive impairments, efforts to ease or cure medical problems may seem to be 'misguided responses to the true problem of disability, and distractions from the work of barrier removal and civil rights' (Shakespeare, 2006, pp. 31–32). This might not be unmitigatedly good news for people who have a medical problem.

In a more restricted sense 'disability' may be used to refer to physical disabilities such as orthopaedic impairments. In medical terminology a disability is 'an incapacity or lack of ability to function normally' (Anderson, 2007, p. 533). It may be mental or physical or both.

(See also, *Learning difficulty* and *classification of disabilities/disorders*)

References

Anderson, D. M. (Chief lexicographer) (2007) (31st edition) *Dorland's Illustrated Medical Dictionary*, Philadelphia, PA, Elsevier/Saunders.
Department for Education and Skills (2001) *Special Educational Needs Code of Practice*, London, DfES.
Shakespeare, T. (2006) *Disability Rights and Wrongs*, New York and London, Routledge.

Further reading

Burke, P. (2008) *Disability and Impairment*, London, Jessica Kingsley.
Brown, I. and Percy, M. (Eds) (2007) *A Comprehensive Guide to Intellectual and Developmental Disabilities*, Baltimore, MD, Brookes.

Address

Office for Disability Issues
www.officefordisability.org.uk
The Office based in London, works across government to improve equality for disabled people.

Discrete trial teaching

Discrete trial teaching, sometimes called discrete trial training, is a structured and therapist-led intervention used with children having autism (Committee on Educational Interventions for Children with Autism, 2001). Behaviourally oriented, it involves the therapist breaking behaviour into small parts, making sure one sub-skill is learned before progressing to another, shaping required behaviours until the child has securely learned them, and gradually reducing prompts that are used to encourage the behaviours required.

Components of the method are: presentation, response, consequence and pause. The adult presents a stimulus such as an instruction which cues the child to carry out a particular action. The child responds as a result of the cue. A consequence such as a reward follows the child's response. There is then a short pause before the next prompt.

The method can be used flexibly. It can form part of another approach as in the Lovaas programme (Lovaas, 1987) or may be used widely and informally. The content of what is taught through discrete trial teaching can vary.

References

Committee on Educational Interventions for Children with Autism (2001) *Educating Children with Autism*, Washington, DC, National Academy Press.
Lovaas, O. I. (1987) 'Behavioural treatment and normal intellectual and educational functioning in autistic children', *Journal of Consulting and Clinical Psychology 55*, 3–9.

Disorder

Medically, a disorder is defined as, 'a derangement or abnormality of function' (Anderson, 2007, p. 555). It is also defined as a 'morbid physical or mental state'. In the United States of America, within the category of 'specific learning disability' is included, 'disorder of written expression', 'reading disorder' and 'mathematics disorder'. In England, classifications include 'autistic spectrum disorder' (Department for Education and Skills, 2005, *passim*). Language disorders is a widely used term (e.g. Schwartz, 2008). More generally, the expression, 'disabilities/disorders' is used to refer to the range of difficulties that may require special education.

References

Anderson, D. M. (Chief lexicographer) (2007) (31st edition) *Dorland's Illustrated Medical Dictionary*, Philadelphia, PA, Elsevier/Saunders.
Department for Education and Skills (2005) (2nd edition) *Data Collection by Special Educational Need*, London, DfES.
Schwartz, R. G. (2008) *Handbook of Child Language Disorders*, New York, Psychology Press.

Further reading

Farrell, M. (2008) *Educating Special Children: An Introduction to Provision for Children with Disabilities and Disorders*, New York and London, Routledge.

Disorder of written expression

In disorder of written expression an individual's writing skills are substantially below age expectations, measured intelligence and 'age appropriate education'. The writing skills are measured by individually administered standardised tests of these skills or through functional assessment. The disorder hinders academic achievement or daily living activities that require the composition of written texts. There may be errors in grammar and punctuation in written sentences, poor paragraph organisation, many spelling errors, and poor handwriting. However, problems with spelling and handwriting alone do not constitute disorder of written expression (American Psychiatric Association, 2000, pp. 54–56). Interventions include those relating to writing composition and spelling.

Writing composition

To help a child's writing composition, the teacher can create an environment that supports developing self-regulation. Pupils can be encouraged to share their writing with others; and the teacher can ensure there are classroom routines where planning and revising are expected and reinforced (Graham and Harris, 1997). Also, writing for a particular purpose can aid motivation and provide an incentive for the child to produce good quality work. As well as being motivational, writing for a purpose requires the pupil to consider the requirements of different audiences.

Supporting frameworks for writing can help the pupil in several ways. They can get the pupil started, give a sense of direction to the task and improve confidence. The teacher can build up with the pupil an understanding of the processes of developing ideas for writing, composing and editing. In generating ideas for a fictional story, the teacher might suggest framework questions such as, 'Who is in the story?' 'Where does it happen?' 'What happens, first, next, finally?' The pupil gradually assumes increased responsibility for generating ideas.

Software packages can help users develop and organise ideas, sometimes using diagrams. This allows ideas to be arranged, which can help to structure an essay. Templates can be used for different subjects. If a pupil is doing a piece of extended writing, the educator can explicitly teach the necessary presentation skills. Word processing packages can help planning, composition, checking and correcting, and publishing. Talking word processors allow users to hear sentences as they are being typed, reassuring the pupil that what they are writing makes sense. If not, the pupil is able to go back and check accuracy.

Spelling

Simply looking at a word is rarely enough for most learners to be able to learn how to spell it. The contribution of kinaesthetic, speech motor and auditory senses are necessary. In the early stages of learning to spell phonemic aware-ness is important (Torgesen and Mathes, 2000). This enables the different sound units of the word to be linked to the graphic representation. Multisensory work for writing and spelling draws on speech-motor, kinaes-thetic, visual and auditory memory.

In the Directed Spelling Thinking Activity (DSTA) (Graham, Harris and Loynachan, 2000), pupils study words, being helped to contrast, compare and categorise two or more words according to their finding similarities and difference in them. The aim is to raise awareness of spelling patterns and more complex principles relating sounds to written forms.

Targets for improving spelling include high frequency core words, personal words, and patterns words illustrating a spelling principle. The pupil might prepare with the teacher's support, a list of personal words he is likely to use often in the week in various contexts. In consultation with subject specialist teachers, older students might list groups of words often needed in the subjects.

References

American Psychiatric Association (2000) *Diagnostic and Statistical Manual of Mental Disorders Fourth Edition Text Revision (DSM-IV-TR)*, Arlington, VA, APA.

Graham, S. and Harris, K. R. (1997) 'Self-regulation and writing: Where do we go from here?', *Contemporary Educational Psychology* 22, 102–114.

Graham, S., Harris, K. and Loynachan, C. (2000) 'The Directed Spelling Thinking Activity: Application with high frequency words', *Learning Disabilities: Research and Practice* 11, 1, 34–40.

Torgesen, J. K. and Mathes, P. G. (2000) *A Basic Guide to Understanding, Assessing and Teaching Phonological Awareness*, Austin, TX, ProEd.

Further reading

Gunning, T. G. (2002) (2nd edition) *Assessing and Correcting Reading and Writing Difficulties*, Boston, MA, Allyn and Bacon.

Addresses

Learning Disabilities Association of America
www.ldanatl.org
A non-profit volunteer organisation.

National Center for Learning Disabilities
www.ncld.org
Provides information, promotes research and offers advocacy.

Down syndrome

Down syndrome is named after Langdon Down who gave the first clear description of this condition in 1866. It is caused by chromosome abnormalities, usually trisomy 21 (see *Chromosome abnormalities* under *Genetic disorders*). Three-quarters of individuals with Down syndrome have congenital heart disease. In later life there is a greater chance of deafness, leukaemia, and myopia (short sightedness), and mild to moderate cognitive impairment (Candy, Davies and Ross, 2001, pp. 241–243).

Education implications include ensuring a curriculum, pedagogy and resources suitable for any cognitive impairment and making sure suitable care is provided for any health conditions.

Reference

Candy, D., Davies, G. and Ross, E. (2001) *Clinical Paediatrics and Child Health*, London and New York, Elsevier/Saunders.

Further reading

Selikowitz, M. (1997) *Down Syndrome: The Facts*, New York and Oxford, Oxford University Press.

Addresses

Down Syndrome Education International, UK
  www.downsed.org
  Aims to improve the education of young people with Down syndrome.

National Association for Down Syndrome, USA
  www.nads.org
  Serving young people in the Chicago area providing support, information and advocacy in relation to Down syndrome.

Drama therapy/drama therapist

Drama therapy is a form of arts therapy systematically using theatre techniques including drama, mime and role play, to support psychological health and achieve therapeutic goals. Puppets and masks may be used. Drama therapy is used in hospitals, schools, clinics and other settings and may involve an individual or groups including families. The therapeutic effects may be a cathartic release of emotions, or an insight into a problem or issue that was inaccessible through other means. Drama therapy in groups or couples can reveal unhelpful and unhealthy patterns of habitually interacting. Relatedly, role play can be used to explore other possibilities. The therapy can be understood in terms of 'core processes' as well as with regard to different approaches (Jones, 2007, *passim*).

A drama therapist is trained in theatre arts, psychology and psychotherapy and in drama therapy itself. Training includes work with different clients under supervision.

Reference

Jones, P. (2007) *Drama as Therapy: Theory, Practice* and *Research*, New York and London, Routledge.

Further reading

Jennings, S. (Ed.) (1994) *Drama Therapy with Children and Adolescents*, New York and London, Routledge.

Addresses

National Association of Drama Therapy, USA
www.nadt.org
Aims to maintain professional standards, develop registration criteria, and promote the profession of drama therapy.

The British Association of Drama Therapists
www.badth.org.uk
The professional body for drama therapists in the UK.

Early education

Early education refers to education before statutory school age. In early education settings such as playgroups or nurseries, where a child has already been identified and assessed as having a disability/disorder, members of staff will need to know the particular educational and care requirements that arise and receive training and support as necessary to provide it. Where a child has not been identified as having a disability/disorder but where staff members have concerns, a procedure for identification, assessment and provision is needed. A key member of staff may be identified and trained to coordinate a graduated response, which may include seeking the advice of specialists such as a psychologist as necessary. In England, a special educational needs coordinator is responsible for the day-to-day operation of the setting's special educational needs policy and for coordinating provision for children with special educational needs (Department for Education and Skills, 2001, chapter 1, section 39).

In the United States of America, several organisations support early education including for children with disabilities and disorders. The Division for Early Childhood (www.dec-sped.org), a division of the Council for Exceptional Children, produces guidance on best practice in early years special education (Sandall *et al.*, 2005). The National Early Childhood Technical Assistance Centre (www.nectac.org) lists state boards of education and coordinators and up-to-date information. The Center for Social Emotional Foundations of Early Learning is located at Vanderbilt University, Nashville, Tennessee and has a federally funded website with empirically validated strategies for supporting the social, emotional and behavioural well-being of young children (www.vanderbilt.edu/csefel/). The Technical Assistance Center on Social Emotional Intervention for Young Children (www.challengingbehavior.org) draws on research showing practices that improve social-emotional outcomes for young children who have or are at risk of delays or disabilities. It creates free resources to help caregivers, decision makers and service providers apply these best practices. The Technical Assistance Center on Social Emotional Intervention for Young Children uses a pyramid

model to promote social-emotional competence and improve behaviour that
is challenging.

References

Department for Education and Skills (2001) *Special Educational Needs Code of Practice*, London, DfES.
Sandall, S., Hemmeter, M., Smith, B. and McLean, M. (2005) *DEC Recommended Practices: A Comprehensive Guide for Practical Application in Early Intervention/ Early Childhood Special Education*, Missoula, MT Division for Early Childhood (DEC) of the Council for Exceptional Children (CEC).

Further reading

Drifte, C. (2001) *Special Needs in Early Years Settings: A Guide for Practitioners*, London, David Fulton Publishers.

Addresses

The Center for Social Emotional Foundations of Early Learning
www.vanderbilt.edu/csefel/
Its website indicates strategies for supporting the social, emotional, and
behavioural well-being of young children.

The Division for Early Childhood
www.dec-sped.org
The Division for Early Childhood of the Council for Exceptional Children
promotes policies and advances evidence-based practice that support families
and enhance the development of children at risk of or experiencing developmental delays or disabilities.

The National Early Childhood Technical Assistance Centre
www.nectac.org
Aims to strengthen service systems to ensure young children with disabilities and their families receive suitable supports and services.

Technical Assistance Center on Social Emotional Intervention for Young
Children (TACSEI)
www.challengingbehavior.org
The site operates under a grant from the United State Department of
Education, Office of Special Programs.

Early intervention

Early intervention can have a broad meaning and refer to interventions to
help ensure children have as good a start in life as possible (e.g. Odom *et al.*,

2003). In the context of children with possible disabilities and disorders, early intervention is perhaps misleadingly named. It is sometimes mistakenly taken to refer to intervening with a child at a young age who may have a disability or disorder. In fact, early intervention is equally relevant to older individuals, for example where a young person has experienced a traumatic brain injury. Perhaps a clearer term might be 'timely intervention'.

Whatever the term used, a key issue is intervening promptly if there appears to be a difficulty, but not intervening too early to discover later that the child or young person did not have difficulties. This relates to understandings of child development. Children develop at different rates within a band that do not necessarily suggest problems with development. However, at some stage the teacher, parents and others will come to recognise that development is slower than typical and the child may benefit from special education.

An aspect of early intervention is an effective procedure for screening children and young people so that anomalies and possible difficulties can be spotted. This is followed by more detailed assessment.

(See also, *Child development*)

Reference

Odom, S. L., Hanson, M. J., Blackman, J. A. and Kaul, S. (Eds) (2003) *Early Intervention Practices Around the World*, Baltimore, MD, Brookes.

Further reading

Coleman, J. G. (2004) (3rd edition) *The Early Intervention Dictionary: A Multidisciplinary Guide to Terminology*, Rockville, MD, Woodbine House Publishers.

Guralnick, M. J. (Ed.) (2005) *The Developmental Systems Approach to Early Intervention*, Baltimore, MD, Brookes.

Hutchinson, N. and Smith, H. (2003) *Intervening Early: Promoting Positive Behaviour in Young Children*, London, David Fulton Publishers.

Addresses

Early Intervention Association of Aotearoa New Zealand
    www.earlyinterventionassociation.org.nz
    A professional body for early intervention practitioners.

International Society on Early Intervention
    www.isei.washington.edu
    A forum for professionals worldwide to communicate about advances in early intervention. The site is located at the Centre on Human Development and Disability, University of Washington in Seattle, Washington, USA.

Education/educator

Education in a very specific sense may be seen as, 'the process of giving or receiving systematic instruction' (Soanes and Stevenson, 2003) and educating someone involves providing, 'intellectual, moral and social instruction' (Ibid.). More broadly, education concerns social and personal development as well as intellectual progress. Pedagogy involves not just instruction, but modelling, questioning, task structuring and other methods (Tharp, 1993, pp. 271–272).

Education implies that 'something worthwhile is being or has been intentionally transmitted in a morally acceptable manner' (Peters, 1966). What is considered worthwhile may change over time and may differ in various cultures, but could be said to be the skills, knowledge, attitudes and values that a society endorses (Farrell, Kerry and Kerry, 1995, p. 70). Education is 'intentional' not incidental, suggesting it involves structured experiences to help learning. Content is transmitted in a 'morally acceptable manner' implying freedom to consider differing views and information, and forming reasoned conclusions (Ibid. pp. 70–71). Education leads to change for the individual, 'in terms of behaviors towards others, ability to understand the world (or aspects of it) and in ability to do things in the world'. This transformation is, 'integrally related to the concepts of knowledge and understanding' (Barrow and Woods, 1982).

An educator facilitates education through ensuring that suitable knowledge, skills and attitudes are transmitted to a child by effective, morally justifiable methods. The educator may be a trained teacher in a school, a child's parents or other people significant in the child's world.

(See also, *Qualifications, standards and training for teachers*, *Pedagogy*)

References

Barrow, R. and Woods, R. (1982) (2nd edition) *An Introduction to Philosophy of Education*, London, Methuen.

Farrell, M., Kerry, T. and Kerry, C. (1995) *The Blackwell Handbook of Education*, Oxford, Blackwell.

Peters, R. S. (1966) *Ethics and Education*, London, Allen and Unwin.

Soanes, C. and Stevenson, A. (Eds) (2003) (2nd edition) *Oxford Dictionary of English*, Oxford, Oxford University Press.

Tharp, R. (1993) 'Institutional and social context of educational practice and reform' in Forman, A. E., Minick, N. and Stone, C. A. (Eds) *Contexts for Learning: Sociocultural Dynamics in Children's Development*, Oxford, Oxford University Press.

Further reading

Farrell, M., Kerry, T. and Kerry, C. (1995) *The Blackwell Handbook of Education*, Oxford, Blackwell.

Addresses

American Academy of Special Educational Professionals
  www.aasep.org
  A professional organisation for those seeking to enhance the needs of individuals receiving services for their special needs.

Department for Children, Schools and Families
  www.dcsf.gov.uk
  The UK government department aiming to enable children and young people to reach their full potential.

National Association of Special Education Teachers
  www.naset.org
  A national membership organisation based in Washington, DC, for special education teachers and those preparing for the field.

United States Department of Education
  www.ed.gov
  Aims to promote student achievement and preparation for global competitiveness through fostering educational excellence and ensuring equal access.

Elective mutism

Elective mutism, also called selective mutism, has been defined as a 'persistent failure to speak in specific social situations ... where speaking is expected, despite speaking in other situations' (American Psychiatric Association, 2000, pp. 125–127). Typically the child will speak at home but not in school or when with playmates. The disturbance interferes with educational achievement, occupational achievement, or with social communication. In terms of the APA criteria, it must last for at least a month. The first month of school is not included as many children are reluctant to speak until they get used to the new setting. The condition is not diagnosed if the disturbance is better explained by other reasons such as embarrassment because of stuttering or other communication difficulties (Ibid. pp. 125–126). The child may also fear embarrassment, be very shy, socially isolated and withdrawn. He may be clinging, or exhibit compulsive behaviour, temper tantrums, or oppositional behaviour (particularly at home). Social and school functioning may be severely impaired. In clinical settings the child is very often additionally assessed as having an anxiety disorder, for example social phobia (Ibid. p. 126).
  Selective mutism occurs in less than 1 per cent of individuals seen in mental health settings and is slightly more common in females than males. It usually occurs before the age of 5 years, although it may not come to professional attention until the child starts school. It may persist for a few months or for several years.

The child may communicate by gesture, nodding or shaking the head, or pulling and pushing. He may use utterances that are short, monosyllabic or monotone or may use an altered voice (American Psychiatric Association, 2000, p. 126).

Elective mutism is responsive to family-based behavioural treatment (Carr, 2006). The child and a family member with whom the child will speak have planned conversations in a setting where the child usually remains mute. This may be the school classroom initially when it is empty. Incrementally, others in whose presence the child does not speak (pupils, the teacher, and the classroom aide) join the child and the family member. The child becomes increasingly able to continue conversation with the family member in the presence of these others. As this happens, the teacher and pupils begin to join the conversation. Eventually, the child and family member move further apart. In time, the child converses with others in the classroom while the family member stays close to the exit. Finally the child asks the family member to depart and collect him at the end of the school day (Ibid. p. 521).

References

American Psychiatric Association (2000) *Diagnostic and Statistical Manual of Mental Disorders, Fourth Edition, Text Revision*, Arlington, VA, APA.
Carr, A. (2006) (2nd edition) *The Handbook of Child and Adolescent Clinical Psychology: A Contextual Approach*, London, Routledge.

Further reading

Sage, R. and Sluckin, A. (2004) *Silent Children: Approaches to Selective Mutism*, Leicester, University of Leicester.

Addresses

Selective Mutism Group
   www.selectivemutism.org
   Part of the Childhood Anxiety Network, SMG provides information, resources and support to those affected by a child having selective mutism.

Selective Mutism Information and Research Association
   www.selectivemutism.co.uk
   A UK-based charity.

Epilepsy

The nature of epilepsy

Epilepsy is a neurological condition defined by 'clinical manifestations linked to chronic recurrence of paroxysmal discharges within neuronal networks of the brain ...' (Jambaqué, Lassonde and Dulac, 2001, p. 1). These clinical indications are seizures and/or 'progressive deterioration of motor, sensory or cognitive functions' (Ibid.). Seizures are associated with various symptoms: convulsions (violent movements of the limbs or the whole body caused by muscular contractions), muscle spasms, involuntary movements and changes in perception and consciousness.

Under this International Classification of Epileptic Seizures (ICES) system, seizures may be classified as generalised or partial. Seizures may be: partial (affecting only one lobe or part of one side of the brain); and generalised (affecting the whole brain). Partial seizures are further classified as 'simple partial' or 'complex partial'. In simple partial seizures, the child remains conscious and may experience a tingling feeling in the arms or legs, disturbance of feeling, or disturbance of the sense of perception. In complex partial seizures, consciousness is impaired but not completely lost. Complex partial seizures can very quickly generalise to the whole brain. There are further classifications for general seizures. Where possible, epilepsy is also classified according to an epilepsy syndrome. Criticisms have been made of this scheme and modifications have been proposed (e.g. Engel, 2001). Nevertheless, classifications are important in education to the extent they help the parent and teacher better understand the implications for learning, language and cognition.

Epilepsy occurs in about 1 in every 200 children and more frequently among those with cognitive impairment. In the United Kingdom, epilepsy affects 0.7 to 0.8 per cent of all school children aged 5 to 17 years (Appleton and Gibbs, 1998). Often the causes of epilepsy are not established, as with over two-thirds of cases of epilepsy in a United Kingdom community survey (Kumar and Clark, 2005, p. 1221). Known causes comprise various combinations of '... brain damage, genetic predisposition and maturation phenomena characteristic of the child's brain' (Jambaqué, Lassonde and Dulac, 2001, p. 1). In 'photosensitive epilepsy' seizures can be precipitated by watching flashing lights, particularly when tired (Candy, Davies and Ross, 2001, p. 318).

Provision

The teacher needs to know any arrangements for the child to take medication during school times; any side effects of medication; and any changes in medication and their implications for school activities. In school all incidences of seizures are recorded perhaps using seizure description forms. Certain procedures are followed if a child has a seizure. Procedures for tonic-clonic seizures include not moving the child unless he is in danger and placing him in the safety-recovery position. Very occasionally, emergencies arise as where a seizure does not look as though it is stopping after several minutes, or the child has several seizures within a few minutes (status epilepticus). In such instances, an emergency protocol is followed which may involve the administration of rectal Valium or buccal midazolam. Trained members of staff carry this out with parental consent under guidelines and procedures agreed with the school. A child having regular tonic-clonic fits, or myoclonic or drop attacks, may wear a protective helmet. It is helpful for teachers to know the type of seizures the child experiences; their frequency and whether they occur at certain times; potential triggers such as fatigue; and how the seizure should be dealt with should it occur (Johnson and Parkinson, 2002, p. 7). Members of staff need to be able to deal with seizures and to carefully record their progress as it has implications for the management of medication and other matters.

Epilepsy can be associated with difficulties in processing information. A structured framework and routine in which to locate information therefore helps the student with information processing. The teacher can: present information in short chunks; reinforce verbal information with written notes; and directly support a pupil having difficulty maintaining attention. Counselling may be offered where pupils feel frustrated or have low self-esteem. Where there is a possibility that a pupil with tonic-clonic seizures may lose bladder and bowel control, the school should ensure privacy and keep a second supply of the child's clothing. Risk assessments are undertaken for activities such as practical subjects, laboratory-based work and aspects of physical education.

When educating children with frontal lobe epilepsy, a multidisciplinary approach may include medication, tutoring and psychological support (Hernandez et al., 2001, p. 109). The child may be impulsive and have difficulty sustaining effort throughout an activity. He may respond best when goals are clear and information is provided step-by-step, checking understanding along the way. A child with frontal lobe epilepsy may require help organising and planning work and leisure. Behaviour modification may be effective. Training in self-management and 'positive feedback' can enable the child to become more autonomous (Ibid.).

References

Appleton, R. and Gibbs, J. (1998) *Epilepsy in Childhood and Adolescence*, London, Dunitz.

Candy, D., Davies, G. and Ross, E. (2001) *Clinical Paediatrics and Child Health*, London and New York, Elsevier/Saunders.

Engel, J. (2001) 'A proposed diagnostic scheme for people with epileptic seizures and with epilepsy: Report of the ILAE Task Force on Classification and Terminology', *Epilepsia* 42, 796–803.

Hernandez, M. T., Sauerwein, H. C. de Guise, E., Lortie, A., Jambaqué, I., Dulac, O. and Lassonde, M. (2001) 'Neuropsychology of frontal lobe epilepsy in children' in Jambaqué, I., Lassonde, M. and Dulac, O. (Eds) (2001) *Neuropsychology of Childhood Epilepsy* (Advances in Behavioural Biology Volume 50), New York, Kluwer Academic/Plenum Publishers.

Jambaqué, I., Lassonde, M. and Dulac, O. (Eds) (2001) *Neuropsychology of*

Childhood Epilepsy (Advances in Behavioural Biology Volume 50), New York, Kluwer Academic/Plenum Publishers.

Johnson, M. and Parkinson, G. (2002) *Epilepsy: A Practical Guide*, London, David Fulton Publishers.

Kumar, P. and Clark, M. (Eds) (2005) (6th edition) *Clinical Medicine*, New York/London, Elsevier/Saunders.

Further reading

Wallace, S. J. and Farrell, K (2006) (2nd edition) *Epilepsy in Children*, New York, Oxford University Press.

Addresses

Epilepsy Action
   www.epilepsy.org.uk
   Aims to improve the quality of life and promote the interests of people living with epilepsy.

Epilepsy Foundation of America
   www.epilepsyfoundation.org
   A voluntary agency concerned with the welfare of people with epilepsy in the USA and their families.

The International League Against Epilepsy (ILAE)
   www.ilae-epilepsy.org
   An association of health professionals seeking better care and well-being for those with epilepsy and related conditions.

Equality of opportunity

Egalitarian theories may suggest support for equality of opportunity. Rawls' 'justice as fairness' theory (1971) proposes that if an individual were denied any knowledge of his abilities and given the choice of living in an egalitarian or inegalitarian society, he would tend to choose the former. The hope of being rich would be countered by the fear of being poor persuading him to choose a society that is 'fair' (Ibid, p. 148). In this view different treatment is justifiable only when inequality benefits the least advantaged by improving incentives and increasing the size of the social pot. Individuals who cooperate for mutual advantage have an equal claim for the outcomes of their cooperation and should not be penalised for factors beyond their control including genetic inheritance. Redistribution, constituting fairness is therefore considered to be a just procedure. Similarly, regarding equality of opportunity, those who through no fault of their own do not have the ability to achieve as easily as others would be given support enabling them to do better than they otherwise might. People more fortunate in their level of ability fund this, as property is redistributed to make opportunities more equal.

Another view is that distributive perspectives such as 'justice as fairness' violate property rights and compromise freedom (Nozick, 1974). Nozick's 'rights' view relates to a libertarian conception of the state. From initial and rudimentary 'private protection associations' emerges the 'ultra minimal' state having a monopoly of the use of force in a territory. This is transformed into a 'minimal' state, involving redistribution for the 'general provision' of protective services (Ibid. p. 52). The process by which this occurs is morally permissible and does not violate anyone's property rights (Ibid. pp. 113–119). However, no state that is more powerful or extensive than the minimal state is legitimate or justifiable. Consequently, developments such as 'equality of opportunity' going further than the minimal state are neither justifiable nor legitimate. Justice is not about equality but about entitlement in relation to individual property rights (Ibid. p. 150). 'Justice as fairness' views assume that everyone has some entitlement on the totality of natural assets in as a 'pool', with no one having differential claims. While Nozick accepts that in a free society, people's talents do not benefit themselves only but others too, he questions extracting even more benefits from others (Ibid. p. 229).

In Nozick's (1974) view, equal opportunity can be achieved either by deliberately worsening the circumstance of those who are better favoured with opportunity, or improving the situation of those less well favoured. As the latter requires resources the implication is still that someone else will have to accept a worse situation. People have to be convinced to give some of their property by choice to help achieve greater equality of opportunity, for example through charitable giving or paying taxes for which the population has voted. However, there is no social obligation to 'rectify' inequalities. The pursuit of equal opportunities violates property rights and compromises freedom (Ibid. p. 238).

In special education, equality of opportunity is sometimes evoked to support mainstreaming. It may be claimed that a child should have an equal opportunity to learn with other children in mainstream classrooms. This may or may not ensure that a child benefits from such opportunities in terms of learning optimally and developing well.

(See also, *Rights*)

References

Nozick, R. (1974) *Anarchy, State and Utopia*, Oxford, Blackwell.
Rawls, J. (1971) *A Theory of Justice*, Cambridge, MA, Harvard University Press.

Further reading

Cavanaugh, M. (2002) *Against Equality of Opportunity*, Oxford, Oxford University Press.
Roemer, J. E. (2000) *Equality of Opportunity*, Harvard, MA, Harvard University Press.

Addresses

Equality and Human Rights Commission, UK
   www.equalityhumanrights.com
   Aims to eliminate discrimination, reduce inequality, and protect human rights in the UK.

Human Rights and Equal Opportunities Commission, Australia
   www.humanrights.gov.au
   Aims to promote and protect human rights in Australia.

Evidence-based practice

In special education, evidence-based practice refers to the approach of drawing on interventions which have been evaluated. Its usefulness depends on the quality and reliability of the evidence and how it is adapted in practice. Those who have a commercial interest in promoting a particular approach may not always be the best source of information about its efficacy. Neither might the evidence of someone arguing anecdotally for an approach that was successful in his experience be universally applicable. There is always a danger of 'fad' treatments being promoted (Hornby, Atkinson and Howard, 1998).

One way of understanding and rationalising evidence-based practice is through considering approaches that work for different types of disability and disorder. Some of the approaches are presented in the present volume under headings of the types of disability and disorder. Fuller examples are available in other sources applying to special education (e.g. Farrell, 2008) and to psychosocial treatments (Fonagy *et al.*, 2005). Evidence ranges from very carefully controlled experimental trials with large numbers of children to groups of case studies. It includes correlational research, group experimental and quasi-experimental research, single subject research, and qualitative studies (see, for example, www.cec.sped.org).

In 2001, in the United States of America, the *Elementary and Secondary Education Act* (ESEA) was re-authorised as the *No Child Left Behind Act* (Public Law 107–110). It enacted that provision in the ESEA applied to all students including those with disabilities. Frequent reference is made to 'scientifically based research' and schools are required to use such research to inform approaches in the classroom.

References

Farrell, M. (2008) *Educating Special Children: An Introduction to Provision for Pupils with Disabilities and Disorders*, New York and London, Routledge.
Fonagy, P., Target, M., Cottrell, D., Phillips, J. and Kurtz, Z. (2005) *What Works for Whom? A Critical Review of Treatments for Children and Adolescents*, New York, Guilford Press.

Hornby, G., Atkinson, M. and Howard, J. (1998) *Controversial Issues in Special Education*, London, David Fulton Publishers.

Address

Council for Exceptional Children, USA
www.cec.sped.org

A professional organisation aiming to improve educational outcomes for students with disabilities and others. Their site has accounts of evidence-based practice.

Fragile X syndrome

Fragile X syndrome is one of the most common identifiable inherited causes of cognitive impairment. The term 'fragile' refers to the apparent break at the end of the long arm of the X chromosome. The pattern of inheritance is X linked. A carrier mother will pass on either a normal or an abnormal sex chromosome to her child. Consequently a half of male offspring will be affected and half of female offspring will be carriers (Candy, Davies and Ross, 2001, p. 240).

It is associated with cognitive impairment and physical features such as enlarged jaw and ears (Anderson, 2007, pp. 1855–1856). Speech may involve litany like communication with up and down swings of pitch, and 'cluttering', that is, rapid and dysrhythmic speech. The child may avoid eye contact, cause self-injury such as hand biting when anxious or excited, and show stereotyped and repetitive behaviours (Turk and Graham, 1997).

Effective approaches draw on what works for types of disability and disorder that relate to the condition, for example cognitive impairment, autistic like features and challenging behaviour. Assessments are related closely to the curriculum and what has been taught, with the child being fully aware of the intended learning outcomes. Structured teaching methods carefully reinforce what the child already knows and build on it. The educator insists on appropriate behaviour and provides immediate rewards for suitable behaviour and learning. Principles of behaviour management may be used, including the teacher being aware of the antecedents and consequences of the child's behaviour to better enable the behaviour to be modified. The learning environment is calm and uncluttered where the child responds unfavourably to overstimulation.

References

Anderson, D. M. (Chief lexicographer) (2007) (31st edition) *Dorland's Illustrated Medical Dictionary*, Philadelphia, PA, Elsevier/Saunders.

Candy, D., Davies, G. and Ross, E. (2001) *Clinical Paediatrics and Child Health*, New York and London, Elsevier/Saunders.

Turk, J. and Graham, P. (1997) 'Fragile X Syndrome, autism and autistic features', *Autism* 1, 175–197.

Further reading

Saunders, S. (2001) *Fragile X Syndrome: A Guide for Teachers*, London, David Fulton Publishers.

Addresses

The Fragile X Society
  www.fragilex.org.uk
  A UK-based society providing mutual support for families, raising awareness and encouraging research.

The National Fragile X Association
  www.nfxf.org
  A US-based organisation concerned with raising awareness, support, education, research and advocacy.

Funding

Funding in education generally and funding relating to pupils with disabilities/disorders tries to follow principles that will lead to a fair distribution of resources. However, this is much easier said that done. It is difficult to agree the amount of extra funding that a school educating a child with a disability or disorder should receive. There is debate about whether this funding should be the same or very similar for different types of disability and disorder or whether some disabilities/disorders should attract greater funding. Bands of funding are sometimes used to reflect the latter view. The picture is further complicated by the fact that some disabilities/disorders are harder to identify and assess than others. There may be little disagreement about identifying profound cognitive impairment but rather less agreement about conduct disorder or reading disorder. Lobby groups may press for greater resources for their particular concerns, often a particular disability or disorder and fail to recognise the impact on funds for other children, including those with other disabilities/disorders.

Publicly funded schools, termed public schools in the United States of America and state schools in the United Kingdom, are funded from taxes of the whole population filtered through local bodies.

In the United States of America, federal government provides a comparatively small percentage of special education funding. The remainder is borne by the particular state and local school districts. Where funding varies from state to state, it is not always discernable to what extent this relates to 'real' differences in the incidence of disabilities/disorders and the degree to which it might be influenced by differing practices for identification and assessment. It is argued that special education funding policy is leading to funding formulas that are burdensome to administer and provide insufficient in return in relation to promoting best practice (Parrish and Harr, 2006).

A Special Education Expenditure Project report of the Center for Special Education Finance updated in 2004 (Center for Special Education Finance, 2004) (www.csef-air.org/publications/seep/national/) indicated the range of funding for pupils with different types of disabilities/disorders. For example, the funds per pupil for individuals with specific learning difficulties were almost half of those per pupil for individuals with multiple disabilities.

It has been suggested in the United Kingdom, allocating funding according to the perceived needs of particular pupils favours pupils whose parents are more articulate, persistent and literate than others or certain well-organised pressure groups (Gross, 1996).

References

Center for Special Education Finance (2004) *Special Education Expenditure Project: What are we Spending on Special Education Services in the United States, 1999–2000*, Palo Alto, CA, CSEF.

Gross, J. (1996) 'The weight of evidence: parental advocacy and resource allocation to children with statements of special educational need', *Support for Learning* 11, 1.

Parrish, T. and Harr, J. J. (2006) *Special Educational Funding: Considering Adequacy, Equity and Efficiency*, San Francisco, CA, American Educational Research Association Meeting (American Institutes for Research) (www.air.org/news/documents/).

Further reading

Bowers, T. and Parrish, T. (2000) 'Funding of special education' in McLaughlin, M. J. and Rouse, M. (Eds) *Special Education and School Reform in the United States and Britain*, London and New York, Routledge.

Department for Education and Skills (2001) *The Distribution of Resources to Support Inclusion*, London, DfES.

Farrell, M. (2004) 'SEN funding in a redistributive society' in *Special Educational Needs: A Resource for Practitioners*, London, Sage, 54–66.

Address

Center for Special Education Finance
www.csf.air.org
Addresses fiscal policy issues related to the delivery and support of special education services in the USA.

G

Genetic disorders

Genetics is one of the most rapidly advancing areas of medicine (Candy, Davies and Ross, 2001, p. 239 and chapter 12). Chromosome abnormalities were the earlier genetic disorders to be described because the shape of the whole chromosome could be seen directly under a microscope.

Chromosomes

Chromosome abnormalities may be related to disabilities/disorders. A chromosome is a structure in the nucleus of a cell, which carries genes (which determine hereditary characteristics). There are normally 46 chromosomes in the nucleus of every living cell in the human body. Chromosomes are rod shaped structures arranged in 23 pairs. One of these pairs comprises sex chromosomes and the remaining pairs are known as autosomes. Each member of a pair of chromosomes comprises two threadlike structures which touch but not at their mid point, giving each chromosome a long and a short arm. The long arm is labelled 'q' and the short arm, 'p' (for 'petit' meaning 'small').

In a woman, the sex chromosomes are a matching pair of so called X chromosomes while in a man, the pair are an X chromosome and a Y chromosome. The 22 pairs of autosomes are classified according to size and shape and are numbered 1 through 22 with number 1 being the longest. When female eggs and male sperm are formed the chromosomes in each pair separate, leaving 23 chromosomes in these cells rather than 23 pairs. When a female egg is fertilised the chromosomes from the egg and the male sperm form themselves into pairs. When this process operates incorrectly, abnormalities occur (see also, Kumar and Clark, 2005, p. 171).

Chromosome abnormalities

Around 1 in 200 live-born infants have a chromosome abnormality and some of these may cause disabilities/disorders. An additional chromosome to a pair is called a trisomy, making the total number of chromosomes in such instances 47 rather than 46. The effects of this depend on the chromosome pair that is the site of the additional chromosome.

Trisomy at chromosome pair 21 is associated with Down syndrome (trisomy 21), the commonest chromosome abnormality in live-born infants. In fact around 94 per cent of cases of Down syndrome are associated with an extra chromosome at pair 21.

Partial trisomy (or duplication) in which there is an extra part of a chromosome in each body cell is associated with a wide range of disorders. It may involve a duplication of a long arm (q) of a chromosome or a short arm (p) and the form and degree of severity of the disorder may relate to the position of the duplication and its extent. Partial trisomy is referred to by the number of the arm of the chromosome concerned. For example, Rethorne's syndrome (partial trisomy 9p), involving mild to moderate cognitive impairment, is associated with partial trisomy of the short arm (p) of chromosome 9.

Deletion refers to a chromosome segment being broken off and lost and the effect depends on the particular chromosome affected, the site of the deletion, and its extent. For example, deletion of the short arm (p) of chromosome 5 is the cause of Cri du Chat syndrome. This rare condition associated with moderate to severe cognitive impairment is characterised by the baby having a rather cat-like cry in the first few months of life.

A ring chromosome is usually formed when the ends of both arms of a chromosome are deleted and the remaining ends join to form a ring shape. A ring in chromosome 13 is associated with Orbeli syndrome typified by slow development and moderate to severe cognitive impairment.

In translocation, part of one chromosome becomes joined to another or becomes part of another. If the translocation is unbalanced, this can affect development. Translocation is the cause of the extra chromosome material in 3 per cent of cases of Down syndrome.

Where there is a chromosome mosaic, a number of cells contain chromosome abnormalities while the remainder are normal. This is caused by abnormal chromosome separation in the later stages of cell division after the egg has been fertilised and the nature and extent of the mosaic influences the extent of disorder.

Where there is a sex chromosomes abnormality, this is associated with higher than average incidence of speech and reading difficulties. Turner's syndrome, occurring in girls and characterised by left-right disorientation and difficulties with perceptual organisation, is caused by the absence of one of the sex chromosomes leaving only one X chromosome.

Other inherited syndromes

Some syndromes are not linked to chromosomal abnormalities. For example, Prader–Willi syndrome has an unknown cause although some individuals have deletions of chromosome 15. Named after the two Swiss physicians who first described it, the condition is diagnosed by the clinical signs. It is associated with obesity in older children, and odd eating habits that may require the child's food intake to be reduced. The child may experience developmental delay and have poor coordination. Williams syndrome is a rare condition involving congenital heart abnormalities, small stature and a slow growth rate, cognitive impairment, and abnormal facial features. The cause is unknown (Candy, Davies and Ross, 2001, p. 244).

References

Candy, D., Davies, G. and Ross, E. (2001) *Clinical Paediatrics and Child Health*, Edinburgh, Harcourt/W. B. Saunders.
Kumar, P. and Clark, M. (2005) (6th edition) *Clinical Medicine*, New York and London, Elsevier/Saunders.

Further reading

Searle, B. and Hultén, M. (2002) *The Little Yellow Book Volume 1: A Guide to Rare Chromosome Disorders*, London, Unique Rare Chromosome Disorders Support Group (www.rarechromo.org/fpdl/LittleYellowBook.pdf).

Address

Unique
www.rarechromo.org/html/home.asp
A UK-based support group with an international membership and concerned with rare chromosome disorders.

Graduated response

A graduated response to disabilities/disorders refers to a mainstream school's levels of intervention. Where a disability or disorder is identified, and parents had been consulted, the school would first look to its own resources and consider ways in which it might adjust its curriculum, pedagogy, use of resources, and classroom and school organisation to ensure that the child progresses well academically and develops well personally and socially. If progress and development is not sufficient or is not what the school or parents expected, the school calls on the support of people who normally work beyond the school for advice and support. The 'outside' professional might provide services directly. Those involved might be a psychotherapist, a physical therapist, occupational therapist, speech and language pathologist and so on.

There are often formalised procedures that enable a school or a parent to request that the level of intervention is reviewed. For example, in England a

Special Educational Needs Code of Practice (Department for Education and Skills, 2001) provides such a structure. In early education settings, where a child appears not to be making enough progress, the setting can, 'present different opportunities or use alternative approaches to learning' (Code 4.9). Continuing difficulties may necessitate help beyond what is normally provided in the setting. These levels are respectively known as 'Early Years Action' and 'Early Years Action Plus'.

A similar approach applies to primary (elementary) school and secondary (high) school where the levels of intervention are called 'school action' and 'school action plus'. If outside intervention still does not produce the progress expected, the school or parent can request a multi-professional assessment that may lead to a more formal provision associated with a 'statement' of special educational 'need'.

Reference

Department for Education and Skills (2001) *Special Educational Needs Code of Practice*, London, DfES.

Group communication

Group communication approaches can be helpful to ensure that the relationships within a group, such as a classroom group, are stable and supportive. While this is important for all children, it has particular implications for pupils with anxiety disorders, or depressive disorders and others. An example is circle time, which seeks to develop individual potential and enable emotional and social development within a supportive, structured group setting. It involves activities, tasks and 'conferencing'. Everyone is an equal member of the circle and has a right to speak and to be heard. Games played in circle time do not involve there being winners and losers but involve collaborative tasks. As members of the circle gradually get to know one another, different topics are explored such as feelings or problems associated with different times of the school day. Conference sessions follow the tasks. Circle time can aid communication, modify behaviour and encourage positive relationships. It can raise self-esteem and help develop a child's understanding of interpersonal relationships and sensitivity towards them.

Further reading

Nash, M., Lowe, J. and Palmer, T. (2002) *Language Development: Circle Time Sessions to Improve Communication Skills*, London, David Fulton Publishers.

Handwriting

Writing involves complex skills including organising ideas, forming letters, spelling, and punctuation (Macintyre and Deponio, 2003, p. 67). Interrelationships of reading and writing are recognised (Nelson and Calfee, 1998, *passim*).

Difficulty with handwriting is not synonymous with disorder of written expression. The *Diagnostic and Statistical Manual of Mental Disorders Fourth Edition Text Revision* (American Psychiatric Association, 2000, pp. 54–56) outlines essential features of disorder of written expression. Measured by individually administered standardised tests of writing skills or functional assessment, these skills are substantially below age expectations, measured intelligence and 'age appropriate education'. The disturbance hinders academic achievement or daily living activities requiring the composition of written texts. There is generally a combination of difficulties evidenced by errors in grammar and punctuation in written sentences, poor organisation of paragraphs, many spelling errors, and very poor handwriting. However, disorder in spelling and handwriting alone is not considered to meet the definition of disorder of written expression (Ibid. p. 56).

Handwriting is an area of particular difficulty for some children with a disability or disorder. A pupil with developmental coordination disorder may need support and specific interventions to develop and improve handwriting. This relates to difficulties with learning the motor plan of the letters and problems with spatial orientation. Motor control deficits can make shaping the letters very difficult. The pupils can be encouraged to adopt a comfortable posture and a card template may be used to help the pupil get a good alignment for his writing paper (Benbow, 2002, p. 271). A pencil grip may be used to help the pupil control the writing implement. Special pens that illuminate when too much or too little pressure is applied can be used. These help the child with poor proprioceptive skills to learn the correct pressure for fluent writing. Exercises are sometimes used where the child is helped to place the pen or pencil on a piece of paper, beginning with training the writing implement on a larger area then gradually refining this to a small point. This helps the pupil place the writing implement correctly on a piece of paper to begin writing.

A pupil with a physical or motor disability may use a work processor as well as working on handwriting. Predictive software can help the pupil compose longer pieces of writing where physical effort is very tiring. A pupil with severe cognitive impairment may learn functional literacy including being able to sign his own name and write his name and address.

References

American Psychiatric Association (2000) *Diagnostic and Statistical Manual of Mental Disorders Fourth Edition Text Revision*, Arlington, VA, APA.

Benbow, M. (2002) 'Hand skills and handwriting' in Cermak, S. A. and Larkin, D. (2002) *Developmental Coordination Disorder*, Albany, NY, Delmar Thompson Learning, pp. 248–279.

Macintyre, C. and Deponio, P. (2003) *Identifying and Supporting Children with Specific Learning Difficulties: Looking Beyond the Label to Assess the Whole Child*, New York, Routledge Falmer.

Nelson, N. and Calfee, R. C. (1998) *The Reading–Writing Connection*, Chicago, IL, National Society for the Study of Education.

Further reading

Farrell, M. (2008) 'Disorder of written expression' in *Educating Special Children: An Introduction to Provision for Pupils with Disabilities and Disorders*, New York and London, Routledge.

Health impairment

The nature of health impairment

In the United States of America, a Code of Federal Regulations definition of 'other health impairments' (excluding orthopaedic impairment) is:

> ... having limited strength, vitality or alertness, including a heightened alertness to environmental stimuli, that results in limited alertness with respect to the educational environment, that (i) Is due to chronic or acute health problems such as asthma, attention deficit or attention deficit hyperactivity disorder, diabetes, epilepsy, a heart condition, haemophilia, lead poisoning, leukaemia, nephritis, rheumatic fever and sickle cell anaemia: and (ii) Adversely affects a child's educational performance.
>
> (34 CFR, section 3000.7 [c] [9] [I] [ii], 1999)

Attention deficit hyperactivity disorder is considered under 'other health conditions', while in England, government frameworks (Department for Education and Skills, 2001), classify it as an emotional, behavioural and social disorder.

Provision

Health impairments can lead to functional impairments and disability. Given the stress that serious and chronic illness or disability can place on the child and family, the school supports families wherever possible. Also, collaboration between parent, school and medical professionals can help ensure the child is included in as many curriculum activities as possible. Curriculum flexibility helps ensure a wide and suitable range of learning experiences is provided. Supervised swimming or walking and related activities may be offered where the pupil is at risk from contact sports. Participation in physical education may be restricted by weather conditions, for example for pupils with asthma. Curriculum opportunities may be modified following risk assessments for some activities such as practical subjects, laboratory-based work and aspects of physical education. For some pupils, for example with cystic fibrosis, time may be allocated for physiotherapy.

The child's educational provision needs to be responsive to changes in the child's physical and motor abilities and sensitive to the physical, psychological and any other effects of the condition. A child with epilepsy may require a structured framework and routine in which to locate information to help him with information processing.

Standing aids might be used for a child with a congenital heart defect where lessons require long periods of standing. Where the school building has stairs the school may ensure that the classroom and other facilities are on the lower floor or minimise the necessity of stair climbing or a lift may be used (e.g. for a child with a heart condition).

With agreement with parents and following correct protocols, the school may administer medication. Surgery may be used to correct abnormality or improve function, for example in the case of a congenital heart condition. Teachers and paraprofessionals regularly carry out specialised health care procedures, such as clean intermittent catheterisation, but do not always consider themselves very knowledgeable about the procedures (Heller *et al.*, 2000). This suggests the need for more training, help in developing policies and technical assistance. The individualised health care plan, developed under the guidance and leadership of a health care professional, helps focus coordinated provision. It includes: a description of the condition, basic health status and health care needs, treatments or medication and their side effects, transportation issues, equipment needs, emergency plans and particular precautions or restrictions on activities (Best and Bigge, 2001, p. 82). School staff should be properly trained and have the knowledge and skills to support health care plans, first aid measures and recording procedures. Developing the plan is likely to involve the child, school staff, health personnel, and parents (Clay, 2004). The school may provide opportunities for counselling to raise self-esteem, help teenagers deal with the stress associated with possible delayed sexual maturity, or support pupils with life-limiting conditions.

School buildings can be designed to ensure where appropriate that a child does not unduly exert himself carrying equipment around the school. Risk assessments are made to avoid situations and activities that may affect the child adversely. Flexible timescales for returning homework and possible home tuition may be employed. Extra supervision may be necessary sometimes at mealtimes or recess to ensure pupils follow dietary or medication procedures.

References

Best, S. J. and Bigge, J. L. (2001) 'Multiple disabilities' in Bigge, J. L., Best, S. J. and Heller, K. W. (2001) (4th edition) *Teaching Individuals with Physical, Health or Multiple Disabilities*, Upper Saddle River, NJ, Merrill-Prentice Hall.

Clay, D. L. (2004) *Helping Children with Chronic Health Conditions: A Practical Guide*, New York, Guilford Press.

Department for Education and Skills (2001) *Special Educational Needs Code of Practice*, London, DfES.

Heller, K. W., Fredrick, L. D., Best, S. J., Dykes, M. K. and Cohen, E. T. (2000) 'Providing specialised health procedures in the schools: Training and service delivery', *Exceptional Children* 66, 173–186.

Further reading

Bigge, J. L., Best, S. J. and Heller, K. W. (2001) (4th edition) *Teaching Individuals with Physical, Health or Multiple Disabilities*, Upper Saddle River, NJ, Merrill-Prentice Hall.

Health services

In the United States of America, state health services are concerned with children's health. In Florida, Children's Medical Services (www.doh.state.fl.us/cms/) provides care for children having special health care needs and their families. A division of this service, the CMS Network and Related Programs, offers family centred services for families with children having special needs. These are children and young people experiencing serious or chronic physical, behavioural, emotional, or developmental conditions that require care beyond what is typical of individuals of the same age. Georgia's Child Medical Services (www.health.state.ga.us/programs/cms/) provide community based medical and health care for individuals up to the age of

21 years with chronic medical conditions such as hearing disorders, vision disorders, and orthopaedic and neuromuscular disorders.

In England, important parts of the local structure are health authorities, National Health Service Trusts, and primary care groups/trusts. Health authorities provide strategic leadership. NHS Trusts provide most hospital services and community services. Primary care groups comprise general practitioners (general physicians) in the locality and community-based professionals. For schools, the initial contact with health services is likely to be through the school health services represented by the school doctor or nurse. These health professionals will be able to advise the school. Other health care professionals such as speech and language pathologists also give support and advice on children with disabilities/disorders.

Addresses

Department of Health
www.dh.gov.uk
Provides health and social care policy, guidance and publications for the National Health Service and social care professionals.

National Institutes of Health
www.nih.gov
Part of the United States Department of Health and Human Services, the NIH Is the primary federal agency for conducting and supporting medical research.

Office of Citizen Services and Communications
www.usa.gov
The official web portal of the Government of the United States of America, with sections concerning health services including by state.

United States Department of Health and Human Services
www.hhs.gov
The principal government agency for protecting health and providing essential human services especially for those least able to help themselves.

Hearing impairment

The nature of hearing impairment

In understanding hearing impairment, it is necessary to understand the terms frequency and intensity/amplitude. *Frequency* concerns the rate at which sound waves vibrate. It is usually expressed as cycles per second (c.p.s).

Rapidly vibrating sound waves are perceived as high-pitched sounds and slower vibrating waves as low-pitched sounds. The human ear is particularly responsive to sounds between 500 and 4,000 c.p.s, the band associated with speech sounds. With this band, vowels tend to have the lowest frequency range and fricatives (e.g. 's', 'f', 'th' and 'sh') the higher ones. Low frequency loss impairs the ability to hear vowels while higher frequency loss diminishes the capacity to hear fricatives and sibilants. Because consonants make speech intelligible, high frequency hearing loss is usually more serious.

The *intensity/amplitude* of a sound is experienced as loudness. It is measured in a decibel (dB) scale on which normal conversation is carried out at around 40 to 50 dB (Steinberg and Knightly, 1997). Hearing impairment can be measured on the dB scale in terms of dB loss. Categories of hearing impairment are recognised although the cut-off points for the different bands vary from country to country (Westwood, 2003, p. 48). Regarding severe loss and profound loss, a distinction is made between prelingual and post-lingual loss. A child who has experience of hearing and speech may already be speaking and may wish to continue. On the other hand, a child with similar loss occurring before speech developed would be likely to find communication using speech more difficult.

Deafness may be the result of an ear disease or injury, although profound deafness is usually congenital. In sensory-neural deafness, 'sounds' reaching the inner ear are not properly transmitted to the brain because of damage to the structures within the inner ear or to the acoustic nerve. Defects of the inner ear may be: congenital or brought about by birth injury; or damage to the developing foetus. The inner ear may be damaged after birth because of severe jaundice or meningitis. Conductive deafness occurs when sound is not properly propagated from the outer ear to the middle ear, usually because of damage to the eardrum or the bones of the inner ear. Common forms of impaired hearing in children are otitis media (middle ear infection) and otitis media with effusion, sometimes called glue ear, in which sticky fluid collects in the middle ear.

Hearing impairment may be identified through neonatal screening; the child's parent or a community health professional; or later through school screening programmes. Hearing tests determine the extent of any impairment and what part of the ear may be implicated. Among the main contributors to hearing impairment are: heredity (13 per cent) or other causes at birth (22 per cent) meningitis (9 per cent) and maternal rubella (5 per cent) (Moores, 2001). Around 20 per cent of children in the range 2 to 5 years at a specified time are affected by otitis media with effusion (a cause of conductive hearing loss). Sensori-neural deafness occurs in about 1 in a 1,000 babies.

Provision

There is debate about the respective merits and demerits of different approaches to deafness: an oral approach, a sign bilingual approach, and total communication.

An oral approach aims to teach children who have hearing impairment (and whose parents are hearing) to speak intelligibly and understand spoken language (Steinberg and Knightly, 1997). Also some deaf parents support oral education for their child, for example so he can later choose whether to learn sign language. Surgical insertion of the cochlear implant may be made at an early age to encourage the use of residual hearing (Ackley, Decker and Limb, 2007). Timely identification of deafness enhances the opportunity to use an oral approach early, although natural gesture is accepted. Residual hearing is used and enhanced. Children unable to comprehend speech by solely using hearing can gain information from lip reading and natural gesture, although speaking and listening has precedence. Educators emphasise communicating, assuming the rules of language will be learned through their practical use. Language development is encouraged through naturally occurring classroom activities, helping the child to generalise vocabulary and patterns of language to daily life. Efforts are made to provide favourable listening conditions and active listening skills are encouraged. The child is taught to use contextual clues and knowledge of the world to help communication and understanding. A speech pathologist or language teacher may provide speech training and auditory training (Reddy *et al.*, 2000). However, this is diminishing with the availability of better hearing aids, cochlear implants and earlier diagnosis.

Sign bilingualism uses both the sign language of the deaf community and the spoken and written languages of the hearing community. It aims to enable the deaf child to become bilingual and participate fully in both the hearing and deaf society. A sign bilingual approach involves the planned, systematic use of both the sign language of the country concerned (American Sign Language, Auslan Australian Sign Language, British Sign Language) and the spoken language. The balance varies according to individual needs. An aim is that each child becomes sufficiently competent in the sign language and the spoken language for their needs as a child and as an adult. This is likely to require the planned use of sign language and spoken language before the child reaches school age and throughout schooling.

Total communication includes the full spectrum of language modes, child devised gestures, the language of signs, speech, speech reading, finger spelling, reading and writing. The choice of methods relates to the child's individual requirements. In the British context, four broad options in total communication are: spoken English without signing; sign language; sign supported English; and signed English. *Sign languages* have their own vocabulary, syntax and grammar but no written form. In British Sign Language, the subject is stated first and then the verbs, adverbs and adjectives. Most signs do not come directly from English words and cannot always be translated 'one-to-one', although finger spelling is used for technical terms and proper names. As well as the shape of manual signs, the position of the communicator's hands in relation to the body (and other aspects) conveys meaning. *Sign supported English* uses signs derived from British Sign Language to support the use of natural English. *Signed English* is a representation with signs of all aspects of spoken English. The vocabulary, plurals, tenses, gender and other features of natural English are all represented. The communicator tries to sign every aspect of what is spoken, thereby facilitating good English.

References

Ackley, R. S., Decker, T. N. and Limb, C. J. (2007) *An Essential Guide to Hearing and Balance Disorders*, New York and London, Routledge.

Moores, D. F. (2001) (5th edition) *Educating the Deaf: Psychology, Principles and Practices*, Boston, Houghton Mifflin.

Reddy, G. L., Ramar, R. and Kasuma, A. (2000) *Education of Children with Special Needs*, New Delhi, Discovery Publishing House.

Steinberg, A. G. and Knightly, C. A. (1997) 'Hearing: sounds and silences' in Batshaw, M. L. (Ed.) *Children with Disabilities*, Sydney, Maclennan and Petty.

Westwood, P. (2003) (4th edition) *Commonsense Methods for Children with Special Educational Needs: Strategies for the Regular Classroom*, London, Routledge Falmer.

Further reading

Bodner-Johnson, B. and Sass-Lehrer, M. (2003) *The Young Deaf or Hard of Hearing Child: A Family Centred Approach to Early Education*, Baltimore, MD, Brookes.

Marschark, M. (2006) *Educating Deaf Students: From Research to Practice*, New York and Oxford, Oxford University Press.

Power, D. and Leigh, G. (Eds) (2004) *Educating Deaf Students: Global Perspectives*, Washington, DC, Gallaudet University Press.

Addresses

American Society for Deaf Children
   www.deafchildren.org
   Supports and educates families of deaf and hard of hearing children and advocates for high quality programmes and services.

British Association of Teachers of the Deaf
   www.batod.org.uk
   A professional organisation for teachers of the deaf.

History of special education

Texts discussing and interpreting the history of special education may be broad (e.g. Safford and Safford, 1996) or thematic (e.g. Cole, 1989). They may explicitly take a particular view such as a sociological one (e.g. Tomlinson, 1982) or focus on a particular country or period of time (e.g. Pritchard, 1963). When consulting such texts, it may be helpful to ask several questions:

- Who was being educated (rich, poor, blind, deaf, 'idiots')?
- Who was educating them (private tutors, school teachers, men, women, the nation state, charities, the Church, industrialists)?
- To what purpose were they being educated (for independence, for work)?
- When were they being educated (the nineteenth century, the twentieth century, the twenty-first century)?
- Where were they being educated (the United States of America, France, the countryside, industrial towns)?
- For whose benefit were they being educated (for society, for themselves, for industrialists)?

References

Cole, T. (1989) *A Part or Apart? Integration and the Growth of British Special Education*, Milton Keynes, Open University Press.

Pritchard, D. G. (1963) *Education of the Handicapped: 1760–1960*, London, Routledge and Kegan Paul.

Safford, P. L. and Safford, E. J. (1996) *A History of Childhood and Disability*, New York, Teachers College Press, Colombia University.

Tomlinson, S. (1982) *A Sociology of Special Education*, London, Routledge and Kegan Paul.

Home schooling

Some children who are too ill to attend school may be educated at home. Some children with depressive disorder or anxiety disorder including school phobia may be taught at home for a time. Home tuition may be provided by local authorities and home teachers may work for a specified number of half days with a child. They liaise with the pupil's school to facilitate his return, when appropriate.

Some parents choose to educate their child at home in preference to sending him to school, and this sometimes includes pupils with a disability or disorder. Any such disability or disorder must be recognised and provided for as part of the home education. Home schooled children may be registered part time in local school and be educated the rest of the time at home. Home schooling families sometimes pool resources and time to share their children's education, which can help ensure the child has varied experiences of socialising and leisure.

Addresses

Directgov
www.directgov.uk
An official UK government website.

United States Department of Education
www.ed.gov
The site's search engine leads to specific pages on 'home schooling'.

Hospital schooling

Hospital schools help ensure that children or young people staying in hospital for a long time can continue their education. In England for example, a hospital school is designated as a type of special school maintained by the local authority on hospital premises. Most pupils are inpatients, but some chronically ill children attend daily from home. A child may attend hospital school for several days a week and go back home for the remaining days.

An example of hospital schooling in the United States of America is the Children's Medical Center in Dallas (www.childrens.com). Its School Transition and Reintegration Service provides educational services including consultation, tutoring, academic instruction, and psycho-educational and cognitive assessments.

The Children's Hospital, Denver, Colorado, the Neuropsychiatric Special Care programme offers intensive evaluation and stabilisation for children and adolescents with an autism spectrum disorder who are in crisis and may have co-morbid conditions (medical and/or psychiatric). The Neuropsychiatric Special Care provides this service in a short-term day treatment or inpatient hospitalisation setting. It provides a structured Treatment and Education of Autistic and related Communication-handicapped CHildren (TEACCH) environment to treat behavioural, medical, psychiatric and family needs.

Further reading

Department for Education and Skills (2001) *Access to Education for Children and Young People with Medical Needs*, London, DfES.

Impairment

Impairment refers to personal limitations brought about by a degree of loss of physical, sensory or mental functioning. Examples are dual sensory impairment, hearing impairment, language impairment, visual impairment or motor impairment. Where impairment has a substantial effect on an individual, this is related to the definition of disability. For example, in England, under the Disability Discrimination Act 1995 section 1(1), a person has a disability if 'he has a physical or mental impairment which has a substantial or long-term adverse effect on his ability to carry out normal day-to-day activities'.

'Strong' versions of social models of disability/disorder tend to differentiate between 'impairment' and 'disability'. 'Impairment' is seen as the physical, bodily aspect of a condition, and 'disability' as relating to the perceived barriers that an oppressive society places on the individual with an impairment. 'Disability' is regarded as a socially created or constructed phenomenon additional to the impairment (Shakespeare, 2006, pp. 12–13) and can be seen as an interaction between the impairment and social influences.

In the United States of America, among the categories of 'disability' in the broad sense reflected in 'designated disability codes' are, 'speech and language impaired', 'orthopaedically impaired', and 'other health impaired'. In England, a similar classification (Department for Education and Skills, 2005, *passim*) includes, 'hearing impairment', 'visual impairment', and 'multi-sensory impairment'.

References

Department for Education and Skills (2005) (2nd edition) *Data Collection by Special Educational Need*, London, DfES.
Shakespeare, T. (2006) *Disability Rights and Wrongs*, London, Routledge.

Inclusion

Inclusion is sometimes distinguished from integration. While both concern the education of children with disabilities and disorders in mainstream schools, integration is seen as assuming the mainstream school system stays largely the same but that extra arrangements are made to provide for pupils with disabilities and disorders. Inclusion suggests that schools reconsider their curriculum, pedagogy, organisation, use of resources and uses of support so that the school responds to all pupils. It does not necessarily apply only to pupils with disabilities and disorders but is a broader approach seeking to embrace all pupils including those that may not achieve as well as others.

Inclusion in its broad sense refers to ensuring or increasing the participation of members of society in what are considered to be main activities of that society. This is sometimes referred to as 'social inclusion' and applies to society in general as well as to the work of schools (Ben, 2006). With regard to individuals with disabilities or disorders, the term inclusion in the present context applies to increasing participation in education.

Inclusion of children already educated in mainstream schools

Where pupils with disabilities and disorders are already educated in mainstream schools, inclusion may refer to increasing the participation of pupils with disabilities and disorders in the life and learning of the school. This implies encouraging schools to reconsider their structure, teaching approaches, pupil grouping, and use of support so that they respond to the diverse learning requirements of all pupils including those with disabilities and disorders. Inclusive pedagogy, for example, might develop activities that enable pupils with disabilities and disorders to take part and learn in lessons and activities with all pupils.

For example, so called 'adaptations' can be developed with reference to pupils with physical, health or multiple disabilities to act as a guide to help select and design suitable adapted physical activities. Rest periods between sections of a game may be increased or the length of time for each segment of a game may be decreased. The dimensions of a game can be reduced, perhaps having a smaller volleyball court or the goals for a game of soccer might be enlarged. The teacher might raise the number of attempts allowed to successfully carry out an activity, say, raising the limit on three strikes and out in a kickball game. In gymnastics the balance beam might be lowered (Bigge, Best and Heller, 2001, pp. 474–475). Essentially these activities are adapted so that a child with a disability or disorder participates in an activity with the same learning outcomes as other pupils but with adaptations to enable learning and achievement.

Inclusion as mainstreaming

Full inclusion refers to the aim of educating all children in mainstream schools through increased support and resources according to the severity of need (Gartner and Lipsky, 1989). In some uses, inclusion is a euphemism for educating an increasing number of pupils in mainstream schools and fewer in special schools. It is another word for mainstreaming but with the inbuilt implication that the child is participating to a greater extent in a mainstream school than in a special school.

Arguments supporting inclusion have included the claim that special schools are segregating and oppressive, that they deny equal opportunities, and reduce participation in decision-making. Moral claims for inclusion have been that it values human rights (Gallagher, 2001), and is associated with respect and fairness.

Empirical evidence for inclusion and whether it enables better academic progress and personal development has also been reviewed (Lindsay, 2003). For some parents, pupils and teachers it is considered important that pupils with disabilities and disorders be educated in mainstream schools where they can be included. This is seen as presenting the opportunity for pupils with disabilities and disorders to see and learn from other pupils.

However, the assumption that mainstreaming equates with being included in any meaningful sense of the word has been increasingly challenged in recent years as parents, pupils and others have spoken out in favour of special schools. Mary Warnock states, 'I profoundly believe that for many children, not only those with the most severe or multiple disabilities, special schools are their salvation' (Warnock, 2006, p. viii).

(See also, *Mainstream school/classroom, Optimal education, Special school*)

References

Ben, W. (2006) *Social Inclusion in Schools: Improving Outcomes, Raising Standards*, New York and London, Routledge.

Bigge, J. L., Best, S. J. and Heller, K. W. (2001) (4th edition) *Teaching Individuals with Physical, Health or Multiple Disabilities*, Upper Saddle River, NJ, Merrill-Prentice Hall.

Gallagher, D. J. (2001) 'Neutrality as a moral standpoint, conceptual confusion and the full inclusion debate', *Disability and Society* 16, 5, 637–654.

Gartner, A. and Lipsky, D. K. (1989) 'New conceptualisations of special education', *European Journal of Special Needs Education* 4, 1, 16–21.

Lindsay, G. (2003) 'Inclusive education: A critical perspective', *British Journal of Special Education* 3, 1, 3–12.

Warnock, M. (2006) 'Foreword' in Farrell, M. (2006) *Celebrating the Special School*, London, David Fulton Publishers.

Further reading

Bowe, F. (2005) *Making Inclusion Work*, Upper Saddle River, NJ, Pearson.
Cheminais, R. (2001) *Developing Inclusive Practice: A Practical Guide*, London, David Fulton Publishers.
Farrell, M. (2004) *Inclusion at the Crossroads: Special Education – Concepts and Values*, London, David Fulton Publishers.
Nind, M., Rix, J., Sheehy, K. and Simmonds, K. (Eds) (2005) *Curriculum and Pedagogy in Inclusive Education: Values into Practice*, London, Routledge.

Address

Wisconsin Education Association Council
www.weac.org/resource/
The site includes information on special education inclusion.

Incontinence

Incontinence can be associated with types of disability or disorder, for example with anxiety disorders. Incontinence of urine (enuresis) is more common at night (as bedwetting) than it is during the day. By the age of about four years old, most children are dry both day and night. Only at about the age of five years is regular enuresis seen as problematic. Night-time bedwetting creates extra work at home and restricts visits away from home. In residential schools it may be a source of shame and embarrassment with peers. Daytime enuresis can create difficulties with teachers and peers at school.

Treating enuresis involves addressing any physical reasons, reducing fluid intake, encouragement and behavioural training. A widely known form of behavioural treatment for bedwetting is the bell and pad method. A battery operated bell (or buzzer) is placed under the child's bottom bed sheet and a rubber sheet is placed beneath the bell. When the child passes urine, the pad becomes wet and completes an electrical circuit, which sounds the bell. This wakes the child who has to get out of bed to switch off the alarm. The child then goes to the toilet. Eventually in many cases, the bladder pressure, which precedes the alarm, acts as a trigger to wake the child who then goes to the toilet.

Incontinence of faeces (encopresis) usually ceases around the age of three years. If soiling continues after four years old, it is usually regarded as problematic. It creates similar difficulties to enuresis. Treatment involves first tackling any physical causes, providing effective toilet training, and if the condition appears to be related to emotional problems, providing therapy involving the family.

Further reading

The Bladder and Bowel Foundation website (see Addresses) lists many booklets and fact sheets.

Addresses

Bladder and Bowel Foundation
  www.bladderandbowelfoundation.org
  A charity providing advice and support for people with bladder and bowel disorders, their carers, families and health care professionals.

Kiwi Enuresis Encopresis Organisation
  www.kiwifamilies.co.nz
  A New Zealand-based charity.

Individual education programme/plan

In the United States of America, an Individual Education Programme (IEP) is a document that represents the coordination and planning of support for a pupil with a disability or disorder. A team that includes the child's parent or parents and professionals, including teachers, who work with the child, develops the IEP. A representative of the education administration also usually attends the meetings. The IEP itself has to include certain features. It specifies the pupil's current levels of educational performance, referring to the effect of the child's disability or disorder on this performance. A statement of annual goals and short-term objectives showing how the goal will be achieved is set out in all areas in which the child is receiving special education services. The progress towards IEP goals is measured by objective tests. The IEP also includes a statement of all the special education services the child will receive and the extent to which he will participate in regular education programmes.

In England the terminology is slightly different. There is a graduated response to try to ensure the child with a disability or disorder makes sufficient progress. This begins with the child being supported by resources that are normally available within the child's school. This is called 'school action'. If progress is not sufficient, support from outside the school such as a school psychologist or physical therapist may be sought. This is known as 'school action plus'. If progress is still not considered enough, the parent or school can request that the child is given a statutory assessment to see if he requires a 'statement of special educational need' (Department for Education and Skills, 2001). Throughout, the child has an Individual Education Plan (also of course abbreviated to IEP). But although the Individual Education

Plan has similarities to the United States of America Individual Education Program, it is the 'Statement' that is closer.

(See also, *Graduated response*)

Reference

Department of Education and Skills (2001) *Special Educational Needs Code of Practice*, London, DfES.

Further reading

Peter W.D. Wright, and Wright, P. D. (1999) *Wrightslaw: Special Education Law*, Hartfield, VA, Harbor House Law Press.

Ysseldyke, J. and Algozzine, B. (2006a) *The Legal Foundations of Special Education: A Practical Guide for Every Teacher*, Thousand Oaks, CA, Corwin Press.

Intelligence

Intelligent activity involves seeing the essentials in a given situation and responding appropriately to them. The nature and structure of intelligence and the relationships with intelligence tests has been the source of much research and debate. Various methods of 'factoring' the correlations between tests of intelligence through the statistical technique of factor analysis have led to various interpretations of the structure of intelligence. This has included a hierarchical structure involving group factors. Guilford identified some 120 intellectual skills. Such structures have led to tests being developed which aim to assess children's performance in different areas of mental ability, such as spatial, reasoning and verbal abilities. Another approach is that of the theory of multiple intelligences in which various intelligences are regarded as different from one another. Mathematical intelligence is fundamentally different from verbal intelligence in this view.

Some intelligence tests may be administered to groups while others are given to individuals. The latter are sometimes used in the assessment of children with disabilities and disorders. It is necessary that the intelligence test is standardised on a sample of individuals representative of the child being tested so that the scores achieved by the individual child can be suitably compared with those of children of the same age. An important concept in relation to intelligence tests is that of intelligence quotient (IQ). Most modern intelligence tests have a deviation quotient. They are standardised to produce distributions of IQs with a mean of 100 and a standard deviation of 15 points. Intelligence test scores can also be expressed as percentile ranks or other measures.

Raven's Progressive Matrices is an example of an intelligence test which can be administered as a group test. A standard form comprises 60 designs in groups of 12. Each design has a piece omitted and several possible missing pieces are shown from which the correct one has to be chosen. As the individual passes through the test, the logical judgement on which the correct judgement is based becomes more difficult. A coloured form is used for children aged 5 to 11 years or for people with cognitive impairment. There is an advanced form for the very able. Children whose physical or motor impairment may make some intelligence tests less accessible for them may be able to access Raven's Progressive Matrices because the correct response can be given simply by pointing.

A widely used individually administered intelligence test is the Weschler Intelligence Scale for Children (WISC), developed by David Weschler. The most recent version is the WISC-IV produced in 2003. There are ten core tests and five supplemental ones. These produce a full-scale IQ and four 'indices' scores for verbal comprehension, perceptual reasoning, processing speed, and working memory. Such tests are used to contribute to an assessment of cognitive impairment in conjunction with other assessments such as functional assessments (American Psychiatric Association, 2000).

Reference

American Psychiatric Association (2000) *Diagnostic and Statistical Manual of Mental Disorders, Fourth Edition, Text Revision*, Arlington, VA, APA.

Further reading

Kaplan, R. M. and Saccuzzo, D. P. (2005) *Psychological Testing: Principles, Applications and Issues*, Belmont, CA, Thompson Wadworth.
Sternberg, R. R. J. (Ed.) (2008) *Handbook of Intelligence*, Cambridge, Cambridge University Press.
Wilhelm, O. and Engle, R. W. (2005) (2nd edition) *Handbook of Measuring and Understanding Intelligence*, Thousand Oaks, CA, Sage.

Addresses

GL Assessment
    www.gl-assessment.co.uk
    A UK-based test provider.

The Psychological Corporation
    www.psychcorp.co.uk
    A company producing tests including tests of intelligence.

Intensive interaction

Intensive interaction is an approach drawing on early parent–child interactions in which the parent through imitation and turn taking invests meaning into the child's earliest random actions. The adult acts as though the actions of the child were meant as communication and in so responding the child's actions gradually become communicative. A speech pathologist or trained parent or teacher uses one-to-one sessions to help an individual to learn the basics of communication. These include taking turns, making eye contact and facial expressions. It can encourage interaction for its own sake or enable interaction with other children. The intervention can allow the child to gain better access to the curriculum by improving his communication and inter-personal behaviour. Intensive interaction involves 'regular, frequent inter-actions' between the adult and the child with a disability or disorder in which there is no focus on the task or the outcome but in which the attention is on 'the quality of the interaction itself' (Hewett and Nind, 1998, p. 2). The approach may be used, for example, with pupils having autism or severe or profound cognitive impairment.

There is some evidence from small group interventions or individual case studies that the approach might be promising. A group of children with 'profound and multiple learning difficulties' (profound cognitive impairment and other disabilities) were observed over a period of a year. Observations were made of them in teacher-led group time not directly aimed at developing communication and in intensive interaction. In the latter, children showed more consistent and advanced behaviour (Watson and Fisher, 1997). Reports on individual children also suggest that daily intensive interaction sessions can develop communication, increase participation in positive social inter-actions and sometimes reduce stereotyped behaviour (Nind and Kellett, 2002).

References

Hewett, D. and Nind, M. (1998) *Interaction in Action*, London, David Fulton Publishers.

Nind, M. and Kellett, M. (2002) 'Responding to individuals with severe learning difficulties and stereotyped behaviour: Challenges for an inclusive era', *European Journal of Special Needs Education* 17, 3, 265–282.

Watson, J. and Fisher, A. (1997) 'Evaluating the effectiveness of Intensive Interactive teaching with pupils with profound and complex learning difficulties', *British Journal of Special Education* 24, 2, 80–87.

Further reading

Nind, M. and Hewett, D. (1994) *Access to Communication*, London, David Fulton Publishers.

Nind, M. and Hewett, D. (2001) *A Practical Guide to Intensive Interaction*, Kidderminster, British Institute of Learning Difficulties.

International classification of functioning, disability and health for children and youth

The *International Classification of Functioning, Disability and Health (ICF)* (World Health Organisation, 2002) builds on earlier forms. It is a classification system that seeks to concentrate on individual functional difference across several areas. At the same time, it seeks to recognise biological, psychological and social factors relevant to functioning.

In the *ICF*, disability is taken to be a broad term covering impairments, participation restrictions and activity limitations. Causation is seen as relating to biological, psychological and social factors so avoiding caricatures of the medical and the strong social model which can be seen as overemphasising respectively biological and social explanations. Disability is seen as an interaction of three dimensions:

- Bodily functions/structures
- Activities, that is tasks and activities that can be carried out, and
- Participation, namely what an individual can do in his present environment.

These dimensions are influenced by both health conditions and by contextual factors.

ICF identifies an individual in four dimensions.

- Body function (physical and psychological)
- Body structure
- Activity and participation, and
- Contextual factors (environmental and personal).

A version of the *ICF* has been derived for children and young people and uses the same model and assumptions of the earlier ICF (World Health Organisation, 2002). This is the *International Classification of Functioning, Disability and Health: Children and Youth Version* or ICF-CY (World Health Organisation, 2007) which covers ages from birth through 18 years. Being multidimensional, and focusing on activities and participation, is intended to allow *ICF-CY* to monitor change through the life span. The 'one level' classification comprises: body functions, body structures, activities and participation, and environmental factors.

Body functions are: mental functions; sensory functions and pain; voice and speech functions; functions of the cardiovascular, haematological, immunological and respiratory systems; functions of the digestive, metabolic and endocrine systems; genitourinary and reproductive functions; neuromusculoskeletal and movement related functions; and functions of the skin and related structures (World Health Organisation, 2007, pp. 45–105). Body structures comprise: structures of the nervous system; the eye, ear and related structures; structures involved in voice and speech; structures of the cardio-vascular, immunological and respiratory systems; structures related to the digestive, metabolic and endocrine systems; structures related to the geni-tourinary and reproductive systems; structures related to movement; and skin and related structures (Ibid. pp. 107–127). Activities and participation consists of: learning and applying knowledge; general tasks and demands; communication; mobility; self-care; domestic life; interpersonal interactions and relationships; major life areas; and community, social and civic life (Ibid. pp. 129–188). Environmental factors are: products and technology; natural environment and human-made changes to the environment; support and relationships; attitudes; and services, systems and policies (pp. 189–223).

Each of these is further subdivided in a two level classification. For example, under body functions – mental functions, these consist of 'global mental functions' and specific mental functions'. Under body structures – the eye, ear and related structures, are 'structure of the eye socket', structure of the eyeball' structure of the inner ear' and so on. Within activities and participation – self care, is 'washing oneself', 'caring for body parts', 'toileting' and so on. Within environmental factors – support and relationships come 'immediate family', strangers' 'people in subordinate positions' and others.

It is said that among advantages of such a dimensional model, is that it can shift the unit of classification from diagnosis to the functional characteristics of the child. This, assuming that non-dimensional disability classifications are inevitably negative and fragmentary, is seen as in keeping with a 'holistic and non stigmatising' approach to disability (Simeonson, Simeonson and Hollenweger, 2008, p. 217). It has been suggested that the *ICF* and its underlying principles might be used to construct a classification of 'educational disability' with greater relevance to 'curriculum and teaching decisions and practices' (Norwich, 2008, p. 147). At the same time, it is recognised that *ICF-CY* in its current form, '... may not have specific relevance to educational provision, defined in curriculum and pedagogic terms'.

One argument for a dimensional model is that individual children with different categorical disabilities or disorders may share similar functional profiles. For example, a child with 'traumatic brain injury' and one with 'learning disabilities' may share similar profiles of functional limitation in attending, recalling, carrying out academic tasks and participating in class and social activities (Simeonson, Simeonson and Hollenweger, 2008, p. 218). It is these profiles, it is argued that have the more important implications for resources and service delivery than the non-dimensional categories. However, non-dimensional categories can provide information and possible prognoses that dimensional classifications may not. For example, the medical, social, behavioural, psychological, personal, physical and other implications that are commonly associated with traumatic brain injury are well documented (Schoenbrodt, 2001).

It is suggested the principles of multidimensional classification might be useful, for example in relation to multi-professional working and cross professional structures (Norwich, 2008, p. 148). It is possible that dimensional functional descriptions might enable a common language across different professionals. This might however be underemphasizing the reasons why different languages have developed, reflecting different kinds of expertise and contributions to the education and well-being of the child. These perspectives include pedagogic, medical, developmental, behavioural, neuropsychological, psychotherapeutic, psycholinguistic and technological (Farrell, 2009). Also, in the context of present non-dimensional classifications such as 'autism' and 'profound cognitive impairment' it is possible the dimensional approach adopted by *ICF-CY* might enable functioning to be described and progress to be monitored. Recording and monitoring functional descriptions and changes can also inform the provision of resources.

References

Farrell, M. (2009) *Foundations of Special Education: An Introduction*, New York and London, Wiley.
Norwich, B. (2008) 'Perspectives and purposes of disability classification systems: Implications for teachers and curriculum pedagogy' in Florian, L. and McLaughlin, M. J. (Eds) *Disability Classification in Education: Issues and Perspectives*, Thousand Oaks, CA, Corwin Press.
Schoenbrodt, L. (Ed.) (2001) *Children with Traumatic Brain Injury: A Parent's Guide*, Bethesda, MD, Woodbine House.
Simeonson, R. J., Simeonson, N. E. and Hollenweger, J. (2008) 'International Classification of Functioning, Disability and Health for Children and Youth' in Florian, L. and McLaughlin, M. J. (Eds) *Disability Classification in Education: Issues and Perspectives*, Thousand Oaks, CA, Corwin Press.
World Health Organisation (2002*) International Classification of Functioning, Disability and Health: Towards a Common Language for Functioning, Disability and Health*, Geneva, Switzerland, WHO.
World Health Organisation (2007*) International Classification of Functioning, Disability and Health: Children and Youth Version*, Geneva, Switzerland, WHO.

Further reading

Florian, L. and McLaughlin, M. J. (Eds) (2008) *Disability Classification in Education: Issues and Perspectives*, Thousand Oaks, CA, Corwin Press.

Address

World Health Organisation
www.who.int

The organisation is the directing and coordinating authority for health within the United Nations system.

Internet: world wide web sites

The Internet is widely used by parents of children with disabilities and disorders and professionals working with these children. It is impossible to list even a fraction of the sites, but an hour or two spent exploring the better known sites will reveal links which will point towards the wealth of information available on other sites. Among currently available sites the following link to a wide range of related information.

Office of Special Education and Rehabilitative Services (OSERS)
www.ed.gov/about/offices/list/osers/
Part of the United States Department of Education committed to improving results and outcomes for people with disabilities, of all ages.

The National Association of Special Educational Needs
www.nasen.org.uk
A UK-based organisation.

Special Education resources on the Internet
www.seriweb.com
A range of Internet accessible information resources for those involved in special education and related areas.
The websites listed after or within entries in this Handbook provide further information.

The Internet is also being selectively used to educate and aid the participation in learning of pupils with disabilities and disorders (Abbott, 2002).

References

Abbott, C. (2002) *Special Educational Needs and the Internet: Issues for the Inclusive Internet*, London, RoutledgeFalmer.

Journals and other publications

Numerous other journals and publications are published on particular types of disability and disorder. Journals covering a broad range of issues in special education include the following:

Australasian Journal of Special Education
www.informaworld.com/smpp/title~content=t768155443~db=all
The journal of the Australasian Association of Special Education.

British Journal of Special Education
www.blackwellpublishing.com/journal
Covers all types of disability and disorder and special schools and mainstream schools.

European Journal of Special Needs Education
www.tandf.co.uk/journals/routledge/08856257.html
The journal concerns the theory and practice of special education and is intended mainly for teachers and researchers.

Exceptional Children
www.cec.sped.org
Covers research, topical issues and broad perspectives.

Journal of the American Academy of Special Education Professionals
www.aasep.org/aasep-publications
An online journal aiming to advance the professional development of special education professionals through research, policy, and practice.

Journal of Research in Special Educational Needs
www.nasen.org.uk/Journal
An online publication disseminating research in special education.

Journal of Special Educational Technology
www.tamsec.org/jset/
An online publication presenting information and opinions about issues, research, policy, and practice related to the use of technology in special education.

The Journal of Special Education
www.sed.sagepub.com
Published in association with the Division for Research, Council for Exceptional Children.

Learning difficulty

A 'learning difficulty' in the United Kingdom context is not the same as a 'learning disability' in the United States of America. In England, a *Code of Practice* (Department for Education and Skills, 2001) defines special educational needs in terms of the Education Act 1996 312(2) and (3). A child has a 'learning difficulty' if:

a) he has a significantly greater difficulty in learning than the majority of children of his age
b) he has a disability which either prevents or hinders him from making use of educational facilities of a kind provided for children of the same age in schools within the area of the local education authority
c) he is under five and is, or would be if special educational provision were not made for him, likely to fall within paragraph (a) or (b) when of, or over that age.

A child with a learning difficulty does not necessarily have special educational needs under the Act, which states that, 'A child has special needs ... if he has a learning difficulty which calls for special educational provision to be made for him' (section 312).

Essentially, the system in the United States of America lists the disabilities/disorders and then specifies that these have to make learning difficult before special education is applicable. The system in England broadly specifies 'disability' or 'difficulty in learning' which include various disabilities/disorders and then specifies that these have to constitute a 'learning difficulty' before the child can be considered to have 'special educational needs'. These needs in turn call for special educational provision to be made.

The term 'learning difficulties' is also used more loosely to refer to disabilities/disorders requiring special education (e.g. Ayers and Gray, 2006).

References

Ayers, H. and Gray, F. (2006) *An A to Z Practical Guide to Learning Difficulties*, London, David Fulton Publishers.

Department for Education and Skills (2001) *Special Educational Needs Code of Practice*, London, DfES.

Learning disability

Learning disability (or learning disorder) is a term used in the United States of America and elsewhere. Regulations for Public Law 101–476, the Individuals with Disabilities Act define a learning disability. It is a 'disorder in one or more of the basic psychological processes involved in understanding or in using spoken or written language, which may manifest itself in an imperfect ability to listen, think, speak, read, write, spell or do mathematical calculations'. The term excludes certain disabilities/disorders for example, visual impairment, hearing impairment, cognitive impairment, and motor disabilities.

There is no universal agreement about which disorders and disabilities are included under this umbrella term. The term is useful in that it indicates that there is considerable overlap in some of the disorders and disabilities, which might suggest some common underpinning causes. On the other hand, when considering provision, it is often more helpful to consider disorders such as reading disorder and mathematics disorder distinctively.

The term 'learning disability' is not to be confused with the expression 'learning difficulty' as it is used in the United Kingdom. However, in the United Kingdom, the expression 'specific learning difficulties' can refer to dyslexia (reading disorder), dyscalculia (mathematics disorder), and dyspraxia (developmental coordination disorder). The common feature is that these disorders are specific to an area of functioning and not associated with wider cognitive impairment.

Understanding of learning disabilities increasingly takes account of genetic, neural, cognitive and contextual factors and provision draws on evidence-based practice (Fletcher *et al.*, 2006).

Reference

Fletcher, J. M., Lyon, G. R., Fuchs, L. S. and Barnes, M. A. (2006) *Learning Disabilities: From Identification to Intervention*, New York and London, Guilford Press.

Further reading

Pennington, B. F. (2009) (2nd edition) *Diagnosing Learning Disorders: A Neuropsychological Framework*, New York and London, Guilford Press.

Swanson, H. L., Harris, K. R. and Graham, S. (2006) *Handbook of Learning Disabilities*, New York and London, Guilford Press.

Addresses

Learning Disabilities Association of America
www.ldanatl.org
A non-profit volunteer organisation that provides support to people with learning disabilities, their parents, teachers and other professionals.

National Center for Learning Disabilities
www.ncld.org
Provides information, promotes research and offers advocacy.

Legal framework

Anglo-American legislation since the 1970s has sought to: discourage discrimination against pupils with disability/disorder compared with other pupils unless justifiable; increase opportunities for pupils with disability/disorder to be educated in ordinary schools as long as certain conditions are met; and has indicated where different professionals need to work closely together, such as in assessing a child. Legislation and related regulations and guidance have sought to provide a structure of identification and assessment for children with disability/disorder to ensure they receive suitable provision. In the United States of America, types of disability/disorder are listed under 'designated disability codes'. These categories of disability are set out under federal law as amended in 1997 (20 United States Code 1402, 1997). In England, although it initially appears legislation has discouraged such classifications, they are extensively used for example in government guidance to schools on data collection (Department for Education and Skills, 2005, *passim*).

In the United States of America, federal laws enacted since the 1970s, in conjunction with the equal protection clause of the United States Constitution and court cases and decisions, have helped shape modern special educational provision (Ysseldyke and Algozzine, 2006, p. 53). For example, the United States Supreme Court has determined that schools must provide straightforward medical procedures the school nurse can administer (Ibid. p. 48).

Section 504 of the *Rehabilitation Act 1973*, adopted in 1977, made it illegal to discriminate against a person with a disability exclusively because of that disability (e.g. denying participation in activities). This applies to programs or activities 'receiving federal financial assistance'. Those with disabilities have to be given equal access including architectural accessibility to services and programmes. Also, 'auxiliary aids' (e.g. readers for pupils who are blind) must be provided for individuals with impairments in speaking, sensory or manual skills where they would otherwise be excluded.

Under the *Education for All Handicapped Children Act 1975* (Public Law 94–142) students aged 3 through 21 years with disabilities have the right to free, appropriate public education. Any assessments determining the nature of the student's disabilities must be racially and culturally fair. The student has to be educated in the 'least restrictive' environment and removed from a general education environment only when a disability is so severe that general education classes and the use of supplementary aids is not effective. Parents have rights to: inspect school records on their child; receive prior written notice if changes are made to the student's educational placement or programmes; and challenge information held in records and any changes in placement. Schools have to keep an individualised education programme for the student based on a multidisciplinary assessment.

In 1986, amendments (Public Law 99–457) to the *Education for All Handicapped Children Act 1975* extended the rights set out under that Act to preschool children with disabilities. Regarding these children, each school district was required to carry out a multidisciplinary assessment and draw up an 'individualised family service plan'.

The *Individuals with Disabilities Education Act 1990* (Public Law 101–476) added the categories of 'traumatic brain injury' and 'autism' to the previously defined categories of disability. The *IDEA 1990* replaced references to 'handicapped children' with 'children with disabilities'. The Act also states that students with disabilities should have access to assistive technology equipment and related services.

In 1997, amendments (Public Law 105–17) to the *IDEA 1990* included requiring states to report on the progress of all students. It aimed to increase the participation of parents in the process of re-evaluation; placement decisions; and programme planning for students with disabilities. Changes were made to requirements for the composition of the Individual Education Program team to ensure people with necessary expertise were included.

The *Individuals with Disabilities Education Improvement Act 2004* (House Bill 1350) enacted that students with disabilities should be taught by teachers holding full certification in special education or who have passed a state teacher licensing examination and hold a state licence. Special education teachers teaching towards alternative achievement standards in particular core academic subjects must be certified in the relevant subject and in special education. Transition planning must be focused on results. Schools must appoint a parent surrogate for students who are disabled and are homeless or wards of the court.

In 2001, the earlier *Elementary and Secondary Education Act* (ESEA) was re-authorised becoming known as the *No Child Left Behind Act* (Public Law 107–110). It enacted that provision in the ESEA applied to all students including those with disabilities. The Act provided for literacy interventions and gave entitlement to supplementary education services. It included greater accountability and a focus on proven educational methods. A subsequent rewriting of the Act further strengthened accountability.

In England, similar developments occurred. Under section 1 of the *Education Act 1981*, previous categories of handicap were apparently replaced by a generic definition of special educational needs, although as pointed out earlier categories continue to be used in government documents and elsewhere. Special educational provision was defined as 'additional to or otherwise different from' that generally provided for children of the same age by the local authority concerned. Provided certain conditions were met children with a 'statement' of special educational needs were to be educated in ordinary/mainstream schools. Parents' views were to be taken into account. Education in ordinary school was to be compatible with three conditions: the child receiving the special educational provision required; the provision of efficient education for other children; and resources being used efficiently. Children with special educational needs must engage in school activities 'together with children who do not have special educational needs' providing the three conditions above are met and it is 'reasonably practicable'. In assessing the child, the local education authority is required by regulations to seek medical, psychological and educational advice.

The *Education Act 1993* sought to improve the system of provision for children with special educational needs, building on principles established by the *Education Act 1981*. Parents of children with a statement of special educational needs are given rights to have their say in the education of the child. They have a right to express a preference of the maintained (publicly funded) school their child should attend. More emphasis was placed on children who have special educational needs but who do not require a statement. But the Act also strengthened the system for pupils requiring statements and for their parents. It introduced a 'Code of Practice' (Department for Education and Skills, 2001) containing guidance and criteria on the identification and assessment of children with special educational needs to which schools must 'have regard' when dealing with pupils with special educational needs. The Act reaffirmed the principle that pupils should be educated in ordinary schools whenever it is possible and sensible to do so.

The *Special Educational Needs and Disability Act 2001* (SENDA) amended some earlier acts (including the *Disability Discrimination Act 1995* and the *Education Act 1994*). It made further provision against discrimination on the grounds of disability in schools and in other educational establishments. Part 1 strengthened the right of a child with special educational needs to be educated in the mainstream unless this is incompatible with the wishes of his parents or the provision of efficient education for other children. The local education authority has to show there are no reasonable steps they could take to prevent the incompatibility. Part 2 imposes a duty on local education authorities not to treat a disabled pupil less favourably for a reason relating to his disability than someone to whom that reason does not apply, without justification. A further duty is to make reasonable adjustments to admission arrangements and regarding education and related services to make sure disabled pupils are not put at a disadvantage in comparison with non-disabled peers without justification.

References

Department for Education and Skills (2001) *Special Educational Needs Code of Practice*, London, DfES.
Department for Education and Skills (2005) (2nd edition) *Data Collection by Special Educational Need*, London, DfES.
Ysseldyke, J. and Algozzine, B. (2006) *The Legal Foundations of Special Education: A Practical Guide for Every Teacher*, Thousand Oaks, CA, Corwin Press.

Further reading

Farrell, M. (2004) *Special Educational Needs: A Resource for Practitioners*, London, Sage, chapter 3, 'Legal Definitions of SEN, Local Criteria and the SENDIST'.
Jasper, M. (2004) (2nd edition) *The Law of Special Education*, New York and Oxford, Oxford University Press.
Russo, C. J. and Osborne, Jr., A. G. (2007) *Essential Concepts and School-Based Cases in Special Education Law*, Thousand Oaks, CA, Corwin Press.

Low vision devices and lighting

Among resources used with children having visual impairment are low vision devices and different forms of lighting. The most suitable low vision devices for a particular child are agreed in consultation with various people. These include the child, parents, an optometrist, a specialist teacher of the visually impaired and a rehabilitation specialist. There are several ways in which magnification can be achieved. The size of the image of the object can be increased. The distance between the object and the person viewing it can be reduced. The visual angle can be increased by using a multi-lens device such as a telescope. There are many devices to achieve magnification. These include a stand magnifier, a hand magnifier, a line magnifier, spectacle mounted devices, and telescopic devices. A flat bed magnifier can be employed. It has a plane base set against the surface to be viewed and a hemispheric plano-convex top. Closed circuit television may be used involving a television camera attached to a movable table and connected to a video display monitor. So called 'near devices' are used to view items such as printed materials using magnifiers and microscopes. 'Distance devices' are used to view such things as sporting events using bioptic lenses. Large print books may be used. Filter lenses are used for medical conditions such as cataracts or cone dysfunctions where light impairs vision and reduces visual acuity.

Lighting is important for pupils with visual impairment. Important are ambient lighting around school and task lighting to maximise the use of the pupil's near vision while studying. The school lighting needs to be glare free. Artificial and natural lighting are controlled so the level is suitable for particular areas of the classroom. The type of visual impairment influences suitable illumination. Pupils having photophobia require reduced lighting. Other pupils prefer higher levels of illumination. Blinds, louvres and tinted glass are used to control natural light and artificial ambient lighting is adjusted by dimmer switches.

Further reading

Sardegna, J., Shelley, S., Shelley, A. and Steidl, S. M. (2002) (2nd edition) *The Encyclopaedia of Blindness and Vision Impairment*, New York, Facts on File.

Mainstream school/classroom

Most special children are educated in mainstream schools and classrooms. The approach of many countries is to provide a range of provision including mainstream school, special classes in mainstream, and special schools. Where there is debate about whether a particular venue is better than another for a particular child this may be informed by different views. One position is that all children should be taught in mainstream, that is full inclusion. Another view is that the place where the child makes the best progress and develops best is preferred: 'optimal education' (Farrell, 2005, pp. 99–101).

Where a special child is educated in a mainstream classroom, so called inclusive approaches may be used. These may include support provided by an additional teacher or teaching aid, extra or different resources, modifications to the curriculum, access to therapies of various kinds including psychotherapy, and particular pedagogy such as the extensive support for moving from concrete operations thinking to formal operations thinking for pupils with mild cognitive impairment. Particular issues may arise for younger children (Jones, 2006), children in elementary/primary school (Briggs, 2005) and students in high school/secondary school (Briggs, 2006). Close partnership working among professionals is important (Todd, 2006). A specially appointed teacher may act as a consultant to general teachers to help them with new approaches and resources. For example, in England a special educational needs coordinator has such a role.

(See also, *Inclusion, Resource room, Special classes, Special school*)

References

Briggs, S. (2005) *Inclusion and How to Do It: Meeting SEN in Primary Classrooms*, London, Routledge.
Briggs, S. (2006) *Inclusion: How to Do It in Secondary Schools*, London, Routledge.
Farrell, M. (2005) *Key Issues in Special Education: Raising Pupils' Achievement and Attainment*, New York and London, Routledge.
Jones, P. (2006) *Inclusive Pedagogy in the Early Years*, London, Routledge.

Todd, (2006) *Partnerships for Inclusive Education: A Critical Approach to Collaborative Working*, London, Routledge.

Further reading

Knowles, G. (2006) *Supporting Inclusive Practice*, London, Routledge.

Mathematics disorder

The nature of mathematics disorder

Mathematics disorder, sometimes called dyscalculia, is a difficulty in understanding and learning mathematics not associated with general cognitive difficulties. Its essential feature is mathematical ability falling substantially below that expected for the child's chronological age, intelligence and age appropriate education. The disorder 'significantly interferes' with academic achievement of daily living that requires mathematical skills (American Psychiatric Association, 2000, p. 53). Relatedly, 'dyscalculia' is defined in a document relating to a national numeracy strategy in England as, 'a condition that affects the ability to acquire mathematical skills' (Department for Education and Skills, 2001).

A pupil with mathematics disorder may have difficulty performing simple calculations such as addition or knowing how to respond to mathematical information. He may substitute one number for another; reverse numbers; misalign symbols; and wrongly name, read and write mathematical symbols. Some suggested types of mathematics disorder relate to dyspraxia or dyslexia. Spatial dyscalculia may relate to dyspraxic difficulties, while lexical and graphic dyscalculia may relate to dyslexic problems (Jordan, Hanich and Kaplan, 2003).

Because mathematics disorder is often associated with reading disorder or developmental co-ordination, estimates of prevalence are difficult to make. It is not always agreed what degree of difficulty with mathematics constitutes a disorder. Nevertheless, estimates taking into account studies in the United States of America, Europe, and Israel suggest 5 per cent to 7 per cent of school age children show some form of arithmetical disability (Geary, 2003, p. 200).

Foetal alcohol syndrome has been associated with babies being born with the parietal lobes, considered important for numeracy, being underdeveloped. This is associated with the child later having difficulties with mathematical cognition and number processing (Kopera-Frye *et al.*, 1996). Different neural systems contribute to mathematical cognition. For example, visuo-spatial regions may be involved with complex calculations (Zago *et al.*, 2001) where visual-mental imagery may be important.

Provision

Attainment in mathematics will be lower than age average. In response, levels of the curriculum may be lower than age typical in mathematics and related areas such as physics, chemistry, biology, and geography. The balance of subjects may emphasise mathematics so that progress can be encouraged and supported. Assessment will need to be sufficiently refined so that progress in mathematics can be shown.

Regarding classroom organisation, explicit systematic instruction with opportunities for students to respond and to talk through their thinking helps pupils with mathematics disorder. Therefore classroom and group organisation that facilitates this is likely to aid learning. See Instructional Research Group, California (www.inresg.org).

Various general approaches are used for mathematics disorder. For example, using concrete apparatus helps give the pupil experience and understanding of what is being done. A pupil with mathematics disorder may need to use concrete items longer than most pupils. When more abstract methods are used, concrete reminders can still be helpful for some tasks. Number lines or a box of physical shapes that are labelled are examples. Concrete material such as Unifix blocks, if judiciously used and if progress is checked, can be useful in developing understanding of computation and other mathematical understanding. Cuisenaire rods can be useful physical aids where size and colour help pupils' understanding of aspects of mathematics (See Poustie, 2001, pp. 61–63 for further practical ideas).

To develop mathematics understanding and skills requires certain prerequisite skills: classification, number, length, area, volume, weight, position and movement. For example, number sense includes: being able to subitise small quantities (rapidly, accurately and confidently judging number given a small number of items), recognise number patterns, compare numerical magnitudes, estimate quantities, count, and carry out simple number transformations (Berch, 2005). The teacher can check that such precursors are in place and, if they are not, teach them using practical examples and experience.

Because of difficulties with fine motor co-ordination, eye-hand co-ordination and spatial relationships, the child with developmental coordination disorder may have difficulties writing numerals, for example getting the size correct. Among the many approaches possible, squared paper with squares of a size allowing the child to write a number in each can be used to help with the size of numerals. Numerals can be taught in groups avoiding grouping similar looking numerals that may be confused (3 and 5; 6 and 9).

Some difficulties associated with reading disorder may also arise in relation to mathematics problems. For example, there may be a relationship between deficits in processing sounds (a feature of reading disorder) and accessing arithmetical facts from long-term memory (Geary and Hoard, 2001).

Certainly, learning number facts includes counting, which involves number words and the use of the phonetic system. However, it is unclear why children with mathematics disorder and not concurrent reading disorder and who presumably have intact phonetic abilities also have problems retrieving facts (Jordan, Hanich and Kaplan, 2003, p. 834).

References

American Psychiatric Association (2000) *Diagnostic and Statistical Manual of Mental Disorders, Fourth Edition, Text Revision*, Arlington, VA, APA.

Berch, D. B. (2005) 'Making sense of number sense: Implications for children with mathematical disabilities', *Journal of Learning Disabilities* 38, 333–339.

Department for Education and Skills (2001) *The National Numeracy Strategy Guidance to Support Pupils with Dyslexia and Dyscalculia*, London, DfES.

Geary, D. C. (2003) 'Learning disabilities in arithmetic: Problem solving differences and cognitive deficits' in Swanson, H. L., Harris, K. R. and Graham, S. (Eds) (2003) *Handbook of Learning Disabilities*, New York, Guilford Press, 199–212.

Geary, D. C. and Hoard, M. K. (2001) 'Numerical and arithmetical deficits in learning disabled children: Relation to dyscalculia and dyslexia', *Aphasiology* 15, 7, 635–647

Jordan, N. C., Hanich, L. B. and Kaplan, D. (2003) 'A longitudinal study of mathematical competencies in children with specific mathematics difficulties versus children with comorbid mathematics and reading difficulties', *Child Development* 74, 3, 834–850.

Kopera-Frye, K., Dahaene, S. and Streissguth, A. P. (1996) 'Impairments of number processing induced by prenatal alcohol exposure', *Neuropsychologia* 34, 1187–1196.

Poustie, J. (2001) *Mathematics Solutions: An Introduction to Dyscalculia Part B – How to Teach Children and Adults Who Have Specific Learning Difficulties in Mathematics*, Taunton, UK, Next Generation.

Zago, L., Presenti, M., Mellet, E., Crivello, F., Mazoyer, B., and Tzourio-Mazoyer, N. (2001) 'Neural correlates of simple and complex mental calculation', *Neuroimage* 13, 314–327.

Further reading

Campbell, J. (Ed.) (2005) *Handbook of Mathematical Cognition*, New York, Taylor and Francis.

Chin, S. and Ashcroft, R. (2006) (3rd edition) *Mathematics for Dyslexics, Including Dyscalculia*, London, Wiley.

Feifer, S. G. and DeFina, P. A. (2005) *The Neuropsychology of Mathematics*, Middletown, MD, School Neuropsych Press.

Hannell, G. (2005) *Dyscalculia: Action Plans for Successful Learning in Mathematics*, London, David Fulton Publishers.

Addresses

About Dyscalculia
www.aboutdyscalculia.org
Provides research information for parents, teachers, policy makers and individuals affected by dyscalculia.

Learning Disabilities Association of America
www.ldanatl.org
A non-profit volunteer organisation that provides support to people with learning disabilities, their parents, teachers and other professionals.
National Center for Learning Disabilities
www.ncld.org
Provides information, promotes research and offers advocacy.

Medication

Children and youth with disabilities and disorders may take medication as part of the treatment of a condition. Where this is the case, teachers need to know that medication is taken and why. Medication may be taken routinely or in certain circumstances as needs (for example with asthma). Where schools administer medication to a child, procedures are agreed with the school, health authorities and parents and staff are trained as necessary.

Some issues relating to the use of medication may be illustrated with reference to attention deficit hyperactivity disorder. One theory is that hyperactivity results from under arousal of the midbrain causing insufficient inhibition of movement and sensation. Where psychostimulant drugs such as methylphenidate appear effective, they may stimulate the midbrain sufficiently to suppress the over activity. Stimulants can therefore improve the child's capacity to concentrate when hyperactive behaviours are inhibited. Neuroimaging studies have indicated that children taking methylphenidate (Ritalin) have improved attention to auditory and visual stimuli (Seifert *et al.*, 2003). Methylphenidate is taken by mouth in tablet form usually in the mornings and afternoons. It is not used with children under 4 years old and is contraindicated where there is a high risk of cardiovascular disease, or tic disorders. Insomnia and temporary loss of appetite have been reported as side effects. Medication is used in combination with other approaches such as behavioural interventions.

There is debate about whether medication may be over prescribed and those raising such concerns may point to wide differences in use that are not easily explainable. For example, in the United States of America, around 90 per cent of pupils with attention hyperactivity disorders receive medication of some kind (Greenhill, 1998). In the United Kingdom the equivalent figure is about 10 per cent with less than 6 per cent being administered

0

methylphenidate (National Institute of Clinical Excellence, 2000). It is widely accepted that a thorough assessment is necessary before medication is used and that effects are continuously monitored, including monitoring by school and home.

References

Greenhill, L. (1998) 'Childhood ADHD: pharmacological treatments' in Nathan, P. and Gorman, M. (Eds) *A Guide to Treatments that Work*, Oxford, Oxford University Press.
National Institute of Clinical Excellence (2000) *Guidance on the Use of Methylphenidate for ADHD*, London, NICE.
Seifert, J., Scheuerpflug, P., Zillerssen, K. E., Fallgater, A. and Warnke, A. (2003) 'Electrophysiological investigations of the effectiveness of methylphenidate in children with and without ADHD', *Journal of Neural Transmission* 110, 7, 821–828.

Further reading

Candy, D., Davies, G. and Ross, E. (2001) *Clinical Paediatrics and Child Health*, Edinburgh, Harcourt/W. B. Saunders.

Addresses

National Institute for Clinical Excellence
www.nice.org.uk
A UK-based organisation providing national guidance on public health, health technologies and clinical practice.

U.S. Food and Drug Administration
www.fda.gov/cder/
A government body regulating food and drugs.

Medicine

The practice of medicine and the medical profession

Drawing on anatomy, physiology, pathology, pharmacology and a range of other knowledge and skills, clinical medicine (McPhee and Ganong, 2006) concerns the management and treatment of health problems. It includes consideration of aetiology (relating to the causes of conditions) and prevalence (the number of cases of a disease or condition in a specified population at any one time). It involves diagnosis, understanding the likely course of a disease or condition, prognosis (an estimate of the outcome of a disease), and treatment.

Paediatrics is concerned with the development and care of children, and 'the nature and treatment of diseases of children' (Anderson, 2007, p. 1421). It embraces paediatric principles, developmental considerations, and systems perspectives such as neurology, orthopaedics and so on (Candy, Davies and Ross, 2001). Community paediatrician's work as part of a team including therapists and community nurses, with children and families, liaising between education and other professionals and agencies as needed.

Among professions related to medicine whose members may support children with disabilities and disorders are: physical therapy/physiotherapy, occupational therapy, speech and language pathology/therapy, prosthetics and orthotics. In providing an individualised treatment programme, a physical therapist and occupational therapist make a detailed functional assessment of the child's abilities and limitations. She may also advise to the school on matters such as seating and mobility aids. Members of such health professions tend to be employed by health care providers. Also, schools sometimes directly employ and pay their own medical professionals, for example a full time speech pathologist. These staff may maintain links with the health care provider for personal support, professional supervision and training.

Medicine and special education

Some children require medical attention whilst being educated to enable them to benefit from education. Medicine and medical information inform the special education and care of children with certain health related conditions. Continuing efforts are made to build understanding and collaboration between educators and health personnel, despite differences in training, perspectives, and roles of the different people working with a child with disabilities and disorders.

Special educators need to be familiar with basic medical information. For a child with visual impairment, such information is used to help determine the best environment. This embraces the use of suitable lighting and other resources, tactile methods of teaching and learning and other aspects of provision and education (Farrell, 2008, chapter 6). Similar understanding is required for a child with hearing impairment and deafblindness, orthopaedic impairments, traumatic brain injury, and health impairments.

Medical information may relate to the fatiguing effects of conditions or physical constraints on mobility. The school may examine situations where pupils generally use stairs, make long journeys between lessons, or where facilities are spread over a large campus area. The environment might be modified or alternatives used, such as installing an elevator to avoid difficulties climbing stairs.

There may be specific risks to children having a particular condition. In areas of the curriculum where noxious fumes may be involved, care is taken to avoid or minimise their inhalation. For pupils more prone to the effects of such fumes, including children with respiratory problems, greater care is needed.

Support and alternative activities may be suitable for pupils with some medical conditions such as brittle bone syndrome (Candy, Davies and Ross, 2001, p. 346). While some conditions may require the child to avoid rough contact sports, he could participate in alternatives such as swimming. The school may arrange earlier or later starts to lessons, or home or hospital tuition. Specialist resources may be used, such as physical aids to positioning and movement to enable the child to participate as fully as possible in lessons.

For a pupil with orthopaedic impairment or motor difficulties, the contribution of the physical therapist may include assessment, direct therapy, and advice on posture and movement. Physical therapists and teachers may work together on programmes enabling the fullest participation of the child in physical activities and lessons including physical education and games (Black and Haskins, 1996). The occupational therapist similarly may provide assessment, direct intervention and advice.

The use of medication has implications for education. For example, in disorders of conduct, it has been maintained that medication cannot be justified as an initial response (Fonagy *et al.*, 2005, p. 192, paraphrased). Where other strategies are developed and evaluated well, medication may not be needed. Where drugs are used, teachers need to be aware of the intended effects and the potential side effects. Taking the example of conduct disorder, combinations of psychosocial treatments and stimulant medication together, appear more effective than either on their own.

References

Anderson, D. M. (Chief lexicographer) (2007) (31st edition) *Dorland's Illustrated Medical Dictionary*, Philadelphia, PA, Elsevier/Saunders.

Black, K. and Haskins, D. (1996) 'Including all children in TOP PLAY and BT TOP SPORT', *British Journal of Physical Education*, Primary PE Focus, Winter edition 9, 11.

Candy, D., Davies, G. and Ross, E. (2001) *Clinical Paediatrics and Child Health*, Edinburgh, Harcourt/W. B. Saunders.

Farrell, M. (2008) *Educating Special Children: An Introduction to Provision for Pupils with Disabilities and Disorders*, New York and London, Routledge.

Fonagy, P., Target, M., Cottrell, D., Phillips, J. and Kurtz, Z. (2005) *What Works for Whom? A Critical Review of Treatments for Children and Adolescents* New York, Guilford Press.

McPhee, S. J. and Ganong, W. F. (2006) (5th edition) *Pathophysiology of Disease: An Introduction to Clinical Medicine*, New York, Lange Medical Books/McGraw-Hill.

Further reading

Lissauer, T. and Clayden, G. (2007) (3rd edition) *Illustrated Textbook of Paediatrics*, London, Elsevier Mosby.

Addresses

American Academy of Pediatrics
   www.aap.org
   An organisation in the USA for pediatricians seeking the optimum health and well-being of children and youth.

The British Association of Paediatric Surgeons
   www.baps.org.uk
   A UK-based organisation aiming to advance study, practice and research in paediatric surgery.

Mentor for pupils

Mentors for pupils may be adults or other pupils. Adults may be volunteers or be employed by the school. The aim of mentoring is to provide an independent person who can befriend and support the pupil. This may involve contributing to raising self-esteem, helping pupils make important life decisions in cooperation with parents. It is accepted that caring adult–child/adolescent relationships can contribute to positive development in young people (Buckley and Zimmermann, 2003). Where pupils are mentors, they need to be carefully selected, trained and supported.

Reference

Buckley, M. A. and Zimmermann, S. H. (2003) *Mentoring Children: A Guide to the Issues*, Westport, CT, Praeger.

Further reading

Fletcher, S. (2000) *Mentoring in Schools: A Handbook of Good Practice*, London, Routledge.
Mortola, P., Hilton, H. and Grant, S. (2007) *BAM! Boys Advocacy and Mentoring: A Leader's Guide to Facilitating Strength's-Based Groups for Boys – Helping Boys Make Better Contact by Making Better Contact with Them*, New York and London, Routledge.

Address

Association of Mentoring Professionals
   www.mentoringprofessionals.org
   An association based in the USA aiming to empower its members through education, advocacy and resource sharing.

Mild cognitive impairment

The nature of mild cognitive impairment

Mild cognitive impairment is often referred to in the United States of America as 'mild mental retardation' and in England as 'moderate learning difficulties'. There is debate about the usefulness of the category. It is correlated with poorer social backgrounds, suggesting to some that it may be predominantly socially constructed. Mild cognitive impairment may be associated with behavioural difficulties and speech and language disorders. In England, government guidance on pupils with 'moderate learning difficulties' states they are likely to 'have attainments significantly below expected levels in most areas of the curriculum, despite appropriate interventions'. Furthermore, 'Their needs will *not* be able to be met by normal differentiation and the flexibilities of the National Curriculum' (Department for Education and Skills, 2005, p. 6). They 'have much greater difficulty than peers in acquiring basic literacy and numeracy skills and in understanding concepts. They may also have associated speech and language delay, low self-esteem, low levels of concentration and underdeveloped social skills' (Ibid. p. 6).

The *Diagnostic and Statistical Manual of Mental Disorders Fourth Edition Text Revision* (DSM-IV-TR) (American Psychiatric Association, 2000, p. 42) includes diagnostic criteria for mental retardation. These include 'co current deficits or impairments in present adaptive functioning ... in at least two of the following areas: communication, self care, home living, social/interpersonal skills, use of community resources, self-direction, functional academic skills, work, leisure, health and safety' (Ibid. p. 49). 'Mild mental retardation' is associated with an intelligence quotient (IQ) range of 50/55 to 70. These IQ levels are interpreted with care, not being the sole criterion. Children with mild mental retardation tend to 'develop social and communication skills during the pre-school years (ages 0 to 5 years)' (Ibid. p. 43) and by the late teens, can acquire academic skills up to about sixth grade level. In 2002, the American Association on Intellectual and Developmental Disabilities (AAIDD) agreed a supports-based definition. This takes the view that mental retardation is a condition that can be enhanced by the provision of supports rather than as a more static disability. In the population of individuals with 'mental retardation' it is estimated that the group having 'mild mental retardation' constitute around 85 per cent (Ibid.). When assessments are made, care is taken that the prevalence for children of different ethnic or cultural backgrounds is reliably and validly determined (Ibid.).

Provision

The curriculum content for pupils with mild cognitive impairment takes account of the fact that the level of attainment of pupils is significantly below that typical of pupils of the same chronological age. Its content is typical of younger children but presented age appropriately. The curriculum tends to be subject based, with communication, literacy, numeracy and personal and social development being emphasised. These may be allocated more time than is usual in schools or embedded in other subjects through cross-curricular planning. Practical experience is emphasised with structured opportunities for the pupil to make progress from being able to think using practical examples to being able to think in more logical and abstract terms, a transfer that pupils with mild cognitive impairment find very difficult. Assessment tends to have steps small enough to ensure that achievements are recognised and celebrated.

Pupils with mild cognitive impairments tend to find self-regulation difficult, with implications for their learning. Borkowski and colleagues (2006) summarise the importance of self-regulation. It is considered fundamental to most learning problems of individuals with cognitive impairment. Pupils may not use strategies efficiently, or suitably generalise newly acquired strategies, perhaps because of immature forms of self-regulation. The teacher provides encouragement and structures to enable pupils to develop and evaluate their problem-solving strategies.

Pupils with mild cognitive impairment tend to be able to think using practical examples but have particular difficulty moving from this to thinking logically and in more abstract ways. The teacher therefore can provide many supported opportunities and support to assist this. This involves carefully moving from thinking using examples to drawing broader inferences from this. For example a pupil may be able to judge respective height by visualising three progressively taller objects. A red object is taller than a yellow one, which is taller than a green object. The move to logical thinking involves realising in this example that therefore the red object will always be taller than the green one.

Practical use of language skills includes conversational skills, such as introducing a topic, maintaining it and concluding it. Role play and being taught cues that are often used when a conversational partner wants to change the topic might aid this. The *Social Use of Language Programme* (Rinaldi, 2001) can assist the communication skills of young people with mild to moderate learning difficulty. It can be used to assess verbal and non-verbal communication skills and implement interventions. Speech and language therapy may be necessary for some pupils.

Various approaches to literacy appear effective with pupils having mild mental retardation. These include 'Phonological Awareness Training' (Wilson and Frederickson, 1995; Brooks, 2002, p. 106). This uses a pupil's existing knowledge of letter sounds and words so that new words containing identically written endings become less difficult in reading and spelling. 'Reading Intervention' (Hatcher, 2000) uses a combination of phonological training and reading (Brooks, 2002, pp. 38–39, 110). Pupils are helped to isolate phonemes within words. In this way, they come to recognise that sounds can be common between words and certain letters can represent specific sounds.

A programme based on a multi-sensory cognitive-behavioural approach to social skills training has been used in a special school for adolescents having 'moderate learning difficulties'. It aimed to enable them to deal with social situations better in preparation for returning to mainstream school. Sessions involve several activities and last about an hour and 40 minutes each. There were six to ten students and two adults. Pupils also used rehearsal, modelling and reinforcement to encourage the use of inner and external speech to influence their behaviour. They also learned acceptable social behaviour and problem-solving skills (Cornish and Ross, 2003).

Pupils with mild cognitive impairment tend to have difficulties with generalising knowledge and skills (Meese, 2001). The teacher can therefore highlight the relevance of what is learned. This helps in generalisation because the learning can be related to regularly occurring day-to-day experiences. Also, repeated opportunities can be built into the curriculum to develop and apply new skills and knowledge.

References

American Psychiatric Association (2000) *Diagnostic and Statistical Manual of Mental Disorders, Fourth Edition, Text Revision*, Arlington, VA, APA.

Borkowski, J. G., Carothers, S. S., Howard, K., Schatz, J. and Farris, J. (2006) 'Intellectual assessment and intellectual disability' in Jacobson, J. W., Mulick, J. A. and Rojhan, J. (Eds) *Handbook of Mental Retardation and Developmental Abilities*, New York, Springer.

Brooks, G. (2002) *What Works for Reading Difficulties? The Effectiveness of Intervention Schemes*, London, Department of Education and Science.

Cornish, U. and Ross, F. (2003) *Social Skills Training for Adolescents with General Moderate Learning Difficulties*, London, Jessica Kingsley.

Department of Education and Skills (2005) (2nd edition) *Data Collection by Special Educational Need*, London, DfES.

Hatcher, P. (2000) 'Sound links in reading and spelling with discrepancy defined dyslexics and children with moderate learning difficulties', *Reading and Writing: An Interdisciplinary Journal* 13, 257–272.

Meese, R. L. (2001) (2nd edition) *Teaching Learners with Mild Disabilities: Integrating Research and Practice*, Belmont, CA, Wadsworth-Thompson.

Rinaldi, W. (2001) *Social Use of Language Programme*, Windsor, NFER-Nelson.

Wilson, J. and Frederickson, N. (1995) Phonological awareness training: An evaluation', *Educational and Child Psychology* 12, 1, 68–79.

Further reading

Rose, R. (1991) 'A jigsaw approach to group work', *British Journal of Special Education* 18, 2, 54–58.

Switzky, H. N. and Greenspan, S. (Eds) (2006) *What is Mental Retardation? Ideas for an Evolving Disability in the 21st Century*, Washington, DC, American Association on Intellectual and Developmental Disabilities.

Addresses

Council for Exceptional Children
www.cec.sped.org
Based in the USA, this professional organisation aims to improve the outcomes for individuals with disabilities and disorders and those with gifts and talents.

The National Association for Special Educational Needs
www.nasen.org.uk
The association aims to promote the development of children and young people with 'special educational needs' and supports those who work with them.

Moderate to severe cognitive impairment

Moderate to severe cognitive impairment is referred to as 'moderate to severe mental retardation' in the United States of America. In England, a similar term is 'severe learning difficulties'. In Canada, Australia and Malta, the term 'moderate to severe intellectual disability' is used.

The nature of moderate to severe cognitive impairment

In England, government guidance (Department for Education and Skills, 2005, p. 6) states that pupils with severe learning difficulties have, 'significant intellectual or cognitive impairments'. Also, 'This has a major effect on their ability to participate in the school curriculum without support. They may also have difficulties with mobility and co-ordination, communication and perception and the acquisition of self help skills. Pupils with severe learning difficulties will need support in all areas of the curriculum. Some pupils may use signs and symbols but most will be able to hold simple conversations' (Ibid.). For most of their schooling these pupils will be working below a level (that is level 1 of the National Curriculum) usually entered by a typically developing child at about the age of 5 to 6 years.

The *Diagnostic and Statistical Manual of Mental Disorders, Fourth Edition, Text Revision (DSM-IV-TR)* (American Psychiatric Association, 2000, p. 42) gives diagnostic criteria for mental retardation in general. These include 'co current deficits or impairments in present adaptive functioning ... in at least two of the following areas: communication, self care, home living, social/interpersonal skills, use of community resources, self-direction, functional academic skills, work, leisure, health and safety' (Ibid. p. 49). The manual relates 'moderate retardation' to intelligence quotient (IQ) levels of 35/40 to 50/55. 'Severe retardation' is associated with IQ levels of 20/25 to 35/40. The range therefore for moderate to severe cognitive impairment is of IQ levels from 20/25 to 50/55. Importantly, IQ is not the sole criterion (Ibid. p. 42). Some 40 per cent of individuals with an IQ level of 70 have a medical background condition. Of individuals having an IQ below 50, 80 per cent have such a condition (Gillberg and Soderstrom, 2003). Most individuals experiencing *moderate* cognitive impairment gain communication skills in early childhood. With supervision they, 'can attend to their personal care' (American Psychiatric Association, 2000, p. 43). They benefit from social and occupational skills training, but are, 'unlikely to progress beyond second-grade level in academic subjects' (Ibid. p. 43). In early childhood, children with *severe* mental retardation tend to acquire little or no communicative speech. During the school age period they may learn to talk and acquire 'elementary self-care skills'. They profit somewhat from teaching in such skills as 'simple counting' and sight-reading of some survival words (Ibid. p. 43).

Organisation for Economic Co-operation and Development (2000) figures vary from country to country. In Italy, 0.88 per cent of the school population are identified as having severe learning difficulties while in the Netherlands the figure is 0.44 per cent. In the United States of America, of the population with mental retardation (mild, moderate, severe, profound) the group having moderate mental retardation are about 10 per cent, and those having severe mental retardation are around 3 per cent to 4 per cent (American Psychiatric Association, 2000, p. 43). Predisposing factors for mental retardation include heredity, early alterations in the development of the embryo, pregnancy and perinatal problems, and general medical conditions acquired in infancy or childhood (Ibid. pp. 45–46).

Provision

The curriculum for pupils with moderate to severe cognitive impairment tends to have 'functional academic content' (Wehmeyer *et al.*, 2002, pp. 190–203) emphasising practicality and relevance. There is flexibility for children to work on areas of the curriculum at levels typical of much younger pupils, while ensuring activities are appropriate to the chronological age of the pupil. Particularly important are functional and practical approaches to communication, literacy, numeracy, and personal and social development. For example, functional mathematics may involve using money, laying a table, telling the time, writing and using a schedule, reading transport timetables, reading energy meters, and measuring areas for practical activities (Algozzine and Ysseldyke, 2006, pp. 38–42). Cross-curricular links of skills and understanding associated with mathematics can be built into the schemes of work for other areas such as science, physical education and modern foreign languages. Small steps in assessment ensure a pupil's progress is recognised.

In teaching and learning, the comparative visual strengths of pupils are used. For literacy, sight recognition approaches tend to be preferred to phonological ones, especially where the pupil has: poor phonological awareness; problems with auditory memory, and hearing impairment. Sight recognition methods may include the use of graphical symbols. Where manual signing is taught, the visual aspects of this are important. Similarly, in mathematics, visual approaches are likely to be preferred, especially where real life contexts are used promoting problem solving. The classroom can be arranged so pupils can notice and respond to visual cues, ensuring this is maintained if furniture is moved and different groupings are adopted for different activities.

Children with severe cognitive impairment may have limited expressive communication skills (Mar and Sall, 1999). Therefore school needs to encourage the child to communicate through its daily structures and routines. These include brief arrival greeting sessions, snack times and recess activities where communication with other pupils is encouraged, as well as groups or paired activities. Ongoing opportunities are taken to develop pupils' communication spontaneously. Augmentative and alternative communication includes the use of signing, photographs and speech synthesisers, objects of reference and symbols. Visual symbols capitalise on visual input and are often used in connection with computer technology. Symbols are used to support emerging literacy.

Encouraging choice and decision-making contributes to developing autonomy and independence and each lesson or activity plan can be examined to seek opportunities for offering choices. This might include choice of food and drink, leisure activity, or musical instrument. Initially, adult support may be necessary to enable the pupil to choose, but later, more complex decision-making can be encouraged.

McDonnell and colleagues (1993) in a study indicated that vocational instruction can lead to significant student gains for high school students with 'moderate to profound mental retardation'. The school can help the student in following directions, punctuality, staying on task and completing assignments. Such skills can be directly taught and the school can provide opportunities to put them into practice (Algozzine and Ysseldyke, 2006, pp. 49–50).

As necessary, therapy may be provided by the physical therapist and/or the occupational therapist. Speech and language therapy may be necessary to help phonological difficulties and other aspects of language development. The school will closely liaise with therapists. Teachers and therapists may jointly assess pupils, and plan and implement interventions.

References

Algozzine, B. and Ysseldyke, E. (2006) *Teaching Students with Mental Retardation: A Practical Guide for Teachers*, Thousand Oaks, CA, Corwin Press.

American Psychiatric Association (2000) *Diagnostic and Statistical Manual of Mental Disorders, Fourth Edition, Text Revision*, Arlington, VA, APA.

Department for Education and Skills (2005) (2nd edition) *Data Collection by Special Educational Need*, London, DfES.

Gillberg, C. and Soderstrom, H. (2003) 'Learning disability', *The Lancet* 362, 811–821.

McDonnell, J., Hardman, M. L., Hightower, J., Keifer-O'Donnell and Drew, C. (1993) 'Impact of community based instruction on the development of adaptive behaviour of secondary level students with mental retardation', *American Journal on Mental Retardation* 97, 5, 575–584.

Mar, H. M. and Sall, N. (1999) 'Profiles of the expressive communication skills of children and adolescents with severe cognitive disabilities', *Education and Training in Mental Retardation and Developmental Disabilities* 34, 1, 77–89.

Organisation for Economic Co-operation and Development (2000) *Special Needs Education: Statistics and Indicators*, Paris, OECD.

Wehmeyer, M. L., Sands, D. J., Knowlton, E. and Kozleski, E. B. (2002) *Teaching Students with Mental Retardation: Providing Access to the General Curriculum*, Baltimore, MD, Brookes.

Further reading

Drew, C. J. and Hardman, M. L. (2006) (9th edition) *Intellectual Disabilities Across the Lifespan*, Upper Saddle River, NJ, Prentice Hall.

Addresses

Council for Exceptional Children
www.cec.sped.org
Based in the USA, this professional organisation aims to improve the outcomes for individuals with disabilities and disorders and those with gifts and talents.

The National Association for Special Educational Needs
www.nasen.org.uk
The association aims to promote the development of children and young people with 'special educational needs' and supports those who work with them.

Multi-professional working

A continuing though challenging aim in educating and supporting special children is close multi-professional working. For example, in the United States of America, a team including the child's parents and professionals who work with the child develop the Individual Education Program. In England a graduated response to disability or disorder involves as necessary support from outside the school, such as a school psychologist or physical therapist.

Multi-professional working may involve professionals from the same services such as a teacher and a school psychologist both working for the same educational agency. It may also involve professionals from different agencies working together, such as a teacher employed by education services and a nurse or speech-language pathologist employed by heath services and a social worker employed by welfare/social services. The latter may be referred to as multi-agency working. Generally, it is a greater challenge to ensure close multi-agency working than to make sure professionals working for the same agency work together closely.

The wide range of professionals that may be involved with a child and his family include a medical doctor, nurse, physical therapist, occupational therapist, teacher, speech pathologist, psychotherapist, and many others. Where provision lasts over an extended period, the particular personnel may move on making the total number of people involved even larger. Consequently, close collaboration is necessary between those working in health services, social services, education, the voluntary sector and others.

Multi-professional working is important for dyslexia and other specific learning difficulties (Farrell, 2006a, pp. 13–15); autism and communication difficulties (Farrell, 2006b, pp. 8–9); behavioural, emotional and social difficulties (Farrell, 2006c, pp. 13–14); learning difficulties/cognitive impairment (Farrell, 2006d, pp. 8–10); and sensory impairment and physical disabilities (Farrell, 2006e, pp. 9–10). There are some differences in the likely composition of teams according to the type of disability and disorder. For example, for children with visual impairment, an optometrist and a specialist teacher will be involved, and for individuals with hearing impairment an audiologist will contribute. Where communication is impaired, a speech-language therapist has a key role. For pupils with disorders of conduct, anxiety disorders or depressive disorders, psychotherapists may form part of the team. Where a child has orthopaedic impairments or certain health impairments, then surgeons, physicians, nurses, and physical therapists may be involved. The size of the team may vary considerably over time as in the case of traumatic brain injury where the initial team may be very large but, as progress is made, may reduce considerably.

Particular issues arise requiring different personnel depending on the child's age. For example, for older pupils, personnel may be employed to ensure a smooth transition from high school/secondary school to college or work.

Close working is made more difficult if:

• The administrative boundaries of different services do not coincide, for example if the area covered by one health authority coincides with several different social services areas.

170 Multi-professional working

- Different professionals work on different sites, which is often inevitably the case.
- There is competition rather than cooperation between different services, high staff turnover and distrust.
- Different professional legal frameworks, perceptions and priorities are not understood or discussed.
- There are different practices regarding confidentiality.
- There are great differences in approaches to funding the different services without a clear rationale.

Close working is also hindered if services are poorly audited and monitored (Kirby and Drew, 2003, p. 85).

Many projects and developments have been tried to improve the coordination of services. For example, in England, in 2003, an early support pilot programme sought to develop good service provision and assist development in several areas including the coordination of multi-agency support for families and partnership across agencies and geographical boundaries. This involve joint working between the then Department for Education and Skills (since renamed the Department for Children Families and Schools), the Royal National Institute for the Blind, the Royal National Institute for the Deaf, the National Children's Bureau and others (www.earlysupport.org.uk).

A helpful perspective is to focus on the required outcomes for children and young people, to examine the contribution that multi-professional working has to make to assuring these outcomes, and developing services to meet these demands. Outcomes are then monitored to ensure they have been achieved.

Associations such as the Council for Exceptional Children in the United States of America and The National Association for Special Educational Needs in the United Kingdom can be useful forums to bring together professionals from different services and disciplines and parents.

References

Farrell, M. (2006a) *The Effective Teacher's Guide to Dyslexia and Other Specific Learning Difficulties: Practical Strategies*, New York and London, Routledge.
Farrell, M. (2006b) *The Effective Teacher's Guide to Autism and Communication Difficulties: Practical Strategies*, New York and London, Routledge.
Farrell, M. (2006c) *The Effective Teacher's Guide to Behavioural, Emotional and Social Difficulties: Practical Strategies*, New York and London, Routledge.
Farrell, M. (2006d) *The Effective Teacher's Guide to Moderate, Severe and Profound Learning Difficulties: Practical Strategies*, New York and London, Routledge.
Farrell, M. (2006e) *The Effective Teacher's Guide to Sensory Impairment and Physical Disability: Practical Strategies*, New York and London, Routledge.
Kirby, A. and Drew, S. (2003) *Guide to Dyspraxia and Developmental Coordination Disorders*, London, David Fulton Publishers.

Further reading

Anning, A., Cottrell, D. M., Frost, N., Green, J. and Robinson, M. (2006) *Developing Multi/professional Teamwork for Integrated Children's Services*, Buckingham, UK, Open University Press.

Siraj-Blatchford, I., Clarke, K and Needham, M. (Eds) (2007) *The Team Around the Child: Multi-Agency Working in the Early Years*, Stoke-on-Trent, Staffordshire, UK, Trentham Books.

Addresses

Council for Exceptional Children
  www.cec.sped.org
  Based in the USA, this professional organisation aims to improve the outcomes for individuals with disabilities and disorders and those with gifts and talents.

The National Association for Special Educational Needs
  www.nasen.org.uk
  The association aims to promote the development of children and young people with 'special educational needs' and supports those who work with them.

Multisensory environments

Perhaps the most common understanding of a multisensory environment is a sensory stimulation room. These may be used with pupils with moderate to severe cognitive impairment, profound cognitive impairment and others (e.g. Fowler, 2008). Such rooms may include devices, which respond to touch or sound by producing sounds or visual effects. There may be a soft area and a ball pool, an optikinetics projector, bubble tubes, a glass fibre optics light tail, and a transmitter of sound effects or music. This may encourage responses from a pupil by rewarding his perhaps spontaneous actions. The room may offer a therapeutic setting in which children who are anxious can be helped to relax.

Sensory stimulation rooms are sometimes called 'snoezlen rooms'. Snoezlen is a combination of two Dutch words meaning 'sniffing' and 'dozing' and the word was used by pioneers of the approach Hulsege and Verheul. Snoezlen is now a registered trademark of one company that produces multisensory environments and unless one is referring to that company, the term sensory stimulation room is generally used. Schools need to be clear about what outcomes are expected when children experience this environment and monitor whether expected benefits are in fact accruing.

Reference

Fowler, S. (2008) *Multisensory Rooms and Environments: Controlled Sensory Experiences for People with Profound and Multiple Disabilities*, London, Jessica Kingsley.

Further reading

Pagliano, P. (2001) *Using a Multisensory Environment: A Practical Guide for Teachers*, London, David Fulton Publishers.

Address

American Association of Multisensory Environments
  www.aame.us
  Sponsored by companies producing multisensory environments and others, the association promotes awareness, access, education, research and science for people who would benefit from multisensory environments.

Multiple disabilities

'Multiple disability' refers to the co-occurrence of several disabilities and disorders. This term is sometimes used generally to refer to deaf-blindness; or different combinations of disabilities and disorders, for example sensory impairment, cognitive impairment, motor impairment, and speech and language impairment.

In England, one of the categories referred to by government guidance is 'profound and multiple learning difficulties' (Department for Education and Skills, 2005, p. 7). Government guidance states that these pupils have 'severe and complex learning needs' and that 'in addition they have other significant difficulties, such as physical disabilities or a sensory impairment' (Ibid.). One of the categories of disability under federal law as amended in 1997 (20 United States Code 1402, 1997) reflected in designated disability codes is 'multi-handicapped'.

Reference

Department for Education and Skills (2005) (2nd edition) *Data Collection by Special Educational Need*, London, DfES.

Further reading

Aird, R. (2001) *The Education and Care of Children with Severe, Profound and Multiple Learning Difficulties*, London, David Fulton Publishers.

Bigge, J. L., Best, S. J. and Heller, K. W. (2001) (4th edition) *Teaching Individuals with Physical, Health or Multiple Disabilities*, Upper Saddle River, NJ, Merrill-Prentice Hall.

Address

PMLD Network
www.pmldnetwork.org
A group committed to improving the lives of children and adults with profound and multiple learning difficulties.

Muscular dystrophy

Muscular dystrophies are a rare group of genetic, progressive muscular disorders. Muscle fibres break down and muscles become wasted and weak. This is because they are damaged and not regenerated sufficiently, so muscle is replaced by fibrous tissue and fat. Life expectancy is shortened and some individuals die in their late teens. However, life expectancy is increasing owing to developments in scoliosis treatments and pulmonary care. At times the condition may be in remission and at other periods, there may be rapid deterioration. Some types affect both sexes. However, the commonest type, Duchenne muscular dystrophy, is inherited through a recessive, sex-linked gene so that only males are affected and only females can pass on the condition. This affects around one in 3,000 male births (Candy, Davies and Ross, 2001, p. 314).

If a boy with Duchenne muscular dystrophy does not take part in physical activity, symptoms tend to progress faster so he is encouraged and supported to be ambulatory as long as possible (Heller *et al.*, 1996). Pupils may require callipers and walking aids and, as the condition progresses, will need a wheelchair. Children with muscular dystrophy require occupational therapy and physiotherapy.

The pupil is given help with mobility as required. This may include wheelchair access and flexible arrival and departure times for lessons. The pupil may need support in class to help him use equipment and resources.

As the illness progresses, the pupil may be absent from school more often, slowing progress in school subjects. He is likely to tire easily and the curriculum may be reviewed to ensure activities and the balance of lessons over time is not over taxing. Homework is often waived or adapted. Handwriting may deteriorate as the condition weakens the pupils' arms and hands. For practical activities, the teacher ensures work is within the pupil's physical capabilities. Computer technology may be used to record work and adaptations such as keyboards with larger keys and voice-activated computers can help. If the pupil has rods surgically inserted in the back to help posture, contact sports cannot be played. In examinations a scribe may be used and extra time allowed. Careers guidance is given with particular sensitivity.

As the condition progresses, the pupil may need increasing help with self-care. Later, one-to-one support, perhaps from a teaching aide, may be needed throughout the day. As the student reaches adolescence and may be increasingly dependent, as peers are getting more independent, particular sensitivity is needed. With parental consent, counselling may be offered to help the pupil come to terms with shorter life expectancy. Families will require support and practical help.

References

Candy, D., Davies, G. and Ross, E. (2001) *Clinical Paediatrics and Child Health*, Edinburgh, Harcourt/W. B. Saunders.

Heller, K. W., Alberto, P. A., Forney, P. E. and Schwartzman, M. N. (1996) *Understanding Physical, Sensory and Health Impairments: Characteristics and Educational Implications*, Pacific Grove, CA, Brookes-Cole.

Further reading

Bigge, J. L., Best, S. J. and Heller, K. W. (2001) (4th edition) *Teaching Individuals with Physical, Health or Multiple Disabilities*, Upper Saddle River, NJ, Merrill-Prentice Hall.

Dewey, D. and Tupper, D. (Eds) (2004) *Developmental Motor Disorders: A Neuropsychological Perspective* New York, Guilford Press.

Addresses

Muscular Dystrophy Association
  www.mda.org
  A voluntary health agency based in the USA and with projects worldwide, the organisation supports research programmes, medical and community services, and health education.

Muscular Dystrophy Campaign
  www.muscular-dystrophy.org
  A UK charity focusing on all muscular dystrophies and related muscle diseases and providing information, advice and support to those affected.

Music therapy/music therapist

A fundamental aspect of music therapy is the development of a relationship between client and therapist. Music making is the basis of communication within this relationship. Sessions may be for an individual or a group and generally, therapist and client(s) actively participate in sessions by playing, singing and listening. The aim of the therapy is to help the client achieve positive changes in behaviour and emotional well-being, increase self awareness and self esteem and improve quality of life. For those finding verbal communication an inadequate form of expression, music therapy provides the opportunity to express and release feelings. It is used with children with various disabilities and disorders such as cognitive impairment, physical impairment, anxiety disorders, and depressive disorders.

A music therapist may work in a special school, hospital, psychiatric unit, or private centre, or in the community and may be employed by health, education or social services. Therapists may work with children and their families (Oldfield and Flower, 2008).

Reference

Oldfield, A. and Flower, C. (Eds) (2008) *Music Therapy with Children and Their Families*, London, Jessica Kingsley.

Further reading

Lathom-Radocy, W. B. (2003) *Pediatric Music Therapy*, Springfield, IL, Charles C. Thomas.

Addresses

American Music Therapy Association
www.musictherapy.org
Based in Maryland, USA, the association aims to advance public awareness and access to music therapy.

British Society for Music Therapy
www.bsmt.org
This UK-based society organises conferences, workshops and meetings that are open to all.

Needs

The term 'special educational needs' is part of the legal definition of special education in the United Kingdom. In Australia, the expression 'additional needs' may be used as an alternative to special educational needs. The expression 'special needs education' is sometime used.

A distinction may be made between conditional and unconditional needs (Farrell, 2004, pp. 14–17). Needs may be 'conditional'. In that case, it is evident there is a goal, that reaching that goal requires or is conditional upon something to be provided (the 'need') and that the need is justifiable. For different types of disorder/disability, the purported 'need' and the goal can often be specified. For example, a child with profound cognitive impairment may need a small steps curriculum and related assessment in order to progress and have the progress recognised; or a child who is blind may need Braille in order to learn to read.

But 'needs' may be unconditional. A parent or a school may say a pupil 'needs' speech and language therapy but may not specify or specify very loosely what the goal of this is. It may be claimed the child needs speech and language therapy to improve his progress. But this could be said of any child given such an opportunity for intensive one-to-one work with an expert specialist. Therefore to say the child 'needs' speech and language therapy must mean more that it would enable better progress. What is usually meant is that the child is behind other children in speech and language skills and that without therapy may remain so or fall further behind.

If such conditions are not explicit, there is the possibility of the term 'need' being used misleadingly, especially with types of disability/disorder that are harder to identify and assess. Therefore, unless there is at least local agreement among parents, schools and school boards about what is meant by the various types of disability/disorder the term 'special need' can be used too loosely. The child may be said to have a 'special educational need' and certain provision requested because the child is said to 'need' it without explaining why, thereby mistaking unconditional needs for conditional goal-directed needs. Debate can take place about whether the goal in a conditional need is justifiable and if it is whether others should pay for it to be achieved. Unconditional need avoids this scrutiny.

A further potential quagmire can be created by the use of the expression 'meeting needs'. It is sometimes said that it is necessary to ensure that the needs of pupils with disability/disorder are met. Typical of this use of 'needs' and having 'needs met' is an entry on a UK government web site of 2007 (www.everychildmatters.gov.uk/ete/specialschool). This states:

> The government expects the proportion of children educated in special schools to fall as mainstream schools develop the skills and capacity to meet a wider range of *needs*. A small number of children will have such severe and complex *needs* that they will continue to require special provision, but children with less significant *needs* – including those with moderate learning difficulties – should be able to have their *needs met* in a mainstream environment' [Italics added].

Such usage is confusing, as is unclear what the particular needs are, how they are to be met, and how anyone would know if and when they were met.

Categories of 'disability' under federal law in the United States of America, include 'children in need of assessment'. In England (Department for Education and Skills, 2005, *passim*), classification includes, 'speech, language and communication needs'.

(See also, *Special educational need*)

References

Department for Education and Skills (2005) (2nd edition) *Data Collection by Special Educational Need*, London, DfES.
Farrell, M. (2004) *Inclusion at the Crossroads: Special Education – Concepts and Values*, London, David Fulton.

Further reading

Department for Education and Skills (2001) *Special Educational Needs Code of Practice*, London, DfES.

Addresses

European Agency for Special Needs Education
  www.european-agency.org
An organisation whose website provides information on systems in different European countries and contacts in different countries.

The National Association for Special Educational Needs
www.nasen.org.uk
The association aims to promote the development of children and young
people with 'special educational needs' and supports those who work with
them.

Neural tube defects

The nature of neural tube defects

Neural tube defects are congenital malformations of the spine, brain or vertebrae. They are the most common congenital anomalies of the central
nervous system (Candy, Davies and Ross, 2001, p. 309).

In spina bifida ('bifid' means 'divided in two') one or several spinal
vertebrae fail to close properly, exposing the nerves. Types include:

- Encephalocele
- Anencephaly, and
- Myelomenigocele.

In encephalocele part of the brain material finds its way through a malforma-
tion in the skull.

Anencephaly involves the brain failing to develop beyond the brain stem
leading to the baby rarely surviving beyond infancy.

In myelomenigocele, the meninges and spinal cord protrude. It may be
associated with total or partial paralysis of the legs; paralysis of the bladder
and bowel; poor fine motor skills; poor balance; problems with blood circu-
lation; difficulties with activities involving the arms and hands; and visual
impairment. Variations of myelomenigocele include spina bifida occulta and
meningocele. In spina bifida occulta there is only a small defect in the bony
covering of the spinal cord leaving slight if any external signs. With meningocele, membranes around the brain and spinal cord (meninges) protrude
through the malformed spinal opening. Most affected infants also have
hydrocephalus, a condition in which an enlargement of the brain ventricles is
brought about by the obstructed flow of cerebrospinal fluid (Candy, Davies
and Ross, 2001, p. 310). It is controlled by a thin tube (a 'shunt') inserted in
the ventricles to drain cerebrospinal fluid away, usually to the chest or
abdominal cavity.

Provision

For myelomenigocele, surgery soon after birth removes the protruding sac
and closes the open area along the spinal column. Soon after, a 'shunt' may be

surgically placed in the brain, helping avoid brain damage caused by cerebrospinal fluid pushing brain matter against the interior of the skull. Orthopaedic treatment to prevent muscle contractures helps avoid deformities of the spine, hips and legs. Braces and splints help correct or reduce deformities. Braces are often used to support the trunk and legs and aid walking, and children unable to walk may need a wheelchair. The physical therapist assists the child in walking correctly and using mobility aids. An occupational therapist helps the child develop self-care and independence skills. This may include working with the family and others to improve school-related skills and encouraging suitable leisure pursuits, and procedures for tube feeding, catheterisation and colostomy/ileostomy care (Bigge, Best and Heller, 2001, pp. 547–551).

The school might provide adapted toilet facilities, assistance with dressing and help for younger pupils to change their catheter. It is important to have wheelchair access to the school building and classrooms and sufficient room to manoeuvre around the classroom. The child may be seated near the door for easier access to and from the classroom. Lesson arrival and departure times can be varied to avoid periods when the corridors are crowded with pupils.

Motor difficulties and spatial problems may hinder handwriting and number work. A classroom aide may help with practical tasks or act as an amanuensis at the same time as encouraging independence. An amanuensis may be required for academic examinations. Computer technology offers alternative means of presenting and recording work.

Some pupils with spina bifida attain at the same academic levels as other children. Others, especially if they also have hydrocephalus, may have cognitive impairment. Absences from school can also lower attainment. The student may have speech and language difficulties, including difficulties comprehending language, requiring speech-language therapy. Visual impairment may make it difficult for the pupil to judge distance or direction, and multi-sensory teaching, drawing on other senses, can help.

References

Bigge, J. L., Best, S. J. and Heller, K. W. (2001) (4th edition) *Teaching Individuals with Physical, Health or Multiple Disabilities*, Upper Saddle River, NJ, Merrill-Prentice Hall.

Candy, D., Davies, G. and Ross, E. (2001) *Clinical Paediatrics and Child Health*, Edinburgh, Harcourt/W. B. Saunders.

Further reading

Sandler, A. (1997) *Living with Spina Bifida: A Guide for Parents and Professionals*, Chapel Hill, NC, University of North Carolina Press.

Addresses

Association for Spina Bifida and Hydrocephalus
  www.asbah.org
  The association works with people with spina bifida and/or hydrocephalus, their families and carers to promote individual choice, control and
quality of life.

Spina Bifida Association
  www.spinabifidaassociation.org
  Through education, advocacy, research and service, the association serves
adults and children who live with spina bifida.

Neurology/neurologist

Neurology is a branch of medicine dealing with disorders of the nervous system: the central and peripheral nervous systems. The central nervous system
consists of the brain and the spinal cord. The peripheral nervous system
extends beyond the central nervous system and is divided into the somatic
nervous system (concerned with voluntary movement and receiving outside
stimuli) and the autonomic nervous system (which helps maintain the body in
a steady state). Assessments used in neurology include electroencephalography, functional magnetic resonance imaging, and functional near infrared
spectroscopy. Electroencephalography measures brain activity through the
skull, reflecting electrical events generated by neurones. It involves placing
electrodes at specified positions on the child's scalp (Mildner, 2008,
pp. 59–60). The functional magnetic resonance imaging method uses the
response of the protons of hydrogen atoms to a strong magnetic field and
radio waves (Beaton, 2004, p. 204). Functional near infrared spectroscopy
involves the use of 'optodes', sensors optically measuring a specified substance (Goswami, 2008, p. xii). Each of these techniques has strengths and
weaknesses.
  A neurologist is a physician who has undergone additional training in the
diagnosis and treatment of conditions of the nervous system. A neurologist
may contribute to the assessment of children in areas including those related
to speech, memory, and other cognitive abilities.

References

Beaton, A. A. (2004) *Dyslexia, Reading and the Brain: A Sourcebook of Psychological
    and Biological Research*, New York, Psychology Press.
Goswami, U. (2008) *Cognitive Development: The Learning Brain*, New York/Hove,
    Psychology Press.
Mildner, V. (2008) *The Cognitive Neuroscience of Communication*, New York,
    Lawrence Erlbaum Associates.

Further reading

Conn, P. M. (Ed.) (2003) (2nd edition) *Neuroscience in Medicine*, Totowa, NJ, Humana Press.
Kandel, E., Schwartz, J. H. and Jessel, T. M. (2000) *Principles of Neural Science*, New York, McGraw-Hill.

Addresses

American Academy of Neurology
www.aan.com
The academy is an international professional association of neurologists and neuroscience professionals.

The Association of British Neurologists
www.theabn.org
Aims to improve the health and well-being of individuals with neurological disorders through advancing the knowledge and practice of neurology.

Neuropsychology/neuropsychologist

Neuropsychology is 'the study of brain-behaviour relationships' (Dewey and Tupper, 2004, p. xi) involving an understanding of brain anatomy and physiology. It seeks to link observed behaviours to implicated brain areas (Lezak, Howieson and Loring, 2004). School neuropsychology applies knowledge of brain-behaviour relationships to school-aged children. In special education, the focus is on aspects of school neuropsychology relevant to the education and development of children with disabilities/disorders. Exploring possible neuropsychological foundations for disorders and disabilities it is envisaged will have several benefits. It can provide better understanding of conditions including the underlying processes thought to be associated with them. It could support better classifications of disabilities/disorders including the identification of possible subtypes. It could pave the way for better justified and more effective interventions.

A school neuropsychologist has to be aware of brain-behaviour relationships, but also of 'their application in real life settings, both for typical children and those with disabilities' (Hale and Fiorello, 2004, p. 4). She is part of an interdisciplinary team that might include other psychologists, medical doctors and clinic staff, speech-language pathologists, teachers, and others (Ibid. p. 2). This is reflected in the multidisciplinary nature of neuropsychology which seeks to interrelate aspects of several disciplines including neurology, cognitive psychology, genetics and biology. In relation to special education, an aim is to construct a pedagogical theory linking neuropsychological assessment data to effective intervention (Bernstein, 2000).

References

Bernstein, J. H. (2000) 'Developmental neuropsychological assessment' in Yeates, K. O., Ris, M. D. and Taylor, H. G. (Eds) *Paediatric Neuropsychology: Research, Theory and Practice*, New York, Guilford Press, 405–438.

Dewey, D. and Tupper, D. E. (Eds) (2004) *Developmental Motor Disorders: A Developmental Perspective*, New York, Guilford Press.

Hale, J. B. and Fiorello, C. A. (2004) *School Neuropsychology: A Practitioner's Handbook*, New York, Guilford Press.

Lezak, M. D., Howieson, D. B. and Loring, D. W. (2004) (2nd edition) *Neuropsychological Assessment*, New York, Oxford University Press.

Further reading

Beaumont, J. G. (2008) (2nd edition) *Introduction to Neuropsychology*, London and New York, Guilford Press.

D'Amato, R., Fletcher-Jansen, E. and Reynolds, C. (2005) *Handbook of School Neuropsychology*, New York and London, Wiley.

Miller, D. C. (2007) (2nd edition) *Essentials of Neuropsychological Assessment*, Hoboken, NY, Wiley.

Yeates, K. O., Ris, M. D. and Taylor, H. G. (2000) *Paediatric neuropsychology: Research, theory, and practice*, New York, Guilford Press.

Addresses

American Board of Paediatric Neuropsychology
www.abpdn.org
Establishes criteria relating to the definition, education, training, competencies and examination procedures leading to certification in paediatric neuropsychology.

National Academy of Neuropsychology
www.nanonline.org
Based in the USA, the academy aims to advance neuropsychology as a health profession and as a science, promote human welfare, and generate and disseminate knowledge on brain-behaviour relationships.

Objects of reference

Objects of reference are objects invested with a special meaning and used for communication. They can assist memory and aid understanding. The object may be a sign that is part of the event for which it stands, for example a coat for 'going out'. It may relate to the thing for which it stands by physical resemblance, for example, a cup for 'drink'. An object of reference may relate to what it stands for by some arbitrary link such as a three dimensional shape for 'begin'.

An individual who is deafblind or who has a visual impairment and cognitive impairment may use objects of reference. People with communication difficulties may use them if they do not respond to written information, symbols or signs. Children with profound cognitive impairment may use objects of reference whether or not they have a visual impairment.

They may be used in several ways. An object of reference can help a child understand his surroundings including what is going to happen next. For example, a piece of swimming costume may convey that the next activity will be swimming. Similarly, a series of objects can convey the intended plan or timetable for the school day. This might be a sequence of a computer disk, a cup, a ball, and a plate to convey, respectively, computer activities, snack time, physical education and lunchtime. Objects of reference can enable the individual to choose between various options such as a coat for going out or a purse for going to the shops. They may be used in school or at home and in the community, and the school and family work together to achieve consistency in the use of the objects.

Care is taken with the choice of object to ensure it conveys what is intended. The object may be one that is used in an activity such as a piece of soap to indicate 'bath' which is then used for bath time. Models or miniature objects may be used if it is evident that the child makes the link between these and the task or event they are meant to signify. A miniature bus might be used to convey an imminent bus journey. A Look Up (www.lookupinfo.org) fact sheet suggests that objects of reference should be meaningful, motivating and frequent.

Some children may move on from using objects of reference to using communication aids that are more abstract such as symbols or photographs.

Further reading

McLarty, M. (1997) 'Putting objects of reference in context', *European Journal of Special Needs Education* 12, 1, 12–20.
Ockelford, A. (2002) *Objects of Reference: Promoting Early Symbolic Communication*, London, Royal National Institute for the Blind.

Address

Look Up
  www.lookupinfo.org
An information service in the UK involving the charity SeeAbility and the Royal National Institute for the Blind and focusing on eye care and vision for people with learning difficulties. The site includes information about objects of reference.

Observational learning and modelling

The nature of observational learning and modelling

Observational learning and modelling are aspects of social learning theory set out by Bandura (1977, 1986). Four processes govern observational learning. The first is 'attentional processes'. For example, a model that is more attractive or interesting to the observer is likely to gain greater attention. 'Retention processes' involve the observed behaviour being retained in symbolic form for later use. Rehearsing what has been observed, either through action or cognitively, helps learning and retention. 'Production processes' involve 'converting the symbolic conceptions into appropriate actions'. Feedback through corrective modelling can help the learners perform the activity better. Finally, 'motivational processes' influence the performance of observationally learned behaviour. For example, observed outcomes for other people affects learners' behaviours as they vicariously experience the consequences (Bandura, 1986, pp. 51–69).

Modelling involves observing others and forming rules of behaviour so that later this coded information 'serves as a guide for action' (Bandura, 1986, p. 27). Words and images are vehicles of modelling. In gaining skills, modelling is more concerned with learning rules than 'response mimicry'. Modelling influences can change observers' 'behaviour, thought patterns, emotional reactions, and evaluation' (Ibid. pp. 47–48). Modelling tends to influence behaviour where the child identifies with the person being observed and in interventions this identification cannot be guaranteed. The child may also be modelling his behaviour on others whose behaviour is contrary to that intended by the intervention.

Applications of observational learning and modelling

Modelling theory suggests aggression is learned through observation and modelling. Fathers of aggressive boys are themselves typically aggressive. Accordingly, interventions include helping parents to model appropriate behaviour for their children, or providing foster care or residential care. Another intervention, Problem-Solving Skills Training (PSST) (Spivak and Sure, 1978), involves clinic-based individual sessions. In comparison with typically developing children, aggressive children tend to attribute hostile intentions to others and anticipate rejection more. They are limited in creating different solutions to interpersonal problems and working out the motivations of other people. Accordingly, in PSST, a therapist examines the ways in which a child with conduct problems tends to respond to interpersonal situations, encouraging a structured approach to solving problems. Children are taught to recognise and alter how they think about and respond to social situations, perhaps using modelling and role play. PSST uses structured tasks related to real life, encouraging social behaviours by modelling and direct reinforcement. Childhood phobias have been effectively treated through modelling (Bandura, 1977). Participant modelling may be used, involving exposing the individual to the real circumstances he fears or modelling the behaviour of others whom he observes coping with the feared circumstances.

For children with autism, Learning Experiences – An Alternative Program for Preschoolers and Parents (LEAP) (Strain and Hoyson, 2000) uses behavioural methods and observational learning. It is used in preschooling classes where children with autism learn with typically developing children to give them the opportunity to learn from models of appropriate social skills and have more opportunities to interact. Strategies aimed at helping difficulties with comprehension may draw on imitation and modelling. A teacher and teaching aide can set up role play sessions in which they model good listening behaviour while pupils observe. Next, each pupil practises the observed skills with an adult or child partner, while the teacher monitors this and praises the children. Observation and modelling are used to help pragmatic difficulties. For example, role play sessions or video/DVD examples are used to illustrate aspects of non-verbal communication, which are next discussed with a small group of pupils.

References

Bandura, A. (1977) *Social Learning Theory*, Englewood Cliffs, NJ, Prentice-Hall.
Bandura, A. (1986) *Social Foundations of Thought and Action: A Social Cognitive Theory*, Englewood Cliffs, NJ, Prentice-Hall.

Spivak, G. and Sure, M. B. (1978) *Problem Solving Techniques in Child Rearing*, San Francisco, Jossey-Bass.
Strain, P. and Hoyson, M. (2000) 'The need for longitudinal, intensive social skill intervention: LEAP follow-up outcomes for children with autism', *Topics in Early Childhood Special Education* 20, 2, 116–122.

Further reading

Bloomquist, M. and Schnell, M. (2005) *Helping Children with Aggression and Conduct Problems*, New York, Guilford Press.
Gabriels, R. and Hill, D. E. (2007) *Growing Up with Autism: Working with School Age Children and Adolescents*, New York, Guilford Press.

Obsessive-compulsive disorder

The nature of obsessive-compulsive disorder

Obsessive-compulsive disorder is an anxiety disorder involving recurring obsessions and compulsions taking up more than an hour a day or creating significant impairment or distress (American Psychiatric Association, 2000, p. 456, paraphrased). The way the disorder is defined excludes substance abuse or medication as a cause. A distinction is made between obsessions and compulsions. Obsessions are persistent ideas, thoughts, desires or images causing significant distress or worry. The child or young person might have to place items in a certain order. He might experience thoughts about being contaminated through touching others or have impulses to hurt other people. Compulsions are repetitive behaviours or mental acts. A repetitive behaviour might be persistent hand washing, while a repetitive mental act might be counting to one's self. Both of these forms of compulsion are attempts to reduce anxiety or distress. Children may not always recognise that obsessions and compulsions are unreasonable. Community studies of children and adolescents have estimated a lifetime prevalence of 1 per cent to 2.3 per cent and 1 year prevalence of 0.7 per cent (Ibid. p. 460). Twin studies suggest there may be a hereditary element. Obsessive-compulsive disorder may be associated with certain infections such as scarlet fever in a very small number of children.

Provision

Selective serotonin reuptake inhibitors appear effective for obsessive-compulsive disorder. One piece of research involved children and young people aged 8 to 17 years. They were assessed using several measures relating to obsessive-compulsive disorder. Scores on these assessments were significantly lower for those given the selective serotonin reuptake inhibitor fluvoxamine compared with those given a placebo (Riddle *et al.*, 2001). Cognitive behavioural therapy, involving exposure and response prevention, is also used. For example, a small-scale study was conducted with 14 children and adolescents meeting the criteria for obsessive-compulsive disorder. With the therapy, 12 of the children experienced at least a 50 per cent reduction in the severity of symptoms. These gains persisted nine months later (Franklin *et al.*, 1998). The optimum treatment for children with obsessive-compulsive disorder may be a combination of selective serotonin reuptake inhibitor medication and cognitive behavioural therapy (March, 1999).

References

American Psychiatric Association (2000) *Diagnostic and Statistical Manual of Mental Disorders, Fourth Edition, Text Revision*, Arlington, VA, APA.

Franklin, M. E., Kozak, M. J., Cashman, L. A., Coles, M. E., Rhiengold, A. A. and Foa, E. B. (1998) 'Cognitive-behavioural treatment of paediatric obsessive-compulsive disorder: An open clinical trial', *Journal of the American Academy of Child and Adolescent Psychiatry* 37, 412–419.

March, J. S. (1999) 'Psychopharmacological management of paediatric obsessive-compulsive disorder (OCD) Paper presented at the 46th annual meeting of the American Academy of Child and Adolescent Psychiatry, Chicago.

Riddle, M. A., Reeve, A. E., Yaryura-Tobias, J. A., Yang, H. M., Claghorn, J. L., Gaffney, G., Greist, J. H., Holland, D., McConville, B. J., Pigott, T. and Walkup, J. T. (2001) 'Fluvoxamine for children and adolescents with obsessive-compulsive disorder: A randomised, controlled, multicenter trial', *Journal of the American Academy of Child and Adolescent Psychiatry* 40, 222–229.

Further reading

De Silva, P., Rachman, S. and Rachman, J. (1998) *Obsessive-Compulsive Disorder: The Facts*, Oxford, Oxford University Press.

Long, R. (2005) *Obsessive-Compulsive Disorders*, London, David Fulton.

Addresses

Obsessive-Compulsive Foundation
www.ocfoundation.org
An international organisation serving those affected by obsessive-compulsive disorder and other neurobiological spectrum disorders.

OCD-UK
www.ocduk.org
A charity working with and for people with obsessive-compulsive disorder.

Occupational therapy/occupational therapist

Occupational therapy involves assessing requirements arising from physical disabilities, psychological difficulties; and problems with sensory awareness, perceptual skills, and motor coordination. Approaches may be developed for particular conditions, for example Duchenne Muscular Dystrophy (Stone *et al.*, 2007). The therapist then recommends and can provide therapy, aids and adaptations. It may include the provision of training programmes for self-help, work and leisure skills. Occupational therapy for children and youth also involves working with families and teachers to enhance such abilities in the home and at school.

Occupational therapists use a number of approaches in treating these perceptual and motor or motor learning disorders. Assessment might indicate particular learning difficulties associated with inadequate sensory integration. In such instances, the occupational therapist may recommend treatments that include specific movement exercises to stimulate more efficient sensory responses.

Programmes are designed to help a child or young person to progress towards independence in personal, self-help, or leisure skills. These may include developing specific abilities such as the eye-hand coordination and visual perception required for handwriting. Occupational therapists may also advise on aids to assist communication or mobility.

Occupational therapists are trained through degree or diploma courses and most are employed by health services. Paediatric occupational therapists specialise in the assessment and management of childhood disabilities in order to help children and youth to achieve skills needed for activities related to everyday life. Occupational therapists may carry out therapy or recommend specialist equipment and, as necessary, building adaptations. They also work with children with emotional difficulties, helping them develop confidence in coping with everyday needs.

Reference

Stone, K., Tester, C., Blakeney, J., Howarth, A., McAndrew, H., Traynor, N., McCutcheon, M. and Johnson, R. (2007) *Occupational Therapy and Duchenne Muscular Dystrophy*, London and New York, Wiley.

Further reading

Rodger, S. and Ziviani, J. (Eds) (2006) *Occupational Therapy with Children: Understanding Children's Occupations and Enabling Participation*, New York and London, Wiley-Blackwell.

Addresses

British Association/College of Occupational Therapists
www.cot.co.uk
The professional body for occupational therapy staff in the UK.

OT Australia
www.ausot.com.au
Australian Association of Occupational Therapy.

The American Occupational Therapy Association
www.aota.org
The national professional association representing occupational therapy practitioners and students.

Ophthalmology/ophthalmologist

For children and young people with visual impairment, an ophthalmologist may contribute to their treatment and the implications of eye conditions and their treatment would inform the child's education. Ophthalmology is a branch of medicine concerned with diseases of the visual pathways. This includes the eye and the area surrounding it, and the brain. Among conditions with which an ophthalmologist might deal are glaucoma (various diseases of the optic nerve), cataract (clouding of the lens of the eye affecting vision), defects of the iris (such as coloboma, a deformity of the iris), defects of the pupil (such as aniscoria or unequal pupils) and inflammatory conditions (Candy, Davies and Ross, 2001, pp. 339–341).

An ophthalmologist is a medical practitioner who has specialised in the treatment of diseases of the visual pathways, including surgery.

Reference

Candy, D., Davies, G. and Ross, E. (2001) *Clinical Paediatrics and Child Health*, Edinburgh, Harcourt/W. B. Saunders.

Further reading

James, B., Chew, C. and Bron, A. (2007) (10th edition) *Ophthalmology*, New York and London, Wiley-Blackwell.
Khaw, P. T., Shah, P. and Elkington, A. R. (2004) (4th edition) *ABC of Eyes*, New York and London, Wiley.

Addresses

American Academy of Ophthalmology
www.aao.org
Aims to advance ophthalmic education.

The Royal College of Ophthalmologists
www.rcophth.ac.uk
Concerned with setting standards, education and research.

Oppositional defiant disorder

Oppositional defiant disorder and conduct disorder are the main classifications of disruptive behaviour disorders in the *Diagnostic and Statistical
Manual of Mental Disorders, Fourth Edition, Text Revision (DSM-IV-TR)*
(American Psychiatric Association, 2000). The essential feature of
Oppositional defiant disorder is a repeated pattern lasting at least for 6
months of behaviour towards people in authority that is, 'negativistic,
defiant, disobedient, and hostile'. This behaviour leads to significant impairment in 'social, academic or occupational functioning' (Ibid. p. 100).
Attention deficit hyperactivity disorder is a common co-occurring condition
(Ibid. p. 101). Prevalence varies widely from 2 per cent to 16 per cent depending on the nature of the population that is sampled and the methods of assessment. This wide range may also relate to difficulty in a school context of
determining whether apparent oppositional defiant disorder is predominantly a 'within child' disorder or mainly a consequence of poor teaching and
behaviour management. The disorder is usually evident before the age of
8 years and generally no later than early adolescence (Ibid. p. 101). Often,
it is a developmental antecedent of conduct disorder. All the features of
oppositional defiant disorder are usually present in conduct disorder so the
former is not diagnosed if the criteria for conduct disorder are met.

Approaches found effective with some children with disruptive behaviour
disorders include: parent training; social skills training and anger management coping skills training; problem-solving skills; and classroom contingency management.

Reference

American Psychiatric Association (2000) *Diagnostic and Statistical Manual of Mental
Disorders, Fourth Edition, Text Revision*, Arlington, VA, APA.

Further reading

Bloomquist, M. and Schnell, M. (2005) *Helping Children with Aggression and
Conduct, Problems*, New York, Guilford Press.

Address

American Academy of Child and Adolescent Psychiatry
www.aacap.org
The site includes a fact sheet on children with oppositional defiant disorder.

Optimal education

Optimal education is a way of determining the best venue for special education, whether this is a mainstream classroom, a special classroom in a mainstream school, a special school or a combination of these (Farrell, 2005, pp. 99–101). Optimal education takes the view that placement in schools should be informed by the academic progress a pupil makes and his personal and social development. If better progress and development is maintained in a mainstream school, then this is the appropriate setting. If a special school provides better in these terms then this is the best venue. In some instances, the child's education may be a combination of mainstream and special school provision. Progress and development are monitored so that this can inform changes in the proportion of time in special and mainstream settings.

Inclusion is questioned. Pupils in special schools are not seen as oppressed or excluded by being educated there, but by the threat of political correctness forcing a so called 'inclusion agenda' and denying them the opportunity of a good education. It is suggested that the assumed equal opportunity for a child to be educated in a mainstream school may not be an equal opportunity to receive a good education or be included in the usual meaning of the expression. Many pupils with disabilities/disorders speak well of their special schools, have subsequently participated well in society and appear to have benefited from the provision. The supposed 'right' to be educated in mainstream is rejected by many parents and children. Rights are so numerous that they can contradict one another, it is maintained. Deaf people evoke rights to a special school where they can express their minority language while others call for their right to attend mainstream schools. Inclusion is considered an unfair policy because it refuses to discriminate (in the positive sense of the word) on seemingly relevant criteria. Empirical overviews and reviews of inclusion do not give it a ringing endorsement (Farrell, 2006, p. 23).

In differing from inclusion, optimal education involves mainstream schools and special schools working together to jointly optimise the academic progress, personal development and well-being of children and youth with disabilities/disorders. In fact the approach can involve a wide range of settings such as mainstream classrooms, special classes in a mainstream school, special schools, and mainstream school classes where pupils attend for support or for some lessons. There is no assumption that a special school is a quick and temporary placement before the child returns to mainstream where he supposedly really belongs. Good special schools are valued as highly as good mainstream schools. Decisions about time spent in different settings are based on progress and development. If a pupil were taught in a special school all the time or for a large proportion of the time, there would be no implication that his human rights were somehow being eroded (Farrell, 2006).

(See also, *Inclusion*, *Special school*)

References

Farrell, M. (2005) *Key Issues in Special Education: Raising Pupils' Achievement and Attainment*, New York and London, Routledge.
Farrell, M. (2006) *Celebrating the Special School*, London, David Fulton.

Oral/aural approaches

Communication

An oral/aural approach (hereafter an 'oral' approach) is one strategy used to teach children who are deaf or have hearing impairment, to speak intelligibly and to understand the spoken language (Steinberg and Knightly, 1997). Hearing parents tend to prefer this approach. Also, some deaf parents, oral and signing, wish their child to have an oral education, perhaps so later, he can choose whether to learn sign language. A cochlear implant may be made at an early age to promote the early use of residual hearing.

In the oral approach: residual hearing is used and enhanced; providing favourable listening conditions is essential; communicating is emphasised; language rules are assumed to be acquired by using language; and active listening skills are encouraged. The child is encouraged to use contextual clues and knowledge of the world to aid communication and understanding. Also, children unable to comprehend speech, using hearing alone can gain information from lip reading and natural gesture.

Speech training and auditory training (Reddy *et al.*, 2000) may be provided by speech pathologists or language teachers. They use speech and articulation, drawing on behavioural principles as well as social learning principles of imitation and modelling. This type of formal speech and auditory training is declining with the development of more powerful hearing aids, cochlear implants and earlier diagnosis. Also language development will be encouraged through naturally occurring classroom activities. These are intended to improve generalisation of vocabulary and language patterns to daily life.

Literacy

Literacy levels of deaf children tend to be below that of hearing peers, perhaps three or four years behind. In the United States of America, only 3 per cent of

18-year-old deaf students had comparable reading levels to the average for their hearing peers (Karchmer and Mitchell, 2003). Yet many deaf students are very accomplished readers. Better attainment has been reported in reading using an oral approach with a quarter of the sample reading at or above chronological age on reaching school leaving age (Lewis, 1998). The approach uses the reader's previous experience, the context of the reading, and the text, which interact to create meaning.

In phonic work, unless sounds that are part of the deaf child's phonic system are used, phoneme-grapheme correspondence cannot be effectively taught. In later reading, discussing what has been read is beneficial. Pre-teaching can prepare the pupil for ideas that will come up in the text, allowing fuller participation. Lewis (1998, p. 104) has suggested that three conditions need to be satisfied if reading is to progress well: a basic level of linguistic understanding must be established before introducing formal reading programmes; the integrity of reading as a receptive process and a reflective activity is preserved; and the language of ideas used to promote deaf children's earliest reading insights is accessible to them.

The written expression of deaf children can be problematic (Power, 1998). This includes difficulties with sentence structures, verb tenses and plurals and incorrect word order. In early writing, the teacher will consider attempts in relation to what is developmentally appropriate and the context of the pupil's present linguistic functioning. In shared writing activities various purposes are used, such as messages, shopping lists and postcards. From early stages, pupils are encouraged to read back what they have written and correct their own work.

References

Karchmer, M. A. and Mitchell, R. E. (2003) 'Demographic and achievement characteristics of deaf and hard of hearing students' in Marschark, M. and Spencer, P. E. (Eds) *Oxford Handbook of Deaf Studies, Language and Education*, New York, Oxford University Press, 21–27.

Lewis, R., Graves, A., Ashton, T. and Kieley, C. (1998) 'Word processing tools for students with learning disabilities: A comparison of strategies to increase text entry speed', *Learning Disabilities Research and Practice* 13, 95–108.

Power, D. (1998) (3rd edition) 'Deaf and hard of hearing students' in Ashman, A. and Elkins, J. (Eds) *Educating Children with Special Needs*, Sydney, Prentice Hall.

Reddy, G. L., Ramar, R. and Kasuma, A. (2000) *Education of Children with Special Needs*, New Delhi, Discovery Publishing House.

Steinberg, A. G. and Knightly, C. A. (1997) 'Hearing: sounds and silences' in Batshaw, M. L. (Ed.) *Children with Disabilities*, Sydney, Maclennan and Petty.

Further reading

Farrell, M. (2008) 'Hearing impairment' in *Educating Special Children: An Introduction to Provision for Pupils with Disabilities and Disorders*, New York and London, Routledge.

Address

Oral Deaf Education
  www.oraldeafed.org
  Provides information on oral approaches and directory listing for schools in the USA.

Orthopaedic impairment and motor disorders

The nature of orthopaedic impairment and motor disorders

Orthopaedics is a branch of medical science concerned with disorders of the bones and joints and associated muscles, tendons and ligaments. It can involve treating skeletal birth defects; setting fractured bones, applying orthotic devices, treating conditions of the joints such as arthritis; and replacing or repairing joints. Orthopaedic impairments may be congenital or acquired and involve deformity, disease, injury or surgery. Examples are spinal curvature; limb deficiencies; and talipes ('club foot'). Motor disorders may be associated with neuromotor impairment. These are disorders involving the central nervous system and affecting the child's ability to use, feel, control and move parts of his body and include muscular dystrophy, cerebral palsy, neural tube defects and developmental coordination disorder.

Under United States of America federal law an orthopaedic impairment is defined as a severe impairment adversely affecting the child's educational performance. The Code of Federal Regulations definition is: 'impairments caused by congenital anomaly (e.g. club foot, absence of some member etc.), impairments caused by disease (e.g. poliomyelitis, bone tuberculosis, etc.) and impairments from other causes (e.g. cerebral palsy, amputations, and fractures or burns causing contractures)' (34 CFR, section 300.7 [c] [8], 1999). The definition's collating of both orthopaedic conditions and neuromotor impairment might be justified in several ways. Both types of impairments can limit movement, although the type of limitation differs. Also, for both, the provision of education, therapy and care has similarities. Finally, a child with a neurological impairment inhibiting limb movement can develop orthopaedic impairments.

Provision

The school designs the curriculum for a pupil with orthopaedic impairment and motor disorders so he is as fully as possible involved and supported in activities. These include subjects such as art, technology, and science where special equipment may be necessary. Many physical education activities will be safe for pupils with an orthopaedic impairment. Often, games can be adapted to ensure the participation of all pupils, or alternative activities arranged leading to similar learning goals. Any special programmes to develop skills or encourage movement can be timetabled to ensure the pupil still encounters a balanced range of subjects.

Bigge, Best and Heller (2001) provide a comprehensive account of resources and their use. Guidance from the physical therapist or the occupational therapist will often be necessary. To help children's correct positioning, pads and cushions or specially constructed adapted seat inserts may be used. Throughout the day adults can ensure the child adopts alternative positions. He might stand or use a sidelyer, wedge or tricycle with a built up back. For comfortable and correct seating, the position of the pelvis is important and vest type or H strap supports may be used for the trunk and shoulders. An abductor or leg separator may be used (Ibid. pp. 199, 201–204). Care is taken with furniture. In science where pupils might sit on high stools, a stool with a back support and arms may be used. Tables may allow their height to be adjusted and its surfaces tilted.

Hoists and other devices may support safe moving of the student. Among assistive walking devices is a PVC pipe walker and crutches. Wheelchair access ramps and continuous areas of smooth floor surfaces may improve access to classrooms and other facilities. The school may have separate rooms for personal care procedures to be carried out in privacy. Toilets and toilet fittings may be adapted to take account requirements such as changing a colostomy bag. Throughout the school there needs to be sufficient room for a pupil requiring a wheelchair or a walking support to move around unhindered.

To help the pupil locate equipment, a wheelchair backpack may be used or modular stacking trays can allow materials to be stored and be accessible from the pupil's desk. Work surface modifications might be a supine 'stander' with a cut out tray, a wheelchair with elbow supports, or angled work surfaces. Modifications to objects include long handled brushes and combs or large handled cutlery. Home lighting, communication devices and computers can control the environment. They can be operated electrically, by infrared, radio control or ultrasound. Switches to control the environment can be operated by different movements and pressures and activated in various ways such as pushing, tilting, puffing, eye blinking, or voice (Bigge, Best and Heller, 2001, pp. 213–221).

Health professionals contribute to provision for the child, either outside the school or within school, where they work closely with educators. They provide preparatory training for school staff in intimate care procedures such as routines for toileting and hygiene; urostomy and colostomy care; and catheterisation. Counselling may be available, allowing the pupil to come to terms with issues such as restrictions on activities and developing relationships.

Where school trips are planned, pre-visits can help check details of physical access. The teacher can make sure there is access for wheelchairs or ensure that facilities and displays are at a height at which they can be viewed. If a pupil is often unable to attend school, arrangements may be made for home tuition or e-mail and the Internet can be used to support home study.

Moving some pupils with physical disability has potential hazards and risk assessments may be carried out on these procedures, supported by training for the adults involved. Fire procedures take into account such matters as making sure wheelchairs can be easily manoeuvred through fire exits. Adults may help students in wheelchairs with negotiating steps using a 'stair climber' or similar equipment. Procedures and responsibilities for administering medication will be clear and supported by staff training as necessary.

(See also, *Cerebral palsy*, and *Neural tube defects*)

Reference

Bigge, J. L., Best, S. J. and Heller, K. W. (2001) (4th edition) *Teaching Individuals with Physical, Health or Multiple Disabilities*, Upper Saddle River, NJ, Merrill-Prentice Hall.

Further reading

Dewey, D. and Tupper, D. (Eds) (2004) *Developmental Motor Disorders: A Neuropsychological Perspective*, New York, Guilford Press.

Address

Paediatric Orthopaedic Society of North America
  www.posna.org
  Aims for the best education of paediatric orthopaedists to assure the best care for patients.

Orthoptics/orthoptist

Orthoptics concerns the diagnosis and treatment of problems relating to eye movements and their effect on vision. Among the conditions that may be treated are amblyopia (lazy eye) in which vision is reduced because of a defect preventing the eye receiving sufficient stimulation; and diplopia (double vision) brought about by abnormal eye movements or a squint.

An orthoptist follows a graduate training in orthoptics. She may assess the use of low vision aids for children with visual impairment.

Further reading

Rowe, F. (2004) (2nd edition) *Clinical Orthoptics*, New York and London, Blackwell Publishing.

Addresses

International Orthoptic Association
www.internationalorthoptics.org
A worldwide organisation of orthoptic professionals.

Orthoptic Association of Australia
www.orthoptics.org.au
The national body for orthoptists in Australia.

Paediatrics/paediatrician

Paediatrics concerns child development and childhood diseases (Osborn *et al.*, 2005). It involves the development and care of children, and 'the nature and treatment of diseases of children' (Anderson, 2007, p. 1421). Typically, paediatric textbooks may cover paediatric principles using a developmental approach, and paediatric conditions using a systems approach such as neurology, metabolism, and orthopaedics (e.g. Candy, Davies and Ross, 2001). Underpinning paediatrics (and medicine as a whole) are disciplines such as human anatomy and physiology, pathology and pharmacology, which inform clinical medicine as it applies to children. A paediatrician is a physician who has specialised in the treatment of children.

References

Anderson, D. M. (Chief lexicographer) (2007) (31st edition) *Dorland's Illustrated Medical Dictionary*, Philadelphia, PA, Elsevier/Saunders.

Candy, D., Davies, G. and Ross, E. (2001) *Clinical Paediatrics and Child Health*, Edinburgh, Harcourt/W. B. Saunders.

Osborn, L. M., DeWitt, T. G., First, L. R. and Zenel, J. A. (Eds) (2005) *Pediatrics*, Philadelphia, PA, Elsevier/Mosby.

Further reading

Lissauer, T. and Clayden, G. (2007) (3rd edition) *Illustrated Textbook of Paediatrics*, London, Elsevier/Mosby.

Addresses

American Academy of Pediatrics
  www.aap.org
  An organisation in the USA for pediatricians seeking the optimum health and well-being of children and youth.

The British Association of Paediatric Surgeons
www.baps.org.uk
A UK organisation aiming to advance study, practice and research in paediatric surgery.

Parents

Parents are the child's first educators. It is widely acknowledged that partnership between parents, teachers and others where a child has a disability or
disorder is important. Such partnership is structured in the requirement that
parents and professionals are involved in developing Individual Education
Programmes/Plans for example.

Effective provision for certain types of disability and disorder also crucially
involves parents. Where a child has anxiety disorder, it has been found that
family cognitive behavioural work coupled with cognitive behavioural
therapy is effective (Barrett, Dadds and Rapee, 1996). For children with mild
anxiety disorder or dysthymic disorder (involving chronically depressed
mood), focal psychodynamic psychotherapy may be used. This involves
five sessions involving the whole family followed by five sessions solely
with the child followed by a final session with the whole family (Muratori
et al., 2002).

Regarding adolescents with depressive disorder, cognitive behavioural
therapy appears effective especially where the adolescent experienced anxiety
also. But where the mother is clinically depressed, the treatment outcome for
the adolescent is poorer suggesting that any such maternal depression should
be concurrently treated (Brent et al., 1998).

For children with autistic spectrum disorder early interventions involve
parents. Learning Experiences – An Alternative Program for Preschoolers
and Parents (LEAP)(Strain and Hoyson, 2000) was developed in the United
States of America. It involves preschooling classes in which children with
autism learn with typically developing children. Parents are taught how to use
behavioural skills with their child at home and in the community. In the
Children's Talk project, developed in the United Kingdom for children with
autistic spectrum disorder, parents are trained in particular parent–child
communication skills (Aldred, Green and Adams, 2004). They are shown
how to improve parent–child joint attention in order to help a child's capacity for social referencing. Parents are trained to provide a supportive com-
mentary on their child's behaviour. They show their child how language can
be used as an aid by translating the child's non-verbal communication into
words. Parents and preschool children attend monthly sessions for six
months and subsequently attend sessions less frequently for a further six
months. Having learned communication skills, parents can plan daily half-
hour sessions to help their child gain these skills.

References

Aldred, C., Green, J. and Adams, C. (2004) 'A new social communication intervention for children with autism: Pilot randomised controlled treatment study suggesting effectiveness', *Journal of Child Psychology and Psychiatry* 45, 1420–1430.

Barrett, P. M., Dadds, M. R. and Rapee, R. M. (1996) 'Family treatment for childhood anxiety: A controlled trial', *Journal of Consulting and Clinical Psychology* 64, 333–342.

Brent, D. A., Kolko, D., Birmaher, B., Baugher, M., Bridge, J., Roth, C. and Holder, D. (1998) 'Predictors of treatment efficacy in a clinical trial of three psychosocial treatments for adolescent depression', *Journal of the American Academy for Child and Adolescent Psychiatry* 37, 906–914.

Muratori, F., Picchi, L., Casella, C., Tancredi, R., Milone, A. and Patarnello, M. G. (2002) 'Efficacy of brief dynamic psychotherapy for children with emotional disorders', *Psychotherapy and Psychosomatics* 71, 28–38.

Strain, P. and Hoyson, M. (2000) 'The need for longitudinal, intensive social skill intervention: LEAP follow-up outcomes for children with autism', *Topics in Early Childhood Special Education* 20, 2, 116–122.

Further reading

Greenwood, C. (2002) *Understanding the Needs of Parents: Guidelines for Effective Collaboration with Parents of Children with Special Educational Needs*, London, David Fulton Publishers.

Hanson, M. J. and Lynch, E. W. (2003) *Understanding Families: Approaches to Diversity, Disabilty and Risk*, Baltimore, MD, Brookes.

Addresses

Association for Special Children and Families
www.ascfamily.org
Seeks to empower and support families to raise all their children to reach their full potential.

National Association of Parents with Children in Special Education
www.napcse.org
The organisation seeks to support and assist parents whose children receive special education services both in and outside of school.

National Parent Partnership Network
www.parentpartnership.org.uk
Parent partnership services are statutory services offering information, advice and support for parents of children and young people with special educational needs. The National Parent Partnership Network supports all parent partnership services across England.

Pedagogy

Pedagogy is 'the way in which the content of education, whether it is the knowledge, skills or attitudes, is learned by the pupil and taught or facilitated by the teacher' (Farrell, Kerry and Kerry, 1995, p. 4). Different methods of instruction used for pupils with disorder/disability have been identified (Algozzine and Ysseldyke, 2006, pp. 38–48).

- Behaviour therapy including operant conditioning.
- Precision teaching, which involves small steps of teaching and assessment with behavioural underpinnings.
- Ability training which has to do with training in abilities (such as visual tracking) that contribute to broader skills (for example, reading).
- Direct instruction including attack strategy training.
- Cognitive behaviour modification, which involves self-statements to improve performance.
- Cognitive skills training involving knowledge, comprehension and application, analysis, synthesis, and evaluation.
- Critical thinking includes approaches such as evaluating information sources and making judgements about information and beliefs.
- Counselling therapy, which might, for example, seek to raise a child's self-esteem.
- Learning strategies including mnemonics to aid memorisation.
- Cooperative learning perhaps involving small groups of pupils who have to pool information they separately possess in order to complete a task.
- Peer directed learning, which might include peer tutoring.

The teacher may emphasise certain sensory modalities in presenting information. A pupil with moderate to severe cognitive impairment may learn better if information is presented visually rather than aurally. For a pupil with Down syndrome having difficulty with short term auditory memory, a visual icon may assist learning to read by enabling the child to link letter sounds to letter names. Pedagogy may involve approaches distinctive to a particular disability/disorder such as creating a 'responsive environment' for pupils with profound cognitive impairment (Ware, 2003, p. 1). The environment is designed to be sensitive to the learner's movements and sounds so that the environmental responses will in turn elicit a response from the child. Pedagogy for special children may draw on principles used also with children who do not have a disorder/disability, such as a slower pace in lessons for pupils with mild cognitive impairment (Lewis and Norwich, 2005, pp. 5–6).

(See also, *Education/educator*)

References

Algozzine, B. and Ysseldyke, E. (2006) *Effective Instruction for Students with Special Needs: A Practical Guide for Every Teacher*, Thousand Oaks, CA, Corwin Press.

Farrell, M., Kerry, T. and Kerry, C. (1995) *The Blackwell Handbook of Education*, Oxford, Blackwell.

Lewis, A. and Norwich, B. (Eds) (2005) *Special Teaching for Special Children? Pedagogies for Inclusion*, Maidenhead, UK, Open University Press.

Ware, J. (2005) 'Profound and multiple learning difficulties' in Lewis, A. and Norwich, B. (Eds) *Special Teaching for Special Children? Pedagogies for Inclusion*, Maidenhead, UK, Open University Press.

Further reading

Farrell, M. (2008) *Educating Special Children: An Introduction to Provision for Pupils with Disabilities and Disorders*, New York and London, Routledge.

Philosophy

Philosophy involves sustained and rigorous thinking about an area of investigation. While there is no coherent philosophy of special education, there is a great deal of theorising, often along sociological lines (Shakespeare, 2006).

Some approaches to philosophy particularly encourage care with defining concepts so that these are as clearly expressed as possible. One aim in the present context is to be as clear as one can in defining elements of special education so that hidden disagreements about terminology do not cloud arguments and debate. Among terms that repay careful analysis are 'disability', 'impairment', 'special', 'barriers', 'inclusion', 'development', 'needs', 'rights', 'discrimination' and many others. To have a debate about, for example, 'inclusion' and to discover well into the discussion that the debaters are using the term to mean quite different things can be avoided if terms are analysed first.

The area of ethics, of course, arises often in special education. Questions include the extent to which mainstreaming or separate education of pupils with disabilities and disorders can each be justified morally. Some interventions associated with special educational provision in the broadest sense raise moral questions. For example, the extent to which medication is used for pupils with attention deficit hyperactivity disorder and how this can be justified is widely debated. The extent to which deafness is considered an impairment or the degree to which deaf people might be regarded as simply another linguistic group is debated. Other difficult moral questions include the extent of sexual freedom appropriate to someone who may have difficulties understanding and forming meaningful relationships, and the pros and cons of the use of plastic surgery to supposedly normalise the appearance of individuals with Down syndrome or other conditions. The moral basis of educating and caring for individuals who may not be able to participate fully in society is also discussed (Reinders, 2000).

Philosophising about special education makes it more difficult to hold views uncritically. It helps one move towards having a clearer set of coherent concepts and views, which can be discussed and modified in the light of debate. In a more general sense, one can speak of one's philosophy of special education meaning the principled basis of one's actions. The activity of philosophy can clarify our own approach and may uncover inconsistencies in our views. Also the study of ideologies in special education and the ideas of thinkers in special education can be helpful in shaping our own thoughts and beliefs.

References

Reinders, H. S. (2000) *The Future of the Disabled in a Liberal Society: An Ethical Analysis*, Notre Dame, IN, University of Notre Dame Press.
Shakespeare, T. (2006) *Disability Rights and Wrongs*, London, Routledge.

Further reading

Farrell, M. (2004) *Inclusion at the Crossroads: Concepts and Values in Special Education*, London, David Fulton.

Addresses

Philosophy of Education Society
    www.philosophyofeducation.org
    The aims of this US-based society include promoting the fundamental philosophic treatment of the problems of education.

Philosophy of Education Society of Australasia
    www.pesa.org.au
    Seeks to advance educational research, policy and practice.

Philosophy of Education Society of Great Britain
    www.philosophy-of-education.org
    Promotes the study, teaching and application of the philosophy of education.

Phobias

The nature of phobia

A phobia is a type of anxiety disorder manifested as an irrational fear that may be specific or social (American Psychiatric Association, 2000). A specific phobia is a persistent unreasonable fear of certain situations, activities or objects. This leads to the individual avoiding them and the condition can create distress and disrupt social relationships. Claustrophobia is an example. Adults tend to recognise the fear as irrational, but children may not. The fear of a stimulus is usually present for a time before it becomes so distressing and restricting that it can be said to be a specific phobia.

With social phobia the individual has a marked, persistent and unreasonable fear of social situations or situations where the person has to perform and may be embarrassed (American Psychiatric Association, 2000, p. 450). If the individual encounters such a situation, he immediately experiences anxiety. The condition often emerges in the mid teens but previously as a child the individual may have been very shy and inhibited. School phobia may lead to school refusal but separation anxiety where the child fears separating from home may also be implicated.

Regarding prevalence, lifetime estimates of phobia range from 3 per cent to 13 per cent (American Psychiatric Association, 2000, p. 453). For specific phobias, in community samples that include adults as well as children, estimates range from 4 per cent to 8.8 per cent (Ibid. p. 447).

Provision

Cognitive behavioural therapy, including gradual exposure techniques, can be effective in treating circumscribed phobias such as school refusal especially in younger children (King *et al.*, 2001). But behavioural interventions are effective for many phobic children (see the review by Ollendick and King, 1998). Circumscribed phobias may respond to desensitisation through either images of what is feared or the real experience. Modelling (Bandura, 1977) has been effective in treating childhood phobias especially participant modelling using real life exposure and the modelling of exposure by others (Blanchard, 1970). Contingency management drawing on operant conditioning can effectively treat phobias in young children (Menzies and Clarke, 1993). School refusal has been successfully treated by 'flooding' in which the child is rapidly returned to school. However, ethical reservations are expressed about the approach (Fonagy *et al.*, 2002, p. 87). In one study, mainly of school refusers of secondary school age, behavioural treatment was much better in maintaining pupils in school than inpatient treatment and home tutoring (Blagg and Yule, 1984).

References

American Psychiatric Association (2000) *Diagnostic and Statistical Manual of Mental Disorders, Fourth Edition, Text Revision*, Arlington, VA, APA.

Bandura, A. (1977) *Social Learning Theory*, Englewood Cliffs, NJ: Prentice-Hall.

208 Physical therapy/physical therapist

Blagg, N. R. and Yule, W. (1984) 'The behavioural treatment of school refusal: A comparative study', *Behaviour Research and Therapy* 22, 119–127.

Blanchard, E. B. (1970) 'Relative contributions of modelling, informational influences, and physical contact in extinction of phobic behaviour', *Journal of Abnormal Psychology* 76, 55–61.

Fonagy, P., Target, M., Cottrell, D., Phillips, J. and Kurtz, Z. (2005) *What Works for Whom? A Critical Review of Treatments for Children and Adolescents*, New York, Guilford Press.

King, N. J., Tonge, B. J., Heyne, D., Turner, S. M., Pritchard, M., Young, D. and Rollings, S. (2001) 'Cognitive-behavioural treatment of school refusing children: Maintenance of improvement at 3 to 5 year follow up', *Scandinavian Journal of Behaviour Therapy* 30, 85–89.

Menzies, R. G. and Clarke, J. C. (1993) 'A comparison of in vivo and vicarious exposure in the treatment of childhood water phobia', *Behaviour Research and Therapy* 31, 9–15.

Ollendick, T. H. and King, N. J. (1998) 'Empirically supported treatments for children with phobic and anxiety disorders', *Journal of Clinical Child Psychology* 27, 156–167.

Further reading

Rachman, S. (2004) (2nd edition) *Anxiety*, London and New York, Taylor and Francis.

Address

Social Phobia/Social Anxiety Association
www.socialphobia.org
The association's goals include encouraging public awareness of and research into social anxiety and facilitating the use and increasing the number of effective therapeutic strategies.

Physical therapy/physical therapist

Physical therapy (usually called physiotherapy in the United Kingdom) involves treatments to improve posture and movement and particular functions relating to them. Methods include movement, exercises, positioning, physical aids and hydrotherapy and the use of warmth and vibration. Among areas of specialisation within physical therapy are developmental physical therapy with children with disabilities and disorders, orthopaedic physical therapy, respiratory and chest physical therapy and rehabilitative physical therapy. A developmental physical therapist begins by conducting a thorough assessment of a child's level of functioning and physical abilities. A treatment plan is developed which may involve others. For example, those caring for the child will work closely with a physical therapist using her advice on positioning, exercises and the use of aids and appliances. The aids and appliances may be provided in consultation with medical personnel. Paediatric physical therapy includes the treatment of children with specific conditions such as cerebral palsy, spina bifida, and juvenile arthritis (Tecklin, 2007).

A physical therapist (physiotherapist in the United Kingdom) is a health professional who provides treatment to improve a client's physical condition, particularly mobility and posture. They may be based in hospitals or community clinics, and may visit schools and homes. She increasingly works as an advisor alongside teachers, parents and others and undergoes specialist training and certification.

Reference

Tecklin, J. S. (Ed.) (2007) (4th edition) *Pediatric Physical Therapy*, Philadelphia, Lippincott Williams and Wilkins.

Further reading

Porter, A. (2003) *Tidy's Physiotherapy*, London, Butterworth/Heinemann.

Addresses

American Physical Therapy Association
www.apta.org
A professional organisation fostering advancements in physical therapy practice.

The Chartered Society of Physiotherapy
www.csp.org.uk
The society represents Britain's physiotherapists, students and assistants.

Pivotal response training

Pivotal response training is a naturalistic intervention to improve the social-emotional and communicative behaviour of young children aged about three to ten years old with autistic spectrum disorders. It does not teach a single behaviour at a time but targets pivotal areas of a child's functioning. These are such that their development is likely to lead to wider changes in untargeted behaviours. A review of studies suggests this is an effective intervention and that in educational settings, '… a child centred approach to intervention in natural environments can optimise communicative and social-emotional functioning' (Humphries, 2003, p. 5).

Procedures are used to structure the environment to teach these pivotal skills to, in turn, improve broader areas of social and communicative functioning (Koegel and Koegel, 1995). Two pivotal areas are motivation and responsivity to multiple cues. The aim might be to increase a child's motivation to learn new skills and to initiate social contacts and respond to others doing so. More generally the teacher might increase the child's motivation by giving the child choices and reinforcing attempts to enable him to respond to natural daily opportunities to learn and interact.

Pivotal response training uses a model of Applied Behaviour Analysis involving positive procedures that are child and family centred. It may involve short sessions perhaps from 10 minutes to an hour several times a week. Pivotal response training uses varied tasks that encompass mastered and novel activities. It ensures adequate modelling of the required behaviour such as turn taking; using naturally occurring reinforcers such as responding meaningfully to a child's requests. The approach uses activities the child prefers and allows choices within these activities. Such procedures are incorporated into daily pedagogic opportunities in natural settings. The teacher helps provide clear and uninterrupted opportunities for the child to ask questions, receive instructions and to respond.

References

Humphries, T. L. (2003) 'Effectiveness of pivotal response training as a behavioural intervention for young children with autism spectrum disorders', *Bridges Practice Based Research Synthesis* 2, 4, 1–10.

Koegel, L. K. and Koegel, R. L. (1995) 'Motivating communication in children with autism' in Schopler, E. and Mezibov, G. (Eds) *Learning and Cognition in Autism: Current Issues in Autism*, New York, Plenum Press, 73–87.

Play and play areas

Play is an activity followed for its own enjoyment and which normally has no serious aim, being pursued predominantly for pleasure. As a key vehicle for learning and as an indication of a child's development, it is important for children with disabilities and disorders.

For children with oppositional defiance disorder, play can provide an indication of their difficulties and an opportunity for adults to encourage the child to develop social skills such as taking turns, negotiating the rules of a game and complying with the rules once they are agreed. For children with anxiety disorders and depressive disorders, play may give the teacher an indication of the child's concerns. Play can help children with language difficulties begin to use language in a relaxed and undemanding setting, although play alone will not necessarily provide the support to develop language.

Children with autism tend not to play in age typical ways and the open-endedness of play seems to be difficult for them and they may appear to prefer repetitive activities such as spinning items. It is suggested that interactive play can be used to help the development of communication, and social understanding and cognition for children with autism (Seach, 2007).

Play areas can be designed with the needs of pupils with disability and disorder in mind. For example, for children with emotional and behavioural difficulties particular attention can be paid to the layout of equipment to improve safety. Children with emotional and behavioural difficulties may have difficulty sustaining social play and even parallel play close to other children may prove difficult. Therefore the playground could have some comparatively isolated areas along with more social ones. This would offer temporary respite for children who feel unable to join their peers and tends to reduce the number of playground conflicts, which add to the safety dangers. Vigilant supervision is very important too.

Reference

Seach, D. (2007) *Interactive Play for Children with Autism: A Practical Guide for Teachers*, London and New York, Routledge.

Further reading

Macintyre, C. (2002) *Play for Children with Special Needs*, London, David Fulton Publishers.
Widerstrom, A. H. (2003) (2nd edition) *Achieving Learning Goals Through Play: Teaching Young Children with Special Needs*, Baltimore, MD, Brookes.

Address

Kids Active
   www.kidsactive.org.uk
   A UK-based organisation promoting and providing play for disabled children.

Play therapy/play therapist

Play therapy is a process involving a child and a therapist in which the child explores matters affecting his life. These influences may be conscious or unconscious, past or present. The therapeutic relationship helps the child draw on his own resources to bring about change. The approach is child centred and may draw on different underpinning theories and models including systemic and psychodynamic ones. Play therapy may take place in a playroom, perhaps in a centre, hospital, residential setting or a school, or within the family. The child is encouraged to play freely with materials which aid imagination and expression such as miniature objects, clay, puppets and paints. He expresses feelings and fantasies in play and certain themes may recur indicating to the therapist the child's concerns.

Where non-directive approaches are used, this implies the child has the ability to resolve his own problems. Such approaches use the technique of reflective listening in which the therapist refers back to the child the feelings that are being expressed in play. Direct approaches on the other hand tend to involve the therapist in structuring the play situation and impinging on the child's consciousness in a purposeful way. The aim of directive methods is to help the child deal with current feelings rather than to explore early difficult experiences. Attempts have been made to bring play therapy within current concerns and interests of evidence-based practice and it has been argued that play therapy constitutes an effective intervention for a wide range of disabilities and disorders including conduct disorder, anxiety disorders, depressive disorders, and speech and language difficulties (Ray *et al.*, 2001).

A play therapist may have an initial qualification in teaching, social work, occupational therapy or a related field as well as experience working with children. She then undertakes a diploma or masters course in play therapy, which involves study and supervised practice.

Reference

Ray, D., Bratton, S., Rhine, T. and Jones, L. (2001) 'The effectiveness of play therapy: Responding to the critics', *International Journal of Play Therapy* 10, 1, 85–108.

Further reading

McMahon, L. (2009) (2nd edition) *The Handbook of Play Therapy and Therapeutic Play*, New York and London, Routledge.

Addresses

British Association of Play Therapists
    www.bapt.info
    The association registers play therapists and regulates play therapy practice.

Canadian Association for Child and Play Therapy
    www.cacpt.com
    A professional association for play therapists.

Politics

The nature of politics in education

Politics is an activity depending on the expression of diverse opinions about proposed aims and how they should be achieved. It works through debate and compromise to resolve conflicting views and differing aspirations and to arrive at solutions to economic and social problems. Debate and persuasion is a crucial part of the political process. Politics assumes that any state will contain many ways of life and that the responsive political order must enable people to follow their own ways within the rule of law. Essentially, it is ruling by the consent of those who are governed. Some views suggest that politics is a system or mechanism drawing on data to produce theories, and such causal theories might draw on economics, social processes and culture. However, much of the study of politics is historical and descriptive. In this respect, politics may be regarded as autonomous and assumes that people act rationally.

Educational politics may be understood in terms of different levels (Cooper, Fusarelli and Cibulka, 2008). At the structural and institutional level, the underpinnings include democracy, political parties and other considerations. At the micro level, may be considered the political behaviours and cultural factors at work in schools and interest groups. Particular philosophical positions can be seen as informing debates such as those on equity and standards. In particular countries, tensions and compromise operate at different levels of structure, for example in the United States of America at the federal, state and school district levels.

Politics and ideology in special education

In special education, as in other areas of policy, there may be political debate in which different views are held which are amenable to argument and contrary evidence. Some positions may be more ideological. It has been suggested (Minogue, 1995) that ideology may be signalled by the presence of a three-part structure of theory. First, past history is regarded as the oppression of some abstract class of person and particular grievances are gathered into the 'symptomatology' of the determined oppression. Second, supporters must mobilise the oppressed class into a struggle against the oppressive system. Third, the emancipatory aim is to attain a fully just society (Ibid. p. 17). The ideal might be that society is managed so where anyone is not fully accepted; political action is indicated to change attitudes so harmony prevails. Politics becomes the authoritative allocation of values. Those in power become managers of equality, building increasingly greater detail into the rules of life. Those who support such developments might regard it as liberationist while others will tend to see them pejoratively as 'political correctness'.

To take one example, ideological positions may be taken on 'inclusion' (where it means mainstreaming pupils). Such a position might not accept the relevance of any evidence of whether pupils made better academic, personal and social development in mainstream or special schools. Placement in mainstream schools might be seen as a given good, and special schools regarded as 'oppressive'. In line with Minogue's (1995) elements of ideology, the past history of provision for special children may be presented as the oppression of these pupils. Instead of seeking to tackle any particular examples of dissatisfaction with special schools in the real world, specific discontents might be gathered into a vision of structurally determined oppression. Supporters might seek to mobilise adults with disabilities and disorders into a struggle against the perceived oppressive system. The third, liberation aspect of ideology it may be thought will be achieved when all pupils attend mainstream schools.

If ideological views are held, it is less likely they will be amenable to political debate. The same holds true for anyone who supports the continuing development of special schools purely on ideological grounds. For example, it would be just as indefensible to support special school education on the ideological grounds that it is self-evidently good that they represent 'diversity' in schooling.

References

Cooper, B., Fusarelli, L. and Cibulka, J. (Eds) (2008) *Handbook of Education Politics and Policy*, New York and London, Routledge.

Minogue, K. (1995) *Politics: A Very Short Introduction*, Oxford, Oxford University Press.

Further reading

Plank, D. N., Sykes, G. and Schneider, B. (2009) *Handbook on Educational Policy Research*, London, Routledge.

Address

The National Institute on Educational Governance, Finance, Policy Making and Management
    www.ed.gov/offices/OERI

Part of the Office of Educational Research and Improvement in the United States Department of Education, the institute seeks to provide national leadership and support to develop and disseminate information pertinent to governance strategies and other matters to support high levels of learning by all students.

Portage

Portage is a home visiting educational service that may be offered to pre-school special children and their families. The scheme began in the small town of Portage, Wisconsin in the United States of America. It encourages partnership between parents and professionals to enable the parent to work systematically with the child using behavioural principles and practices such as reinforcement and shaping.

A Portage team member visits the home for about an hour a week. The parent is shown how to complete a developmental checklist and to specify a teaching target. This is broken down into manageable steps using task analysis and a series of teaching activities is agreed for the subsequent week. The parent works with the child for short periods each day and records progress. Each week, the visitor reviews the progress and plans activities for the following week.

The approach is used widely in over 60 countries and parents and professionals tend to report favourably on its impact. However, empirical evidence about effects of the Portage Guide to Early Intervention is limited by small sample size, lack of control groups and other constraints. It is suggested that therefore professionals are conservative when discussing the merits of the Portage Guide's effects (Brue and Oakland, 2001).

Reference

Brue, A. W. and Oakland, T. (2001) 'The Portage Guide to Early Intervention: An Evaluation of Published Evidence', *School Psychology International* 22, 3, 243–252.

Addresses

Indian National Portage Association
  www.inpa.org.in
  A non-profit organisation based in Chandigarh, India, focusing on personnel training and research, for children at risk of developmental delays, learning disabilities and cognitive impairment.

National Portage Association
  www.portage.org.uk
  The Portage association for the UK.

Postmodernism

Postmodernism is a broad and often loosely used term to indicate a range of approaches to cultural practices and theory. In the present context it refers to a trend, informed by Continental philosophy and other sources, to be suspicious of overarching theories ('grand narratives') of progress and the Enlightenment 'project'. Among influences in postmodern thought are Michel Foucault's ideas about power and control, and Jacques Derrida's notion of deconstruction, involving close examination of a text's internal logic and contradictions.

General criticisms of postmodernism have included that it is too eclectic and irrational.

Postmodern approaches to special education may be distinguished from arguments often apparent in social models of disability. A social model maintains there is nothing disadvantageous or problematic about the workings or attributes of individual bodies apart from the person's social environment. The social environment may be regarded as having aspects that may be physically or materially disabling but which can often be changed, such as buildings that are inaccessible to physically disabled individuals. Also the social environment can involve relationships between those having disabilities and disorders and others that may involve prejudice or lack of understanding that exacerbate the disability or disorder. That is, the social environment can be said to have 'material-physical' and 'symbolic interactive' dimensions (Young, 2002, p. xii). A postmodern position may go further than a social model. It may question assumptions about people 'socially positioned' as disabled, trying to analyse how such assumptions are developed and sustained. It seeks to challenge and change the way people view the constraints and capacities of people considered disabled (Ibid. p. xiv).

In a social model, a distinction is made between 'impairment' (bodily constraints) and 'disability' (the additional constraints placed on the individual by society). Disability is seen therefore as socially created and constructed 'on top of' impairment. The changing notions of disability are placed 'in the social and economic structure of the society in which it is found'. The social model tends to be concerned with emancipation and perhaps the 'oppositional politics of identity' (Corker and Shakespeare, 2002, p. 3). Postmodernism questions 'foundationalist' assumptions. It focuses not so much on the material factors of economics, but aims to create a shift in how people, 'perceive, think and produce'. It is concerned with how we build inclusive societies and the social role of knowledge in this process (Ibid.). In postmodern views, impairment is not just accepted as being a biological fact but is questioned or 'problematised'. Impairment is theorised as 'a bio-social phenomenon' (Thomas and Corker, 2002, p. 24). It is suggested that so-called, 'oppressive discourses' are part of the problem and efforts should be made to change them.

While the social model may seek to move understanding of disability away from medical perspectives, a postmodern perspective might suggest that the social view has left the impaired body still susceptible to medical interpretation. A postmodern approach might analyse the biomedical practices involved in the emergence of the category of impairment aiming to show that the allegedly real entity of disability is a 'historically contingent effect of modern power' (Tremain, 2002, p. 34).

Some social perspectives may assume that when unequal power relations are overcome, there will be true knowledge and social transparency (Kiel, 1995). For postmodernism, behind appearances in society is more appearance, not the 'real'. Power flows in many directions. Professions in special education are part of the web of power and increase control over people's lives. The disabled individual is controlled by internalising the norms of the disciplinary professions and coming to believe that the perspective of these professions is the sole reality (Ibid. pp. 147–148). For postmodernism, a perspective that distinguishes disability and impairment 'needs to be deconstructed'. Postmodernism seeks to show that impairment and disability are 'coexisting social and political facets of disablement' (Goodley and Rapley, 2002, p. 138). Yet this is not so much an argument, more of a restatement of the postmodern position. Where the supposed 'need' for deconstruction comes from is unclear.

References

Corker, M. and Shakespeare, T. (2002) 'Mapping the terrain' in Corker, M. and Shakespeare, T. (Eds) *Disability/Postmodernity: Embodying Disability Theory*, London, Continuum.

Goodley, D. and Rapley, M. (2002) 'Changing the subject: Postmodernism and people with 'learning difficulties' in Corker, M. and Shakespeare, T. (Eds) *Disability/Postmodernity: Embodying Disability Theory*, London, Continuum.

Kiel, D. C. (1995) 'The radical humanist view of special education and disability: Consciousness, freedom and ideology' in Skrtic, T. M. (Ed.) (1995) *Disability and Democracy: Reconstructing (Special) Education for Postmodernity*, New York, Teachers College Press, Columbia University.

Thomas, C. and Corker, M. (2002) 'A journey around a social model' in Corker, M. and Shakespeare, T. (Eds) *Disability/Postmodernity: Embodying Disability Theory*, London, Continuum.

Tremain, S. (2002) 'On the subject of impairment' in Corker, M. and Shakespeare, T. (Eds) *Disability/Postmodernity: Embodying Disability Theory*, London, Continuum.

Young, I. M. (2002) 'Foreword' in Corker, M. and Shakespeare, T. (Eds) *Disability/Postmodernity: Embodying Disability Theory*, London, Continuum.

Further reading

Drolet, M. (Ed.) (2003) *The Post Modernism Reader: Foundational Texts*, London and New York, Routledge.

Macey, D. (2000) *The Penguin Dictionary of Critical Theory*, London, Penguin Books.

Postural and positional supports

Postural and positional supports may be used for a child or young person with orthopaedic impairment, assisted by advice from a physical therapist or occupational therapist. Correct positioning is supported by pads and cushions or specially constructed adapted seat inserts. Using an aid such as a sidelyer, wedge or tricycle with a built up back or by standing helps ensure that the child adopts different positions as necessary throughout the day.

To help the child sit comfortably and properly the pelvis needs to be correctly positioned and the trunk and shoulder correctly supported, for example by vest type supports or H straps. For seating, an abductor or leg separator may be used as either a distinct piece of equipment or as part of the seat. Examples of alternative seating are a chair without legs, a chair with arms and a footrest, and corner seats (Bigge, Best and Heller, 2001, pp. 199, 201–204). Some subjects are associated with particular furniture such as high stools often used in science, which may require a back support and arms. Assistive walking devices include a PVC pipe walker and forearm or underarm crutches. An occupational therapist can advise and help arrange a specially moulded toilet seat where this is needed.

Reference

Bigge, J. L., Best, S. J. and Heller, K. W. (2001) (4th edition) *Teaching Individuals with Physical, Health or Multiple Disabilities*, Upper Saddle River, NJ, Merrill-Prentice Hall.

Prader–Willi syndrome

Prader–Willi syndrome is a congenital condition named after the two Swiss paediatricians, A. Prader and H. Willi who first identified it. It is characterised by severe cognitive impairment, delay in speech and walking, underdeveloped genitals and excessive appetite. The child often develops diabetes mellitus. Behavioural difficulties may develop in relation to wanting food. The syndrome and its associated medical, nutritional, psychological, social, educational and therapeutic implications require support from a range of professionals working closely together (Whittington and Holland, 2004).

Reference

Whittington, J. and Holland, T. (2004) *Prader–Willi Syndrome: Developments and Manifestations*, Cambridge, Cambridge University Press.

Further reading

Butler, M., Lee, P. D. K. and Whitman, B. Y. (Eds) (2006) (3rd edition) *Management of Prader–Willi Syndrome*, New York, Springer.

Addresses

Prader–Willi Syndrome Association
www.pws-uk.demon.co.uk

The association offers a range of services to help families, individuals with Prader–Willi syndrome and professionals.

Prader–Willi Syndrome Association
www.pwsausa.org
An organisation of families and professionals aiming to promote and fund research, provide education, and offer support.

Prevalence and incidence

Prevalence refers to the total number of instances of a disability or disorder in a specified population at one particular time. It is often presented as the number of instances in every 100,000 people. Disabilities or disorders may be described according to their relative commonness. In a country asthma may be common, blindness fairly common, Down syndrome uncommon and autism rare (Anderson, 2007, p. 1505).

Incidence refers to the number of new instances in a specified period. There may be 100 new cases of a disorder per 100,000 people per year. If these continue, year-on-year prevalence will exceed incidence unless people with the condition die at the same rate that new cases appear (Anderson, p. 919).

Reference

Anderson, D. M. (Chief lexicographer) (2007) (31st edition) *Dorland's Illustrated Medical Dictionary*, Philadelphia, PA, Elsevier/Saunders.

Problem-solving skills training

An intervention that may be used with aggressive children is problem-solving skills training (Spivak and Sure, 1978). Aggressive children compared with non-aggressive children are more likely to attribute hostile intentions to others and to anticipate rejection. Children with conduct problems are not very good at producing various solutions to interpersonal problems and lack insight into other people's motivations. Accordingly, problem-solving skills training is intended to develop essential interpersonal and cognitive problem-solving skills.

Through techniques such as modelling and role play children are taught to recognise and alter how they process and react to social situations. Problem-solving skills training involves around 20 clinic-based individual sessions with a therapist who examines the ways the child tends to respond to interpersonal situations and encourages the child to take a structured approach to tackling problems. The therapist uses structured tasks related to real life. Social behaviours are encouraged by modelling and direct reinforcement.

A cognitive behavioural approach was used for children aged 2 to 13 years with conduct disorder which involved child problem-solving skills training methods such as using 'stop and think' self statements. Parent management training including using positive reinforcement was also used (Kazdin, 2003, pp. 241–262). Important individual aspects included cognitive and behavioural repertoires and predispositions to respond to situations that could be problematic. Antecedents of the child's behaviour and the responses of others were also influential. All these were used to encourage 'pro-social behaviour' (Ibid. p. 258). The evidence indicated that problem-solving skills training can be effective, particularly in combination with parent training. The more severe the dysfunction, the smaller tended to be the positive effect (Kazdin and Wasser, 2000).

References

Kazdin, A. E. (2003) 'Problem-solving skills training and parent management training for conduct disorder' in Kazdin, A. E. and Weisz, T. R. (Eds) *Evidence Based Psychotherapies for Children and Adolescents*, New York, Guilford Press, 241–262.
Kazdin, A. E. and Wasser, G. (2000) 'Therapeutic changes in children, parents and families resulting from treatment of children with conduct problems', *Journal of the American Academy of Child and Adolescent Psychiatry* 39, 414–420.
Spivak, G. and Sure, M. B. (1978) *Problem Solving Techniques in Child Rearing*, San Francisco, Jossey-Bass.

Profound cognitive impairment/profound and multiple learning difficulties

The nature of profound cognitive impairment

In England the equivalent term to 'profound cognitive impairment' is 'profound and multiple learning difficulty' (Department for Education and Skills, 2005, p. 6). In the United States of America, the expression 'profound mental retardation' is widespread, defined in terms of limitations in both intellectual functioning and in adaptive behaviour (American Psychiatric Association, 2000, p. 42). While it is associated with an intelligence quotient (IQ) range of below 20 or 25, IQ levels are not the sole criterion. Mental retardation is associated with 'co current deficits or impairments in present adaptive functioning ... in at least two of the following areas: communication, self care, home living, social/interpersonal skills, use of community resources, self-direction, functional academic skills, work, leisure, health and safety' (Ibid. p. 49). In 2002, the American Association on Intellectual and Developmental Disabilities agreed a supports-based definition.

Prevalence is about 0.6 per cent and 0.8 per cent (Rumeau-Rouquette *et al.*, 1998). Almost all children with profound cognitive impairment have organic brain damage and there is evidence of, 'considerable impairments' in sensory motor functioning (American Psychiatric Association, 2000, p. 44). Very many individuals with profound cognitive impairment are also multiply disabled and conditions that do not cause profound cognitive impairment may be associated with it.

Provision

Reflecting the very early developmental level of those with profound cognitive impairment, the curriculum is informed by knowledge of typical early infant development. Planning ensures a rich variety of curriculum experiences. Essential requirements such as therapy, medical care, and special programmes are integrated into provision. Priorities in an Individualised Education Programme tend to involve the acquisition of basic and fundamental skills. The curriculum also involves practical, functional activities in such areas as: 'communication, self-care, home living, social/interpersonal skills, use of community resources, self-direction, functional academic skills, work, leisure, health and safety' (American Psychiatric Association, 2000).

Communication is central. Turning towards a sound or fixing one's gaze are potentially ways of communicating and vocalisations may indicate feelings or preferences. But some behaviour may be ritualistic or obsessive. Where an adult responds with patience and sensitivity, to certain early gestures, looks and sounds they can acquire communicative significance. Some students with profound cognitive impairment may respond to and use symbolic communication, allowing communication about absent items or people or about proposed activities. Objects of reference may be tried. The student may learn to use and understand visual symbols conveying activities, places, preferences, choices and feelings. Any use of simple language is encouraged. Manual sign language is used to communicate and to supplement verbal communication.

Task analytic instruction can inform teaching and learning for tasks such as teaching a child to drink from a covered cup holding it in both hands. The required learning goal is that when the child is thirsty and a covered cup containing drink is placed on a tray before him, he will pick up the cup and drink from it. Task elements are to look at the cup, place both hands round it, raise it to the lips and tilt it to drink. Subtasks might be taught in this order or through 'backward chaining', where the child is prompted for all but the final part of the sequence and progressively encouraged to complete earlier parts unsupported.

Multisensory approaches can stimulate the senses to encourage responsiveness in a child who may be less able than other children to explore his environment. But, more effectively, they can incorporate sensory experiences based on learning priorities into activities with their own 'structure and meaning' such as exploring cookery ingredients. They can enable participation in subject-related activities such as mathematics or history. However, if the topic is outside the pupil's understanding, the sensory experiences may be fragmented or fail to convey what is intended (Ouvry and Saunders, 2001, p. 245). Sensory experiences can be extended to give opportunities for conceptual learning and to help the pupil to better understand his surroundings, daily activities and everyday experiences (Carpenter, 1994).

For older students, as part of the transition from school to post-school settings, vocational instruction including community-based vocational instruction is important. It can help the development of adaptive behaviour. A study with high school students with 'moderate to profound mental retardation' found such instruction helped them become more independent (McDonnell, *et al.*, 1993). The coordination of the school, potential employers, rehabilitation counsellor, transport managers and volunteers helps maximise potential benefits. Planning takes account of local circumstances and job opportunities and training schedules help students develop employment skills. Task analyses may be made of the main tasks required such as cleaning procedures, or packing skills.

Activities may be enhanced and structured using the visual and auditory capabilities of digital videodiscs or interactive compact disks. Choice-making leading to greater autonomy may be taught using adult prompting and/or using a switch-activated reinforcer. Prompting may be used to teach switch activation or/and discrimination between different choices. Multiple micro switches can enhance different responses in children. A digital still or video camera can record interesting activities and its images transferred to a computer and projected, if the pupil is able to recognise these. For students able to use symbolic communication, electronic communication systems may be used that speak programmed messages when the pupil activates locations marked by symbols.

Developing a 'responsive environment' (Ware, 2003, p. 1) can enable pupils to get responses to their actions, respond to others, and lead an interaction. The environment has to be sensitive to movements and sounds made by the pupil so that these environmental responses will in turn bring a response from the child. Pupils should be enabled to act to control aspects of their surroundings. Related to this is encouraging choice and decision making, such as choice of whether to go out or stay in the classroom, and with whom to sit. Establishing that the child is aware of the link between his behaviour and its consequences is important. Using switch operated reinforcers, the child may be prompted to use the switch so that he will experience his action and its consequences repeatedly and link the two.

References

American Psychiatric Association (2000) *Diagnostic and Statistical Manual of Mental Disorders, Fourth Edition, Text Revision*, Arlington, VA, APA.

Carpenter, B. (1994) 'Finding a home for the sensory curriculum', *PMLD Link* 19, 2–3.

Department of Education and Skills (2005) (2nd edition) *Data Collection by Special Educational Need*, London, DfES.

McDonnell, J., Hardman, M. L., Hightower, J., Keifer-O'Donnell and Drew, C. (1993) 'Impact of community based instruction on the development of adaptive behaviour of secondary level students with mental retardation', *American Journal on Mental Retardation* 97, 5, 575–584.

Ouvry, C. and Saunders, S. (2001) 'Pupils with profound and multiple learning difficulties' in Carpenter, B., Ashdown, R. and Bovair, K. (Eds) *Enabling Access: Effective Teaching and Learning for Pupils with Learning Difficulties*, London, David Fulton Publishers, 240–256.

Rumeau-Rouquette, C., du Mazaubrun, C., Cans, C. and Grandjean, H. (1998) 'Definition and prevalence of school-age multi-handicaps', *Archives of Paediatric and Adolescent Medicine* 5, 7, 739–744.

Ware, J. (2003) *Creating a Responsive Environment for People with Profound and Multiple Learning Difficulties*, London, David Fulton Publishers.

Further reading

Aird, R. (2001) *The Education and Care of Children with Severe, Profound and Multiple Learning Difficulties*, London, David Fulton Publishers.

Mednick, M. (2007) *Supporting Children with Multiple Disabilities*, London, Continuum.

Address

PMLD Network
   www.pmldnetwork.org
   A UK-based group committed to improving the lives of children and adults with profound and multiple learning difficulties.

Progress

A broad view of progress

The progress of pupils with disabilities and disorders is central to determining and evaluating provision for them. The judgement is informed by many factors and it conveys little to say that the child's 'needs' are being met, whatever these are perceived to be. Definitions of progress vary, but perhaps a useful starting point is to consider it to apply to both academic progress and development. Academic progress may apply to school subjects or areas of the curriculum such as mathematics, literacy, science, physical education and so on. Development may refer to areas such as personal and social development, including self-esteem and well-being. Determining progress involves making an assessment of attainment or development level at one time and another assessment at a later time and judging whether the rate of improvement is sufficient.

Ways of determining progress

Progress can be determined in different ways. It can be approached using standardised assessments of attainment or development. It can be judged according to progress on a specified curriculum. Levels of accreditation and examination results also contribute to judgements of progress. For students who may make very slow progress, assessments are made using very small steps so that progress can be recognised and celebrated. For example with a child with developmental coordination disorder, assessment needs to be detailed enough to show small increments of progress in coordination, movement and balance. In England there are several assessments that are used to show very small steps of progress for pupils with cognitive impairment and others. These include commercial assessments, ones developed originally by local authorities, and ones developed under the auspices of government bodies.

Judging whether progress is sufficient

A central and complex issue, however, is how the extent of progress made by a child with a disability can be judged. What amount of progress can be deemed to be satisfactory? What would constitute excellent progress? How would educators, parents and others know when progress was unsatisfactory? These are important in themselves. They are also helpful to substantiate or contradict notions that a particular approach or location or teacher might lead to aspirations for a child being too low.

Very broad attempts to deal with these issues can be seen in attempts in the United States of America to develop standards-based reforms and accountability programmes. Under provisions of the No Child Left Behind Act (20 U. S. C. 6301 et seq.) children with disabilities participate in state accountability testing and assessments. The legislation also requires that these children are provided with reasonable modifications and accommodations. The scores for these students have to be included with the scores of all students and are disaggregated so that the performance of pupils with disabilities can be assessed for school accountability. A 2004 reauthorisation of the *Individuals with Disabilities Education Improvement Act* (House Bill 1350) enacted that some students with disabilities were exempted from taking assessments that most students took. Regulations and other measures allowed increasing variations in the types of participation of special children in assessments and the calculation of the 'adequate yearly progress' in relation to academic performance made (for a fuller summary of these developments see Pullin, 2008). This can be viewed as a regrettable move away from supposed inclusion in the same systems. Alternatively, it can be seen as an inevitable recognition that some special pupils will not be able to show what they can do in assessments used for all. A more important issue, perhaps, is whatever assessments are used, how can it be established that special pupils are making sufficient progress.

In making a rounded judgement about progress, other factors that can influence progress are taken into account such as gender, ethnicity and social background. Also important when judging progress is the amount of time a child has been receiving special education and support.

One approach is to try to evaluate the progress made by special children in relation to that expected of children without a disability or disorder. By definition a special child has a disability or disorder and the disability or disorder makes education more difficult. Therefore, broadly, if a special child were to make the same progress as that expected for all children, or better, then this could presumably be considered excellent progress. Somewhere below such a level of progress, other judgements might be placed. For example, would less than half the progress expected of all children represent unsatisfactory progress? Would some point a little above such progress be seen as satisfactory? Would a point perhaps midway between satisfactory and excellent progress constitute 'good' progress? Another factor that would be included would be the attainment level of the child in relation to his age. If a young person aged 16 years old with profound cognitive impairment were functioning on an assessment at a level typical of a child of one or two years old, expectations of, for example, 'satisfactory' progress would be likely to be much lower than half the progress of a typically developing individual. This is not to lower expectations randomly but to take account of the rate of progress already made in the student's development and bring this to bear on judgements of progress and expectations.

Types of disability and disorder

It is not the case that a particular type of disability or disorder determines progress because there are variations within categories of disability and disorder. Neither is it the case that disabilities and disorders have no bearing on progress.

Consider a pupil with mathematics disorder. His progress in mathematics and in areas where similar underpinning processes might be involved would be likely to initially be slower than that of other pupils. But in areas less related to mathematics and less related to the supposed underpinning processes associated with mathematics disorder, his progress may be similar to that of other pupils. Taking such considerations into account could help ensure that expectations for these subjects are as high as they should be. To take another example, the progress in reading of a blind child using Braille tends to be slower than that of a sighted child. This is partly because there is no touch equivalent to the peripheral vision a sighted child uses to look ahead and prepare for the next words he is going to read, thereby speeding up his reading. However, schools will still have high aspirations for reading progress for a child using Braille although this may not be as fast as for sighted children. With some disabilities and disorders, progress can vary over time. A child with hearing impairment may progress slower than others children in language skills in early stages then progress much more rapidly later, making up for previously lost ground. Issues of interpretation sometimes relate to a particular disability or disorder. When assessing reading with children with autism, particular care is needed to ensure that the child fully understands what he is reading. He may have mastered the mechanics of reading, but when questioned about the content, understand much less that might at first appear, especially where the content involves complex social meanings. Very occasionally, a special child may make no progress or may regress over time, for example because of a debilitating condition.

Data on pupils with different types of disability and disorder may be gathered and used to aggregate progress over a specified period of say one year. The progress of an individual pupil can then be considered in relation to average progress for the group. The annual progress of pupils with moderate to severe cognitive impairment ('severe learning difficulties' in England) could be collated. Evaluations could then be made of the relative progress of individual pupils, groups of pupils and other cohorts. In England, such information is available through the organisation 'Equals' and elsewhere. Some local authorities gather such information so that parents can see the progress that is being made in the school their child attends in terms of the types of disability and disorder. In the large county of Hampshire, for example, parents can examine for say pupils with mild cognitive impairment ('moderate learning difficulties' in the English system) the typical progress made by these pupils on average in local mainstream schools and local special schools to inform their decision about their child's placement (Farrell, 2006, pp. 59–61). These are broad judgements and require interpreting carefully because within a category such as mild cognitive impairment, there is a band of ability and attainment. This requires that the starting points of individual pupils also be also taken into account when considering their progress.

Consistency and moderation

Whatever the forms of assessment used to determine starting points and subsequent progress, it is necessary that those administering them are consistent from one administering to the next. Also where several people are administering the assessments, for example several teachers in a school, it is important they too are consistent. Training and practice in applying the assessment and some form of moderation are often used. Where national accreditation is used the issue of whether the grades achieved in these are high enough is determined with reference to the pupils' starting points and previous progress.

Attempts are made to improve progress and ensure it is sufficient by setting targets of progress for individual pupils in their Individual Education Programmes/Plans and for cohorts of pupils. However, individual targets on their own do not provide evidence that progress is sufficient unless they are related to wider evaluations of expected progress as outlined earlier. Schools, including special schools, also compare the progress of their pupils with that of other schools educating pupils with similar disabilities and disorders in a process sometimes called benchmarking. This can help a school identify what it is doing well and learn from other schools what it might do better.

Using data to improve progress and provision

A summary of the complex task of ensuring progress of special children is sufficient to indicate that there are no fixed and agreed benchmarks at national or any other level that can unequivocally show what progress can be expected. But neither can any level of progress be considered acceptable. High aspirations are informed by a broader view of how other children with similar disabilities and disorders progress and other factors.

The purpose of all this is to make sure special pupils are progressing well enough. Where they are not, then the systems of assessment can identify this and the school can decide on the steps that need to be taken to improve matters. Is slower progress associated with a particular class teacher? Is it linked to a particular group such as girls with disabilities and disorders, or boys, or pupils in a particular age group? Is teaching poorer in English than in mathematics or vice versa? Does pupils' written work indicate that they are not covering different areas of the subject in equal and sufficient depth? Where this sort of analysis is undertaken, the school can take steps to improve matters.

References

Farrell, M. (2006) *Celebrating the Special School*, London, David Fulton Publishers.
Pullin, D. C. (2008) 'Implications for human and civil rights entitlements: Disability classification systems and the law of special education' in Florian, L. and McLaughlin, M. J. (Eds) *Disability Classification in Education*, Thousand Oaks, CA, Corwin Press.

Further reading

Farrell, M. (2001) *Standards and Special Educational Needs*, London, Continuum.

Address

Entitlement and Quality Education for Children with Learning Difficulties
(Equals)
   www.equals.co.uk
   An organisation aiming for improved provision for children and young
people with learning difficulties and disabilities through supporting high
quality education.

Prosthetics and orthotics

Prosthetics concerns the bringing together of mechanical devices and the
human body to help motor control. A prosthesis is therefore an artificial
device fitted to the human body. An example is an artificial arm for a person
whose arm has been amputated because of injury or disease or who has been
born without the limb. A prosthetist measures, designs, makes, fits and looks
after prostheses. She works with a physician to ensure the best prosthesis is
developed for the individual's requirements.

   Orthotics derives its name from the Greek 'ortho' meaning to straighten.
Orthoses are pieces of equipment supporting or rectifying musculoskeletal
deformities and improving physical functioning. Orthotics involves designing, making and fitting such devices. Orthotics may contribute to the
treatments of various conditions including cerebral palsy, muscular dystrophy and congenital deformities arising in childhood (Morris and Dias,
2007). An orthotist is a member of an allied health care profession whose
training draws on anatomy and physiology, materials engineering, and other
sources.

Reference

Morris, C. and Dias, L. (Eds) (2007) *Paediatric Orthotics: Orthotic Management of
   Children*, New York and London, Blackwell Publishing.

Further reading

Ott, K., Serlin, D. and Mihm, S. (2001) *Artificial Parts, Practical Lives: Modern
   Histories of Prosthetics*, New York, New York University Press.

Addresses

American Academy of Orthotists and Prosthetists
   www.oandp.org
   Aims to promote professionalism and advance standards of patient
care.

International Society for Prosthetics and Orthotics
www.ispo.ws
The society based in Copenhagen Denmark, is a multidisciplinary organisation of people with a professional interest in prosthetics, orthotics and
related areas.

Protective appliances and clothing

The aims of using protective appliances including clothing are to protect individuals with self-injurious behaviour and/or emotional and behavioural
problems. These appliances are used as part of a behavioural programme
seeking to decrease harmful behaviour and to replace it with alternative
behaviour. They can prevent tissue damage, and are usually preferable to
human restraint, which can reinforce the unwanted behaviour. On the other
hand, the appliances too can reinforce the unacceptable behaviour, can
restrict activities, and can make the special child dependent on them.
Protective appliances are best reserved for emergency use. Good practice
includes that there are clear instructions about their use, and that records are
kept of the circumstances, and the frequency and duration of their use.

Before protective appliances are employed, a functional analysis is made of
the behaviour and the environment. Behaviour is monitored before and after
the appliance is used. Staff aim for the minimal use of the appliances to avoid
hindering motor development. The appliance should cause minimal restric-
tion and as far as possible should allow participation in activities. If the appliance is quickly and easily put on, it is less likely to involve the adult giving the
child attention for the inappropriate behaviour, which could reinforce it.
Clear plans are formed for gradually dispensing with the use of the appliance.
The appliance is only fitted when the unacceptable behaviour occurs.

Protective environments include cot padding (usually to prevent damage
from head banging), padded chairs and plastizote cushions. Minimum physical restraints can take various forms. Muffs are used particularly where the
individual uses his own clothing as a form of self-restraint. Mittens stop the
child biting his hands, fingers and wrists and can prevent probing with the fingers into the nose, mouth or anus. But it can be difficult to keep mittens on
and they restrict manual activities. Elbow splints are used where the child
may damage his head, face or eyes with his fists or fingers or where he picks
slow healing scars. They allow the full use of the hands and may be made of
plastizote, canvas or foam. Variable hinged arm splints can allow the elbows
to be flexed in order to eat. Palm splints prevent hand biting, wrist biting and
hair pulling. Capes stop the child using his fists to hit his head or striking his
head onto his shoulders. The individual can use his hands to eat, employing
long-handled cutlery but cannot reach the face. A mouth guard or lip splint
prevents lip biting.

Protective helmets guard against head banging and hitting the head or face, and chin protection can be added. An orthotic helmet is made and fitted by an orthotist, a specialist appliance maker. It is expensive and for longer-term use and tends to be more secure than a commercial helmet.

Further reading

Morris, C. and Dias, L. (Eds) (2007) *Paediatric Orthotics: Orthotic Management of Children*, New York and London, Blackwell Publishing.

Address

British Association of Prosthetists and Orthotists
  www.bapo.com
  The association encourages high standards of prosthetic and orthotic practice.

Psychodynamic therapy

The term 'psychodynamic' relates to emotional tensions taking place in the person's unconscious. Several arts therapies including some approaches to music therapy, art therapy, drama therapy and movement therapy, draw on psychodynamic perspectives. Some play therapy approaches are psychodynamic in their orientations. The notion of the unconscious, it is suggested, has been, 'central to some areas of the arts therapies: their thinking and their methodology' (Jones, 2005, p. 126).

An example of one successfully evaluated therapy is 'focal psychodynamic psychotherapy'. This has been evaluated with children with relatively mild anxiety disorder or dysthymic disorder (involving chronically depressed mood). The dynamic formulation of the child's conflicts are explored with the whole family, then sessions take place involving only the child, before finally the whole family are seen again (Muratori *et al.*, 2002).

In line with psychodynamic principles, settings for special education may encourage children to communicate openly and may provide communicative and expressive activities such as drama, aspects of physical education, and play. Nevertheless, important differences remain between activities such as drama and their therapeutic counterparts such as drama therapy. Each has different aims and the training and perspectives of educators and therapists differ considerably.

In some specialist settings psychodynamic interpretations may be used in day-to-day living as well as in individual sessions. The Mulberry Bush School in the United Kingdom (www.mulberrybush.oxon.sch.uk) is a special school, whose provision developed from the work of its founder the psychotherapist Barbara Dockar-Drysdale (1991) who was in her turn influenced by the psychoanalyst and paediatrician Donald Winnicott (1965).

Discrete nurture groups (Boxall, 2002) based in mainstream settings were influenced by the attachment theory of John Bowlby (1969, 1973, 1980). These early intervention groups are intended for children whose emotional, social and behavioural 'needs' cannot be supported well in a mainstream classroom. It is suggested these children have not had early experiences enabling them to function socially and emotionally in a way typical of their age. The nurture group might consist of a teacher and an assistant and about twelve children. The relationship between the child and the adults is important to help the child develop a sense of self. Social development is encouraged and concentrates on the emotional aspects of interactions between child and caregiver. The children return to mainstream classes when appropriate.

References

Bowlby, J. (1969) *Attachment and Loss Volume 1: Attachment*, London, Hogarth Press.

Bowlby, J. (1973) *Attachment and Loss Volume 2: Separation, Anxiety and Anger*, London, Hogarth Press.

Bowlby, J. (1980) *Attachment and Loss Volume 3: Loss, Sadness and Depression*, London, Hogarth Press.

Boxall, M. (2002) *Nurture Groups in School: Principles and Practice*, London, Paul Chapman Publishing.

Dockar-Drysdale, B. (1991) *The Provision of Primary Experience: Winnicottian Work with Children and Adolescents*, London, Free Association Press.

Jones, P. (2005) *The Arts Therapies: A Revolution in Health Care*, Hove, Brunner-Routledge.

Muratori, F., Picchi, L., Casella, C., Tancredi, R., Milone, A. and Patarnello, M. G. (2002) 'Efficacy of brief dynamic psychotherapy for children with emotional disorders', *Psychotherapy and Psychosomatics* 71, 28–38.

Winnicott, D. W. (1965) *The Maturational Process and the Facilitating Environment*, London, Hogarth Press.

Further reading

Gurman, A. S. and Messer, S. B. (Eds) (2003) (2nd edition) *Essential Psychotherapies: Theory and Practice*, New York, Guilford Press.

Lanyado, M. and Horne, A. (1999) *Handbook of Child and Adolescent Psychotherapy: Psychoanalytic Approaches*, London, Routledge.

Midgley, N., Anderson, J. Grainger, E., Nesic-Vuckovik, T. and Urwin, K. (Eds) (2009) *Child Psychotherapy and Research: New Approaches – Emerging Findings*, London, Routledge.

Address

Association of Child Psychotherapists
www.acp-uk.eu
The professional association for child psychotherapists in the UK.

Psycholinguistics

The nature of psycholinguistics

Psycholinguistics is a multidisciplinary subject drawing on psychology, neuroscience, phonetics, language pathology, and computer modelling. It has been said to help us understand how we put together our own speech and writing and how we understand the speech and writing of other people. It gives insights into '... how we store and use vocabulary; into how we manage to acquire a language in the first place; and into how language can fail us' (Field, 2004, p. ix).

There is a focus on underlying processes. In assessment, psycholinguistics investigates underlying skills. In interventions it seeks to target, 'the underlying sources of the difficulties rather than the symptoms alone' (Stackhouse and Wells, 2001, p. 412). There is an attempt to understand children's speech difficulties in terms of 'underlying points of breakdown in a speech processing chain or model' (Pascoe, Stackhouse and Wells, 2006, p. 4). The aim of psycholinguists has been said to be 'to find out about the structures and processes which underlie a human's ability to speak and understand language' (Aitchison, 2008, p. 1).

Some applications of psycholinguistics

A psycholinguistic framework may be used in relation to children with specific phonological impairment, verbal dyspraxia and a wide range of communication difficulties, which appear to relate to speech processing problems. These include children with semantic pragmatic difficulties or autistic features (Popple and Wellington, 2001, pp. 299–329).

For example, intonation is an area where a psychodynamic approach may be used. Prosody may be understood as combining the features of tone, duration and intensity (Mildner, 2008, p. 185). Where prosody is atypical, the approach seeks to identify the underlying level of deficit by examining different levels of processing. A battery assessing children's intonation, the *Profiling Elements of Prosodic Systems – Children (PEPS-C)* is described in a published article (Peppé and McCann, 2003).

Turning to word finding difficulties, these are evident when a target word is in a child's receptive vocabulary but he cannot produce it promptly and easily when required. A psycholinguistic approach aims to establish how the difficulty arises in lexical development; and what it is that makes certain words hard to find (Constable, 2001, p. 334). In a single word naming task, problems may arise at different levels: semantic representation; the motor programme; or motor execution (Ibid. p. 336). Teaching and therapy targets may address: underlying input and output processing skills, memory, improving the accuracy of stored information, and strategies that enable the child to cope better (Ibid. p. 355).

References

Aitchison, J. (2008) *The Articulate Mammal: An Introduction to Psycholinguistics*, New York and London, Routledge.

Constable, A. (2001) 'A psycholinguistic approach to word-finding difficulties' in Stackhouse, J. and Wells, B. (Eds) *Children's Speech and Literacy Difficulties Book 2: Identification and Intervention*, London, Wiley, 330–365.

Field, J. (2004) *Psycholinguistics: Key Concepts*, New York and London, Routledge.

Mildner, V. (2008) *The Cognitive Neuroscience of Human Communication*, New York, Lawrence Erlbaum Associates.

Pascoe, M., Stackhouse, J. and Wells, B. (2006) *Children's Speech and Literacy Difficulties Book 3: Persisting Speech Difficulties in Children*, London, Wiley.

Peppé, S. and McCann, J. (2003) 'Assessing intonation and prosody in children with atypical language development: The PEP-C test and the revised version', *Clinical Linguistics and Phonetics* 17, 4/5, 345–354.

Popple, J. and Wellington, W. (2001) 'Working together: The psycholinguistic approach within a school setting' in Stackhouse, J. and Wells, B. (Eds) *Children's Speech and Literacy Difficulties Book 2: Identification and Intervention*, London, Wiley, 299–329.

Stackhouse, J. and Wells, B. (Eds) (2001) *Children's Speech and Literacy Difficulties Book 2: Identification and Intervention*, London, Wiley.

Further reading

Schwartz, R. G. (Ed.) (2008) *Handbook of Child Language Disorders*, New York and London, Routledge.

Traxler, M. and Gernsbacher, M. A. (Eds) (2006) (2nd edition) *Handbook of Psycholinguistics*, San Diego CA, Academic Press.

Addresses

American Speech-Language Hearing Association
www.asha.org
ASHA is a professional and accrediting association for speech-language pathologists and audiologists in the USA and elsewhere.

The Royal College of Speech and Language Therapists
www.rcslt.org
The professional body for speech and language therapists in the UK maintaining high standards of ethical conduct, clinical practice and education of therapists.

Psychology/psychologist

Psychology is the study of mental processes and behaviour. It is a broad area covering many types of psychology including child psychology, research psychology, counselling psychology, cognitive psychology and others. Important fields are clinical psychology and educational psychology.

Cognitive psychology concerns areas of cognition such as attention, perception, memory, thinking and language and relates to clinical disorders such as aphasia and agnosia (Groome *et al.*, 2006).

Clinical psychology concerns the study and application of psychology to prevent and treat psychological problems and encourage psychological health. It embraces research, assessment and treatment, for example, through psychotherapy. A clinical psychologist is a psychology graduate who has undertaken further training to specialise in applying psychology to the clinical sphere. She applies psychological principles to the treatment and management of individuals with emotional and behavioural difficulties and other disorders and disabilities. She may treat clients individually or as members of a group, including a family. A clinical psychologist has skills in observation and assessment, diagnosis and treatment.

Educational psychology concerns studying how individuals learn in educational venues, in the present context, this particularly applies to how children learn in schools. It includes assessing the effectiveness of educational interventions and the psychology of teaching. The social psychology of groupings and the wider organisation of schools are also included. Within educational psychology, its application to special children is important.

In the United States of America, and elsewhere, school psychology refers to applications of clinical psychology and of educational psychology to assessing and intervening to help children and young people learn and develop better. Problem solving approaches informed by data are increasingly advocated (Merrell, Ervin and Gimpel, 2006). School psychology is psychology applied to children's education and development in the context of their schooling. It involves close teamwork with teachers and others. It encompasses assessing pupils, including assessing their cognition and functional skills. A school psychologist combines training and skills relating to education, child and adolescent development, learning, personality, and what constitutes effective teaching and learning. They may carry out assessment and provide advice about interventions. In the United Kingdom school psychology is known as educational psychology and a school psychologist is known as an educational psychologist.

References

Groome, D., Brace, N., Dewart, H., Edgar, G., Edgar, H., Esgate, A., Kemp, R., Pike, G. and Stafford, T. (2006) (2ⁿᵈ edition) *An Introduction to Cognitive Psychology: Processes and Disorders*, New York and London, Guilford Press.

Merrell, K. W., Ervin, R. A. and Gimpel, G. A. (2006) *School Psychology for the 21ˢᵗ Century: Foundations and Practices*, New York and London, Guilford Press.

Further reading

Carr, A. (1999) *Handbook of Child and Adolescent Clinical Psychology: A Contextual Approach*, London and New York, Routledge.

Slavin, R. E. (2003) (8ᵗʰ edition) *Educational Psychology: Theory and Practice*, Columbus, OH, Allyn and Bacon.

Addresses

Association of Educational Psychologists
www.aep.org.uk
The professional organisation and trade union for educational psychologists in the UK.

National Association of School Psychologists
www.naspweb.org
An association based in the USA which represents school psychology and supports school psychologists to enhance the learning and mental health of children and young people.

Psychometric tests and testing

Psychometric tests enable the tester to report, compare and gather objective information to inform teaching and learning. Among the uses of assessments are to: evaluate the effectiveness of a teaching strategy; lead to a record of information about a child that is suitable for passing on to an employer or another school; monitor the progress of a particular pupil; identify pupils who need help or special supervision; and check a child's understanding of specified topics.

Tests need to be suitable for the purpose for which they are being used. They should be valid, that is they should measure what it is said they are measuring. Tests should be reliable so that they consistently measure the same thing at different times. There are tests of intelligence, aptitude and ability. Some are administered individually, others to groups. Some tests are diagnostic while others provide global assessments. When considering ordering a test from a provider, teachers and others may wish to consider the following questions. Is the test really necessary? Will it give any substantial information not already apparent from one's own knowledge of a particular child? When was the test previously standardised? Was it standardised in the country of its intended use? Is the cost in terms of time and money justified?

Further reading

Phelps, R. (Ed.) (2005) *Defending Standardised Testing*, Mahwah, NJ and London, Lawrence Erlbaum Associates.

Rust, J. and Golombok, S. (2008) (3rd edition) *Modern Psychometrics: The Science of Psychological Assessment*, London, Taylor and Francis.

Address

National Council on Measurement in Education
  www.ncme.org
  Based in the USA, the council's aims include to advance the science of measurement in the field of education, improve measurement instruments and related procedures, and improve applications of measurement.

Psychotherapy/psychotherapist

Different types of psychotherapy, for example behavioural, psychodynamic, or systemic, can be understood in terms of key features (Gurman and Messer, 2005, pp. 4–20). These include: the concept of personality that is implied; psychological health and pathology; the process of clinical assessment; and the practice of therapy. It also includes the therapeutic relationship and the stance of the therapist; curative factors or mechanisms of change; and treatment applicability.

A psychotherapist is trained in psychotherapy, which can be informed by various approaches. Psychotherapists treating children and adolescents work with other colleagues as part of a multidisciplinary team in a clinic or in a community setting such as a school or a medical practice. A long-established definition of psychotherapy is: 'the informed and planful application of techniques derived from established psychological principles' delivered by, 'persons qualified through training and experience to understand these principles and to apply these techniques' (Meltzoff and Kornreich, 1970, p. 4). The aim is to help individuals, to 'modify such personal characteristics as feelings, values, attitudes and behaviours which are judged by the therapist to be maladaptive or maladjustive' (Ibid.).

References

Gurman, A. S. and Messer, S. B. (Eds) (2003) *Essential Psychotherapies: Theory and Practice*, New York, Guilford Press.

Meltzoff, J. and Kornreich, M. (1970) *Research in Psychotherapy*, New York, Atherton.

Further reading

Farrell, M. (2009) 'Psychotherapeutic' chapter in *Foundations of Special Education*, New York and London, Wiley.

Fonagy, P., Target, M., Cottrell, D., Phillips, J. and Kurtz, Z. (2002) *What Works for Whom? A Critical Review of Treatments for Children and Adolescents*, New York, Guilford Press.

Address

Association of Child Psychotherapists
www.acp-uk.eu
The professional association for child psychotherapists in the UK.

Pupil 'voice'

Pupil voice refers to attempts to increase the involvement of pupils in their education. In relation to pupils with disorders and disabilities, it concerns a range of approaches. At the root of good participation is effective communication with and among pupils. This may require considerable support, for example for children with autism, or cognitive impairments. The use of aids to communication might include signing, symbols and other means.

It is considered good practice to gather the views of pupils regularly, to collate these, present the results to pupils and others and to take action as necessary. For example, if a school carries out a survey about the quality of lessons, and finds that many pupils are unhappy that resources are not stimulating enough, this should lead to a review of the policy and practice of ordering resources. Pupils themselves of course may suggest topics for surveys or other forms of consultation. The school may have a council of pupils who make decisions about certain aspects of school life. They may report back to and discuss their business with the principal or head teacher. Systems of pastoral care or counselling as well as an ethos in which pupils are valued is likely to improve pupil participation and satisfaction with their education.

Establishing pupils' views and responding to them is a concomitant of pupil voice. Lewis (2004) identifies methods relevant to children who are chronologically or developmentally young. These include permitting 'don't know' responses and requests for clarification, and using statements rather than questions to trigger fuller response. Children may assume the adult already knows the answer to questions so it is important to stress not knowing about events or views. More accurate responses tend to be generated if the adult uses open or moderately focused questions, for example with children with cognitive impairment. The adult will avoid questions that can attract a yes or no answer especially with children with cognitive impairment to avoid acquiescence. The aim is to encourage an uninterrupted narrative.

(See also, *Advocacy*)

Reference

Lewis, A. (2004) 'And when did you last see your father? Exploring the views of children with learning difficulties/disabilities', *British Journal of Special Education* 31, 1, 3–9.

Further reading

Cheminais, R. (2008) *Engaging Pupil Voice to Ensure that Every Child Matters: A Practical Guide*, London, David Fulton.

Ruddock, J. and Flutter, J. (2004) *How to Improve Your School: Giving Pupils a Voice*, London, Continuum.

Flutter, J. and Ruddock, J. (2004) *Consulting Pupils: What's in it for Schools?*, London, RoutledgeFalmer.

Qualifications, standards and training for teachers

The preparation of teachers of special children tends to relate to categories of disorders and disabilities. For example, in the United States of America, to the extent that there has been support for continued classification by disability category, this can involve a relationship between classification and access to free appropriate public education. A loss of such categorisation and funding associated with it, for example for pupils eligible for government funded special programmes, might lead to a diminution of services for special children, it may be argued. Relatedly, the preparation of teachers in universities and colleges has tended to offer different preparation for special teachers and general teachers. More recently, it has been suggested that all teachers should receive collaborative preparation enabling general teachers and special education teachers to work together in teaching all children (Hardman and McDonnell, 2008, p. 161). This might assume a considerable overlap between education and related provision for children that do and do not have disabilities and disorders. Or it may assume that provision, especially education, can be divided meaningfully and pragmatically into content knowledge (mainly held by the general teacher) and specialist pedagogic skills to individualise instruction (mainly held by the special education teacher).

There may be special qualifications for teachers who educate children with disabilities and disorders. These teachers may have additional qualifications to those held by other teachers, for example a post graduate degree in special education. Specialist qualifications may be required for certain types of disability and disorder.

For example, in England regulations specify that a person employed by a school as a teacher of a class of children with visual impairment, hearing impairment or deafblindness must have a 'mandatory qualification' (www.tda.gov.uk). Relatedly, professional standards may be set to try to ensure that teachers with responsibilities in special education have the necessary skills and knowledge. In England, for example, standards have been developed for 'specialist teachers'. Core standards set out the professional knowledge and understanding, skills and attributes needed by effective special educational needs teachers. Specialist standards set out the additional skills needed in various areas of specialist work: autism; emotional and behavioural difficulties; deafness; blindness; deafblindness; physical disabilities; severe and profound learning difficulties; specific learning difficulties; speech, language and communication difficulties; and visual impairment. Using the standards, specialist teachers should be enabled to plan and monitor their professional development, their training and their performance. This should allow them to set targets to improve their effectiveness. Similarly, there are standards for special educational needs coordinators (SENCOs), teachers having responsibilities for coordinating special education (www.tda.gov.uk).

In the United States of America, state-licensing systems set entry-level standards for special education professionals. The American Academy of Special Educational Professionals (AASEP) Professional Board Certification in Special Education sets advanced standards. It represents a professional's qualifications in a specific field of professional practice in special education. Five certificates of advanced professional development must be obtained to achieve an AASEP Professional Board Certification in Special Education. These are: review of the major principles of special education; principles of IEP development; understanding assessment in special education; understanding response to intervention; and special education eligibility (www.aasep.org).

Reference

Hardman, M. L. and McDonnell, J. (2008) 'Disability classification and teacher education' in Florian, L. and McLaughlin, M. J. (Eds) *Disability Classification in Education: Issues and Perspectives*, Thousand Oaks, CA, Corwin Press.

Further reading

Jones, F., Jones, K. and Szwed, C. (2001) *The SENCO as Teacher and Manager: A Guide for Practitioners and Trainers*, London, David Fulton Publishers.

Addresses

American Academy of Special Educational Professionals
www.aasep.org
A professional organisation for those seeking improvements for individuals receiving services for their special needs.

National Association of Special Education Teachers
www.naset.org

A national membership organisation based in Washington, DC, for special education teachers and those preparing for the field.

Training and Development Agency for Schools
www.tda.org.uk
In England, a national agency responsible for the training and development of the school workforce.

Reading disorder

The nature of reading disorder

In reading disorder, reading achievement is 'substantially below' what is expected given the child's age, measured intelligence and education (American Psychiatric Association, 2000, pp. 51–53). Reading achievement is assessed by individually administered standardised tests of reading accuracy, speed, or comprehension. Reading disorder 'significantly' hinders the academic achievement of daily living activities requiring reading skills. Oral reading is characterised by 'distortions, substitutions or omissions' (Ibid. p. 52); reading tends to be slow and errors are made in comprehension whether reading is silent or not. Developmental delays in language may occur with reading disorder. The American Psychiatric Association (Ibid. pp. 51–53) criteria imply that reading disorder can be present when there is an age typical level of reading but where there is a discrepancy between reading attainment and intelligence quotient. Another view is that reading disorder has to be associated with reading achievement below age expectations. In research 'dyslexia', may still be defined in terms of a discrepancy view so it is important to be clear about the position of the researchers. So-called exclusionary definitions of dyslexia exclude general intellectual impairment, sociocultural constraints or emotional factors as possible causes.

Definitions of reading disorder and dyslexia may differ. Dyslexia may include disorder of written expression. On the other hand, the American Psychiatric Association (2000) criteria separate these while acknowledging the two often occur together. Mathematics disorder is also often associated with reading disorder. Types of dyslexia such as 'visual dyslexia' and 'verbal dyslexia' have been suggested. In the United States of America and some other countries, reading disorder/dyslexia is considered a 'learning disability' along with dysgraphia, dyscalculia and (as an associated disorder) attention deficit hyperactivity disorder. Prevalence studies do not always distinguish disorders of reading, written expression and mathematics. Rates vary in different countries depending on how strict are the criteria. In the United States of America it is estimated that about 4 per cent of school-aged children experience reading disorder. More boys than girls are referred but this may relate to boys' associated behaviour difficulties. When careful diagnostic procedures are used there is a more equal gender balance (Ibid. p. 52).

Loci on chromosomes 2, 3, 6, 15, and 18 (Fisher and DeFries, 2002) may be implicated in the heritable transmission of phonological awareness deficits and subsequent difficulties with reading. Functional brain imaging with children and adults with dyslexia indicates that the left hemisphere posterior brain systems may not function correctly during reading (Paulesu *et al.*, 2001).

Possible underlying factors

Various underlying factors have been associated with reading disorder. For example, phonological difficulties may relate to a phonological deficit (Snowling, 2000). Where there are serious phonological difficulties, a speech pathologist may work with the teacher to develop and oversee suitable programmes. The child may be taught to be more aware of and to use in spoken language, sounds and sequences of sounds that conveying meaning in speech. In his own speech, the pupil may practise sounds he often misses.

Other underlying factors include visual difficulties and visual processing difficulties. Also implicated are auditory perception and auditory processing difficulties; short-term verbal memory difficulties; and difficulties with temporal order. If a child has difficulties with one or several sub-skills he may find it hard to improve the problematic skill while maintaining the other. In reading, the pupil has to visually focus on words effectively and track words across a written page. He must retain information in short-term memory while processing it; and organise information. He has to auditorily discriminate, sequence, blend and segment sounds in words. The pupil may find it difficult to improve such skills while sustaining other skills, so some skills may be tackled distinctively. Stronger skills may be used to compensate for weaker ones. For example, a pupil's difficulties with auditory processing and blending and segmenting sounds in words may be helped by teaching phonics, linking visual and kinaesthetic modes with word sounds.

Provision for reading skills

Brooks (2002) reviewed and evaluated the effectiveness of various reading schemes. Particularly effective was Phonographix™ (www.readamerica.net). It develops the notion that written English is a phonemic code with each sound in a spoken word being represented by some part of the written version. It teaches the phonological skills such as blending and segmenting needed to use a phonemic code, explicitly teaching correspondences in sound-to-symbol relationships. Also effective was 'Reading Intervention'

(Brooks, 2002). It combines phonological training with reading, enabling pupils to isolate phonemes in words, to recognise words can have sounds in common, and specific sounds can be represented by certain letters.

Foorman and colleagues (1998) studied the effectiveness of approaches with children in first and second grade classrooms scoring in the lowest 18 per cent on an early literacy assessment. The more effective programme was a direct code approach, providing direct instruction in letter–sound correspondences and practise in decoding text. This led to better word identification skills and steeper learning curves in word reading than implicit code instruction, especially for children entering the programme with the lowest levels of phonological awareness.

In another study (Lovett, Lacerenza, Borden, 2000), children aged 7 to 13 years having severe reading disability were found to respond particularly well to a Phonological Analysis and Blending/Direct Instruction programme followed by Word Identification Strategy Training. It appears optimal approaches in instructing children with learning disabilities combine direct instruction and strategy instruction methods (Swanson and Hoskyn, 1998). A programme, the PHAST Track Reading Programme (Phonological and Strategy Training) for younger 'struggling readers' integrates the two approaches (Lovett, Lacerenza and Borden, 2000). It has been extended to include reading comprehension, writing and spelling lessons. An adaptation was developed for older readers and young adults.

A programme to improve reading fluency RAVE-O (Retrieval, Automaticity, Vocabulary elaboration, Engagement with language, Orthography) has been devised (Wolf, Miller and Donnelly, 2000). It is taught in combination with a systematic phonologically-based programme (teaching for example letter-sound knowledge) while remediating speech-based phonological processes. RAVE-O encourages children to learn to play with language through animated computer games, building word webs, instruction in playful but systematic word retrieval strategies, and reading one-minute stories.

Reading comprehension involves getting the main idea from a text so one can then draw further inferences from it. Difficulty with reading comprehension may be the result of lack of fluency in word recognition. But it may also be related to cognitive processing problems. These include limitations in lexical processing difficulties, working memory, poor inference making and poor monitoring of comprehension (Gersten et al., 2001). Following research into how pupils understand the theme of a story, an instructional model for pupils with learning disabilities was developed. It involves teacher explanation and modelling, guided practice, and independent practice.

References

American Psychiatric Association (2000) *Diagnostic and Statistical Manual of Mental Disorders, Fourth Edition, Text Revision*, Arlington, VA, APA.

Brooks, G. (2002) *What Works for Reading Difficulties? The Effectiveness of Intervention Schemes*, London, Department of Education and Science.

Fisher, S. E. and DeFries, J. C. (2002) 'Developmental dyslexia: Genetic dissection of a complex cognitive trait', *Nature Reviews, Neuroscience* 3, 10, 767–780.

Foorman, B. R., Francis, D. J., Fletcher, J. M., Schatschnieder, C. and Mehta, P. (1998) 'The role of instruction in learning to read: Preventing reading failure in at risk children', *Journal of Educational Psychology* 90, 1, 37–55.

Gersten, R., Fuchs, L. S., Williams, J. P. and Baker, S. (2001) 'Teaching reading comprehension strategies to students with learning disabilities: A review of research', *Review of Educational Research* 71, 279–320.

Lovett, M. W., Lacerenza, L., Borden, S. L. (2000) 'Putting struggling readers on the PHAST track: A program to integrate phonological and strategy based remedial reading instruction and maximise outcomes', *Journal of Learning Disabilities* 33, 5, 458–476.

Paulesu, E., Demonet, J. F., Fazio, F., McCrory, E., Chanoine, V., Brunswick, N., Cappa, S., Cossu, G., Habib, M., Frith, C. and Frith, U. (2001) 'Dyslexia – cultural diversity and biological unity', *Science* 291, 2165–2167.

Snowling, M. J. (2000) *Dyslexia*, Oxford, Blackwell.

Swanson, H. L. and Hoskyn, M. (1998) 'Experimental intervention research on students with learning disabilities: A meta-analysis of treatment outcomes', *Review of Educational Research* 68, 3, 277–321.

Wolf, M., Miller, L. and Donnelly, K. (2000) Retrieval, automaticity, vocabulary elaboration, orthography (RAVE-O): A comprehensive, fluency-based reading intervention program', *Journal of Learning Disabilities* 33, 4, 375–386.

Further reading

Beaton, A. A. (2004) *Dyslexia, Reading and the Brain: A Sourcebook of Biological and Psychological Research*, London, Psychology Press.

Swanson, H. L., Harris, K. R. and Graham, S. (Eds) (2003) *Handbook of Learning Disabilities*, New York, Guilford Press.

Addresses

British Dyslexia Association
www.bda-dyslexia.org.uk
Offers various services including a national helpline, early identification, and education.

Learning Disabilities Association of America
www.ldanatl.org
An organisation advocating for individuals with learning disabilities.

Referral and evaluation

Referral and evaluation are part of the process of establishing that a child has special educational needs. In the United States of America, parents who consider their child is making insufficient progress at school can make a written request to the local school district that they carry out an evaluation. This is a 'referral for evaluation'. A meeting is then held with parents and representatives of the school board. Following this, a team of professionals including a teacher and a specialist knowledgeable in the child's disability carries out an evaluation. This is likely to include administering tests and making observations of the child in school. Once the evaluation information is gathered it is reviewed at a meeting of the Individual Education Program team who establish whether the child is eligible for special education services. If so, they classify the child as having a particular disability/disorder. Categories of disability under federal law as amended in 1997 (20 United States Code 1402, 1997) reflected in subsequent 'designated disability codes' are:

01 Mentally Retarded (mild, moderate, severe, profound)
02 Hard-of-hearing
03 Deaf
04 Speech and Language Impaired
05 Visually Handicapped
06 Emotionally Disturbed
07 Orthopaedically Impaired
08 Other Health Impaired
09 Specific Learning Disability
10 Multi-handicapped
11 Child in Need of Assessment
12 Deaf/Blind
13 Traumatic Brain Injury
14 Autism.

In England, a similar process takes place. This is carried out under the remit of 'identification and assessment'. A *Code of Practice* (Department for Education and Skills, 2001) is followed. The local education authority has to make sure the child's needs are identified and assessed and matched to suitable provision (Ibid. 1.11). The code proposes a graduated approach to assessment and provision. A parent or teacher or others may express initial concerns about the child's progress and support may be provided from within the school's resources. If this does not lead to better progress, other professionals may be involved and a multi-professional statutory assessment undertaken. An early level of intervention is 'school action' or for younger children, 'early years action' where the school or early years setting intervenes from within its own resources. A later possible intervention is 'school action plus' or 'early years action plus' where the setting draws on outside help. If progress is still a concern the local authority may make a 'statutory assessment' of the child's needs which may lead to a 'statement' of special educational needs being agreed. A similar classification (Department for Education and Skills, 2005, *passim*) is adopted to that in the United States of America. It comprises:

- Learning difficulty (moderate, severe, profound)
- Hearing impairment
- Speech, language and communication needs
- Visual impairment
- Behavioural, emotional and social difficulty
- Physical disability
- Specific learning difficulties (e.g. dyslexia, dyscalculia, dyspraxia)
- Multi-sensory impairment
- Autistic spectrum disorder.

References

Department for Education and Skills (2001) *Special Educational Needs Code of Practice*, London, DfES.
Department for Education and Skills (2005) (2nd edition) *Data Collection by Special Educational Need*, London, DfES.

Regional and local organisation

In the United States of America, the Office of Special Programs (OSEP) (www.ed.gov/about/offices/list/osers/osep) aims to improve results for individuals aged birth to 21 years with disabilities. At state level, state Boards of education support schools in their areas to comply with federal and state legislation including concerning the education of pupils with disabilities. For example, the Illinois State Board of Education (www.isbe.stae.il.us) supports the work of schools, policy makers and residents with regard to Illinois public schools. The Board sets state education policies and guidelines for schools and disburses state and federal funding. The Georgia State Board of Education (www.doe.k12.ga.us) provides statewide leadership encouraging local schools and systems to develop suitable policies to support students, teachers, parents and communities. Intermediate school districts (associated with counties or groups of counties) and their boards implement state education policy. Local school districts are administered by elected local school boards, which own and run public primary and secondary schools.

In England, the education services of a local authority have a role between the schools in its area and the government Department for Children, Schools and Families (www.dcsf.gov.uk). Local authority education services have various legal duties including ones relating to the support and education of pupils with disabilities and disorders. The education service in Birmingham City Council education services (www.birmingham.gov.uk) has sought to ensure in its plans and services that all schools including special schools have key roles. Hampshire County Council education services (www.hants.gov.uk/learning) developed a special education policy to ensure change is led by principles of quality of provision. Individual schools are managed by voluntary governors who represent parents, the local authority, local business and the community.

Further reading

Sweet and Maxwell (2007) *2007 Directory of Local Authorities*, London, Sweet and Maxwell.

Timm, M. H. (2002) *State and Local Government in the United States*, Hauppage, NY, Nova Biomedical.

Addresses

Local Government Association
www.lga.gov.uk
A voluntary lobbying association acting as a voice for the local government sector.

National Association of State Boards of Education
www.nasbe.org
An organisation in the USA which aims to serve and strengthen state boards of education.

Research

Research in special education provides helpful information on the success or otherwise of national and local policies and the extent to which a policy is having the intended effect. A researcher in the area of special education may be involved in gathering, collating and analysing data on such matters as policy and provision including teaching and therapy. Other focuses of research include the psychological, sociological, psychiatric, communication, motor and other aspects of disability and disorder. The interest in evidence-based practice draws on good pieces of research that evaluate various interventions.

Among the institutions involved in research in special education are universities and foundations such as the National Foundation for Education Research in the United Kingdom. Research into the causes of and provision for disorders and disabilities is carried out in schools, clinics and research units.

A common issue is that there is not always sufficient interaction between practice and research in special education. Of course some research appropriately focuses on areas with no immediate practical application. Even so, research does not always sufficiently emerge from practical issues and concerns. Neither are the results of research always effectively conveyed to practitioners. Important vehicles that can go some way to rectifying this are good review articles, which draw together previous research in a circumscribed area and synthesise it. Links can be further developed between researchers and practitioners. Also, practitioners themselves may conduct research, for example, when studying for a research degree.

Further reading

Cohen, L., Mannion, L. and Morrison, K. (2007) (6th edition) *Research Methods in Education*, London and New York, Routledge.
Rose, R. and Grosvenor, I. (2001) *Doing Research in Special Education – Ideas into Practice*, London, David Fulton Publishers.

Addresses

National Council on Measurement in Education
    www.ncme.org
    Based in the USA, the council's aims include to advance the science of measurement in the field of education, improve measurement instruments and related procedures, and improve applications of measurement.

National Foundation for Educational Research
    www.nfer.ac.uk
    The Foundation aims to improve education and training by carrying out research and related activities.

Resource room

A resource room is a classroom in which special education programmes are provided for children with a disability or disorder. The pupil spends part of the day in the resource room learning individually or as part of a small group, perhaps concentrating on study skills. The pupil's Individual Education Program Plan will specify the provision and the likely time needed in the resource room, for example about an hour a day. For the remainder of the day the child will be in regular classes with modifications or accommodations to the provision to help ensure he learns and develops well.

A pupil with opposition defiance disorder may find time in the resource room helpful if he receives support in managing his behaviour through, for example, anger management techniques. A child with mild cognitive impairment might concentrate on key subjects such as literacy, numeracy and computer use in the resource room and join lessons with other children with support.

Where the term is common in the United States of America and Japan, in other countries other terms are used to convey a similar approach. In the United Kingdom, such provision might be called a special class base.

(See also, *Special classes, Special school, Mainstream school/classroom*)

Rett syndrome

A rare condition, Rett syndrome almost exclusively affects girls. First described in the 1960s by Austrian Andreas Rett, the syndrome was medically recognised in the 1980s. Symptoms usually occur when the child is 12 to 18 months old after the child has apparently developed normally. Skills such as walking and talking that had been previously acquired gradually decline and the rate of head growth declines. Other characteristics are odd, repeated hand movements and unexplained outbursts of laughter.

Affecting about 1 in every 105,000 baby girls (Candy, Davies and Ross, 2001, p. 18), Rett syndrome is caused by mutations on a gene located on the X chromosome. There is presently no cure for the condition, which is associated with learning difficulties and requires constant care and attention. Physical therapy, occupational therapy and speech therapy all contribute to provision. Medication may be prescribed, for example anti-psychotic drugs may help with self-harming behaviour.

(See also, *Syndromes*)

Reference

Candy, D., Davies, G. and Ross, E. (2001) *Clinical Paediatrics and Child Health*, Edinburgh, Harcourt/W. B. Saunders.

Further reading

Hunter, K. (2007) (2nd edition) *The Rett Syndrome Handbook*, Clinton, MD, International Rett Syndrome Association Publishing.
Lewis, J. and Wilson, D. (1998) *Pathways to Learning in Rett Syndrome*, London, David Fulton Publishers.

Addresses

International Rett Syndrome Foundation
   www.rettsyndrome.org
   Funds research for treatment and cure and provides information, programmes and services.

Rett Syndrome Association
www.rettsyndrome.org.uk
Supports girls and women affected by the disorder, and their families and carers.

Rights

The concern with rights can be argued to have helped articulate the needs of many in society who may be vulnerable or open to exploitation. It may be said to have given a positive face to requests for greater consideration or extra funding for particular groups. Rights have been expressed in all areas of life including in education and special education. The language of rights has been used to highlight such abuses as torture and genocide. Attempts have been made to ensure any new rights are more fundamental. A United Nations resolution adopted in 1986 set out compliance criteria for international human rights instruments. This stated that they should, 'be of fundamental character and derive from the inherent dignity and worth of the human person'. However, given different ideas and practices about what constitutes the value and worth of a person, such a statement is nebulously broad.

Concern has long been voiced that an expanding list of rights may trivialise any core rights that may exist (Glendon, 1991), while doing little to advance the numerous further causes that have been claimed to be rights. Benn and Peters (1959, pp. 88–89) argued that rights and duties have a reciprocal relationship. If an individual claims a right, they suggested, this implies a correlative duty on someone else. The right might imply non-interference while the correlative duty might lie in doing nothing to interfere. A right may impose an active duty on someone else, as when a person's right to claim a debt of another implies the duty of that person to repay it. The correlation between rights and duties is logical (Ibid. p. 89) because a right and a duty are different names for 'the same normative relation' seen from different points.

It is suggested that 'the more the fight for human rights gains in popularity the more it loses any concrete content' (Kundera, 1991). Everything has become a right. 'The desire for love the right to love' and so on (Ibid. p. 154). It is argued that, 'there is very little agreement regarding *which* needs, goods, interests, or values should be characterised as "rights"'. Similarly, there is little consensus about what to do when 'various rights are in tension or collision with one another' (Glendon, 1991 p. 16). Rights rhetoric is accompanied by 'a near silence concerning responsibility, and a tendency to envision the rights-bearer as a lone autonomous individual' (Ibid. p. 45).

A treatise adopted in 2006, *The International Convention on the Rights of Persons with Disabilities* concerned the right to make decisions, marry, have a family, work and receive education. While it may be accepted that many people might like to marry or want to marry, it is less clear whether anyone, having a disability/disorder or not, has a 'right' to marry. Again, while some people might want children, it is not clear that anyone has a 'right' to have a family. The supposed right for anyone to marry suggests the rights-bearer is an autonomous individual and the arrangement no longer depends on someone else wanting to marry the rights bearer.

In special education, as in other areas of life, supposed rights have proliferated. It might be thought there is a 'right' to receive provision such as speech and language therapy and the 'right' to one-to-one tuition if a child is falling behind. A 'right' to be educated in the mainstream may be claimed by those who might depict special schools as segregating and oppressive. Simultaneously there may be claims for a 'right' for deaf children to be educated in a special school for those who believe that deaf people form a linguistic minority whose form of communication should be encouraged.

References

Benn, S. I. and Peters, R. S. (1959) *Social Principles and the Democratic State*, London, George Allen and Unwin.

Glendon, M. (1991) *Rights Talk: The Impoverishment of Political Discourse*, New York, The Free Press.

Kundera, M. (1991) *Immortality*, London, Faber and Faber.

Further reading

Cole, M. (Ed.) (2006) *Education, Equality and Human Rights: Issues of Gender, 'Race', Sexuality, Disability and Social Class*, London and New York, Taylor and Francis.

Address

Equality and Human Rights Commission
  www.equalityhumanrights.com
  This UK-based commission works to eliminate discrimination, reduce inequality, protect human rights and build good relations, ensuring everyone has a fair chance to participate in society.

Semantic pragmatic disorder

Semantics refers to the meaning of words or phrases. Semantic disorders may be considered as disorders of receptive language and of higher-level language. Difficulties for children with such problems tend to relate to working out what a sentence is about, for although they may understand the possible meanings of a word, their difficulty lies with working out how the word is being used on a specific occasion. One particular difficulty is with metaphorically used words or phrases such as 'give me a hand'.

Pragmatics concerns knowing what to say, when to say it and how to say it. Children with pragmatic difficulties find it hard to use language in a social context. They tend to have problems with social conventions like taking turns in conversations or indicating to the speaker signs of interest in what is being said. Others often feel that the conversation of such children is irrelevant or inappropriate.

Children with semantic and pragmatic disorders have unusual characteristics of language. They find understanding certain words and sentences difficult, and use others inappropriately or oddly. Their social development and play may be limited. Appropriate educational provision involves effective assessment, and close working partnerships between teachers, parents, speech pathologists and school psychologists. There is debate about the extent to which semantic pragmatic disorder may be considered a useful diagnostic concept and the degree to which it is viewed as high functioning autism (Gagnon, Mottron and Joanette, 1997).

Reference

Gagnon, L., Mottron, L. and Joanette, Y. (1997) 'Questioning the validity of the semantic–pragmatic diagnosis', *Autism* 1, 1, 37–55.

Further reading

Botting, N. and Adams, C. (2005) 'Semantic and inferencing abilities in children with communication disorders', *International Journal of Language and Communication Disorders* 40, 1, 49–66.

Address

Semantic Pragmatic Disorder Support Group
⬩www.spdsupport.org.uk
An Internet-based voluntary organisation of parents and professionals providing information, advice and support to those supporting children with semantic pragmatic disorder.

Sign bilingualism

In communication, sign bilingualism uses both the sign language of the deaf community and the spoken and written languages of the hearing community. The aim is to enable the deaf child to become bilingual and participate in both hearing and deaf society. The approach involves the systematic use of both the sign language and the spoken language of the country, balanced in line with individual needs. This is to help each child become sufficiently competent in the sign language and the spoken language for their present and future needs, requiring the planned use of sign language and spoken language before school and throughout schooling.

In literacy, where sign language is the preferred or main language for some children who are deaf, it is used for teaching and learning, including of spoken and written English. But because sign language has no orthography, bilingual deaf children have not had the chance to develop literacy skills in their primary language. It is important a pupil's sign language skills are innovatively and interestingly used in literacy teaching for 'presentation, discussion, analysis and explanation of tasks in a way that can bring reading and writing alive for deaf children' (Swanwick, 1998, p. 113). Metalinguistic understanding and awareness developed in sign language is in constructing the second language (e.g. English). Deaf and hearing adults teaching literacy in a sign bilingual approach need to understand the structure of both languages so they can make explicit comparisons and anticipate potential areas of difficulty (Swanwick, 2003, p. 135).

Various activities support a sign bilingual approach. Directed Activities Related to Text (DARTS) offers strategies to tackle a text. Dialogue journals where a pupil and adult communicate through a shared writing journal allows the adult to model correct written English for the pupil. Video analysis (Partridge, 1996) to make a bilingual version of a reading scheme can help raise metalinguistic awareness and improve skills through comparing the two languages.

References

Partridge, S. (1996) 'Video stories for 7 to 11s' in Galloway, C. (Ed.) *Using Videos with Deaf Children*, Manchester Centre for Audiology, Education of the Deaf and Speech Pathology, University of Manchester.

Swanwick, R. (1998) 'The teaching and learning of literacy within a sign bilingual approach' in Gregory, S., Knight, P., McCracken, W. Powers, S. and Watson, L. (Eds) *Issues in Deaf Education*, London, David Fulton Publishers.

Swanwick, R. (2003) 'Sign bilingual deaf children's writing strategies: Responses to different sources for writing' in Galloway, C. and Young, A. (Eds) *Deafness and Education in the UK – Research Perspectives*, London, Whurr Publishers.

Further reading

Turkington, C. and Sussman, A. E. (2001) (2nd edition) *Encyclopaedia of Deafness and Hearing Disorders*, New York, Facts on File.

Sign language/signing

A sign language is any system of communication using bodily signs, hand and finger movements, facial expression and bodily movements. Among sign languages are those used by deaf people in different countries, for example British Sign Language, which is used in the United Kingdom. 'Signed (Exact) English' is a system using signs from deaf sign languages, which are used in the same order as in spoken English. Further signs and finger spelling indicate such features as tense. Signed (Exact) English can be used alongside spoken English to give a parallel representation of speech and to complement lip reading. The Paget-Gorman sign system is designed to parallel as exactly as possible the grammar, morphology and syntax of spoken English. It is meant both to complement speech and to enhance the ability to write in a grammatically correct way. 'Signs supporting English' uses signs only for some aspects of spoken English and gives an extra aid to understanding spoken English. 'Cued speech' is a system of shapes made with one hand around the lips. It aids lip reading by providing information about sounds, which are not conveyed by lip reading alone. Cues speech is used by children who have some understanding of speech. It also opens up the possibility of learning to read using phonetic approaches.

Makaton is a nine-stage vocabulary of about 350 manual signs taken from British sign language and used with learners who experience moderate to severe cognitive impairment, hearing impairment and cognitive impairment, or severe language impairment. Signalong, based on British Sign Language, is sign supporting system developed for individuals with cognitive impairment. It is used by people with cognitive impairment who find British Sign Language too complex; children whose language is delayed and who may use the signs as a visual prompt to help develop word selection and comprehension; and others who have communication difficulties. The basic vocabulary comprising about 1,600 signs is taught in four phases. Decisions about whether to use a signing system, and if so which one, are informed by the aim of enabling the child to communicate with as many people as possible.

Further reading

Tennant, Richard (1998) *The American Sign Language Handshape Dictionary*, Pittsburgh, PA, Laurent Clerc Books.

Addresses

Makaton Vocabulary Development Project
    www.makaton.org
    A charity based in the UK that promotes the use of Makaton to teach communication, language and literacy skills to people with communication and learning difficulties.

The Signalong Group
    www.signalong.org.uk
    A charity based in the UK aiming to enable children and adults with impaired communication to understand and express themselves.

Skills

A skill is the practised capacity to carry out an activity or task. In terms of the curriculum, three areas of skills are key skills, functional skills and life skills.

Key skills

The curriculum can be considered as including various components. These include the subjects of the curriculum such as mathematics and science. Permeating the whole curriculum are certain skills that arise in many subject areas and contexts and which are known variously as 'key skills', 'curriculum strands' or 'basic skills'. Examples are literacy, numeracy, computer skills, and problem-solving skills. There is sometimes debate about whether these skills are better taught in dedicated sessions or in the context of other activities. This is probably not a question of either one approach or the other, but of finding the right balance of dedicated teaching sessions and application. If this is correct, then to take one example, computer skills will be best learned if there are sessions in which the pupil can concentrate on the skill building coupled with practice sessions in which the newly learned skills can be usefully applied.

Functional skills

Functional skills are skills associated with carrying out specified activities. These include personal care skills such as preparing food, dressing and washing oneself. Social skills are learned such as shopping, participating in leisure activities and taking turns in conversation. Functional skills relating to recreation help the individual participate in leisure activities, for example learning the basics of playing a board game, or dancing. Where literacy skills are not developing fluently, the student may be taught functional aspects of literacy that will help in practical situations (Carpenter, Ashdown and Bovair, 2001). This could be learning to read signs such as 'danger', 'toilet', 'entrance', 'exit' and so on. In functional writing the student may learn to write his own name and address or to write a shopping list. Social skills relating to mathematics would be such activities as using money for small purchases, counting the correct number of items needed when shopping, dividing food portions equally and so on. Functional literacy, numeracy and health-related skills are sometimes known as functional academic skills.

Aspects of functional social skills may be taught to pupils with developmental coordination disorder. Because of proprioceptive difficulties, the child may not be able to position himself the usual acceptable distance from someone he is speaking with and this may need to be taught. Pupils with severe cognitive impairment where they are not making progress in more fluent literacy and numeracy may be taught related functional skills. The motivation for the pupil is often that he can see a clear, practical outcome for learning. These may not develop to the extent that the student could be said to have attained functional literacy in the sense that he can read a newspaper, use a dictionary or meaningfully sign a contract. But even basic functional literacy skills contribute towards greater autonomy.

Life skills

Life skills are ones leading towards an individual being able to function autonomously in adult society. They include self-help skills such as feeding, dressing, personal hygiene and health care; household skills like shopping, cooking and cleaning; social skills including using a post office or bank or being able to travel on local transport. Part of education leading towards independence, life skills aim to prepare the individual for life as an adult. Where a pupil has, for example, profound cognitive impairment, and there is no expectation that he will be independent, the aim is to achieve comparative independence in particular skills such as feeding.

Schemes exist to accredit life skills and enable a student to demonstrate what he has achieved in this area. For example, in England, some of the Award Scheme Development Accreditation Network (ASDAN) awards involve life skills.

Reference

Carpenter, B., Ashdown, R. and Bovair, K. (Eds) (2001) (2nd edition) *Enabling Access: Effective Teaching and Learning for Pupils with Learning Difficulties*, London, David Fulton Publishers.

Address

Award Scheme Development Accreditation Network (ASDAN)
www.asdan.co.uk
A UK-based accreditation body.

Social skills training

Helping develop social skills has particular implications for pupils with disabilities and disorder. For example, social skills may need to be explicitly taught to learners with moderate to severe cognitive impairment. In particular every effort is made to explain the reasons behind the social behaviour so that this is not learned just as a superstitious ritual.

To take another example, with pupils with disorders of conduct the issue is often one of developing social skills in the context of respect for others. One package, Equipping Youth to Help One Another brings together social skills training with anger management, moral reasoning training and problem-solving skills training in a group setting (Gibbs *et al.*, 1996). With a small sample of incarcerated male offenders aged 15 to 18 years, a year after their release the recidivism rate for the Equipping Youth to Help One Another group was 15 per cent compared with 41 per cent for the control group.

Reference

Gibbs, J. C., Potter, G. B., Barriga, A. Q. and Liau, A. K. (1996) 'Developing the helping skills and prosocial motivation of aggressive adolescents in peer group programmes', *Aggression and Violent Behaviour* 1, 283–305.

Social work/social worker

Social work seeks to apply social theory and research to understand and improve the lives of individuals, groups and communities. Research and evaluation is an important aspect relating to evidence-based practice (Grinnell and Unrau, 2007). The discipline has links with other areas of social science such as sociology, social studies, political science, psychology, and economics. Social work is often associated with applications to people perceived as vulnerable.

A social worker having studied and qualified in social work is employed to try to improve the quality of life of individuals and groups in society, and ameliorate social problems. The qualification may be a professional degree in social work. In England, for example, a social worker is registered with the General Social Care Council. In relation to children and young people with disabilities and disorders, the role of social workers may involve family counselling and support, providing advice on services and funding to help the family, and liaison with the child's school and the local authority. Multi-professional working with education and health services and others is central.

Reference

Grinnell, R. and Unrau, Y. (2007) (8th edition) *Social Work Research and Evaluation: Foundations of Evidence-Based Practice*, New York and Oxford, Oxford University Press.

Further reading

Butler, I. and Roberts, G (2003) (2nd edition) *Social Work with Children and Families: Getting into Practice*, London, Jessica Kingsley.

Addresses

British Association of Social Workers
   www.basw.co.uk
   The association helps, supports, advises and campaigns on behalf of its members.

National Association of Social Workers
   www.socialworkers.org
   A professional association in the USA providing guidance, research, information, and advocacy for its members.

Sociology

The nature of sociology of special education

Sociology applied to special education seeks to challenge what are seen as the 'recipe' approaches of other disciplines such as psychology, medicine and some aspects of pedagogy. It brings perspectives to bear on the social structures, social processes, policies and practices that make up special education. It describes, analyses, explains and theorises about social interactions and relationships. Applying general principles and findings from sociology to the administration and processes of special education, the sociology of special education seeks to do three things. Firstly, it deals with concepts such as society, culture, social class, community, status and role. Secondly, it compares the contexts in which special education takes place within a particular society and between one society and another. Thirdly, it analyses the sociological processes within educational institutions.

The concerns of sociology of special education include the effects of the economy on the sorts of special education provided by the state. It is interested in the social institutions such as the family involved in the process of special education. Another focus is the school as a formal organisation, and social change in relation to special education. The sociology of special education seeks to understand special education as a social process in a social context.

Perspectives in sociology of special education

The different perspectives taken towards special education reflect the broader perspectives of sociology more generally. These represent functionalist, structural functionalist, conflict theory, interpretative, social constructionist and social creationist views.

A functionalist view attempts to explain why social structures exist in relation to their role in society as a whole. It starts with an analysis of society rather than of the individual, recognising the importance of the interrelationships of interdependent parts. The way in which the parts function is seen as vital to the well-being of the whole. Values are regarded as the key determinants of behaviour. In special education, a functionalist approach includes the use of methods like the social survey aiming to determine such 'facts' as the number of individuals with disabilities and disorders requiring special education. It may see disability and disorder as a social problem and focus on organisation, management, provision and direction. The functionalist perspective rests on the assumption that consensus in society is a normal state. While it is recognised that conflict arises from time to time, this is regarded as an evolutionary phenomenon. One criticism of the functionalist view is that it takes insufficient account of disorder and conflict, such as that arising from time to time among those involved in special education (for example children, parents, teachers, the local authority or school board, health personnel) who may take different views.

Another perspective is a structural-functionalist one. This is a form of functionalism concerned with order and equilibrium in society. In this view, structures in society interact to perform positive roles for society as a whole.

Everything in society is seen as having a positive function. A criticism is that some structures such as those associated with organised crime are hard to justify in this way. As it might apply to special education, this view would point to special education as having a positive role in fitting pupils with disabilities and disorders into society, including finding suitable employment for those leaving school. Conflict theory provides yet another view, emphasising the struggles in society between different groups. These struggles are thought to centre on access to limited economic resources or power. Where there is a Marxist emphasis, this concentrates on class conflict about economic resources. Neo-Marxist approaches to conflict in education may regard the existing educational structure as the result of social class struggles. Class interests are thought to lie behind any pattern of educational organisation, and economics is seen as the key determinant of behaviour. Some aspects of disability theory have elements of neo-Marxist theory. Approaches relating to the work of Max Weber concentrated more on the struggle between different groups over power and status as well as resources. In this view, one group's dominance over another can arise in various ways and authority is seen as an important aspect of dominance. Accordingly, group interests are considered to permeate education and dominant interest groups could, it is thought, reform educational structures for their own ends. Regarding special education, this perspective leads to considering the nature of historical development and economic, social and political climates in which special education developed, and the way such developments help to maintain a particular order in society.

An interpretative view starts its analysis from the level of the individual and works its way up to the level of society as a whole. Research tends to focus on small-scale interactions in everyday life. The interpretative view developed from phenomenological perspectives. These relate to the social construction of the 'world' and its maintenance, and the interactions of its participants. Phenomenology views social reality as the creation of participants in it. Communication and interaction between people are believed to produce social categories and social knowledge. Reality is 'socially constructed'. In special education, such views might inform small-scale research into interactions, for example between teachers and pupils with a disability or disorder.

Relatedly, a social constructionist perspective attributes the causes of disability predominantly to environmental factors, including teaching methods and the attitudes of those who interact with the child. It discourages labelling and categorisation which is seen as problematic. The problem of disability is considered to be in the minds of able bodied people and is manifested in prejudice and social policies reflecting a tragic view of disability. A criticism of this view is that there is a fine line between identifying a disability and disorder and potentially negative labelling and there is a danger that a social constructionist view could make invisible those who may need support.

Finally, a social creationist standpoint regards disability as a problem within the institutional practice of society. Disability is seen as a form of

Further reading

Barnes, C., Mercer, G. and Shakespeare, T. (1999) *Exploring Disability: A Sociological Introduction*, Cambridge, Polity Press.
Meighan, R. and Harber, C. with contributions by Barton, L., Siraj-Blatchford, S. and Walker, S. (2007) (5th edition) *A Sociology of Educating*, London and New York, Continuum.

Addresses

American Sociological Association
www.asanet.org
Aims to advance sociology as a scientific discipline and a profession.

The British Sociological Association
www.britsoc.co.uk
The professional association for sociologists in the UK.

Special children

Special children (Farrell, 2008, *passim*) refers to children with disability/disorder who are receiving special education. In the United States of America, categories of disability under federal law as amended in 1997 (20 United States Code 1402, 1997) are reflected in subsequent 'designated disability codes' as follows: mentally retarded, hard-of-hearing, deaf, speech and language impaired, visually handicapped, emotionally disturbed, orthopaedically impaired, other health impaired, specific learning disability, multi-handicapped, child in need of assessment, deaf/blind, traumatic brain injury, and autism.

In England, a similar classification (Department for Education and Skills, 2005, *passim*) comprises: specific learning difficulties (e.g. dyslexia, dyscalculia, dyspraxia); learning difficulty (moderate, severe, profound); behavioural, emotional and social difficulty; speech, language and communication needs; autistic spectrum disorder; visual impairment; hearing impairment; multisensory impairment; and physical disability.

In the United States of America's system, mental retardation is broadly equivalent to the English classification of moderate, severe and profound learning difficulties (see also, Farrell, 2001, pp. 1–5).

References

Department of Education and Skills (2005) (2nd edition) *Data Collection by Special Educational Need*, London, DfES.
Farrell, M. (2001) *Standards and Special Educational Needs*, London, Continuum.

Farrell, M. (2008) *Educating Special Children: An Introduction to Provision for Pupils with Disabilities and Disorders*, New York and London, Routledge.

Special classes

A special class generally refers to a class in a mainstream school in which pupils with disabilities and disorders are taught separately from pupils who do not have a disability or disorder. However, the term can mean different things in different countries and within a single country. The proportion of time a child spends in the special class and in mainstream classrooms can vary. A child may spend a period full-time in a special class and gradually spend increasing amounts of time in other mainstream classrooms over a transition period. The pupil may be timetabled into a special class for certain aspects of the curriculum and join other mainstream classes for other curriculum periods.

Data from the Organisation for Economic Cooperation and Development (OECD) presents the location of education of students who fall in a category of 'disability' (other categories were 'learning disability' or 'social disadvantage'). Locations were, 'regular classes', 'special classes' or 'special schools'. The students were those receiving additional resources over the period of their compulsory education. Countries considered were Spain, England, Mexico, the United States of America, Turkey, France, the Netherlands, Slovak Republic, Japan, Germany, Hungary, Czech Republic, and Korea and the regions of Flanders in Belgium and New Brunswick in Canada. In different countries and regions the proportion of students educated in special classes was highest for Japan, Korea, the United States of America, and Hungary and France. Also, Turkey, Mexico, the Slovak Republic and the Czech Republic had proportions of students in special classes although smaller.

(See also, *Mainstream school/classroom, Resource room, Special school*)

Reference

Organisation for Economic Co-operation and Development (2005) *Equity in Education: Students with Disabilities, Learning Difficulties and Disadvantages*, Paris, OECD.

Address

Organisation for Economic Cooperation and Development
www.oecd.org
A Paris-based organisation bringing together governments to support economic growth and related purposes and provides comparable statistics, and social and economic data.

Special education

Special education refers to distinctive education and related provision made for children with disabilities and disorders to ensure they learn and develop as well as possible. It draws on a range of disciplines. The aims of special education include:

- Identifying and assessing pupils with disability/disorder and evaluating whether the disability/disorder hinders or potentially hinders learning and development
- Identifying the distinctive provision that best promotes learning and development
- Identifying foundational disciplines that contribute to promoting learning and development
- Ensuring that elements of provision informed by these foundations promotes learning and development.

(Farrell, 2009)

In special education, as with general education, the expectation is that provision will enhance learning and development (Farrell, 2001, 2005). Academic progress includes progress in school subjects and in areas of the curriculum such as problem-solving skills. Personal and social development embraces personal and social skills, life skills, high self-esteem, and concern for others.

Elements of provision that promote the learning and development of special children are: curriculum, pedagogy, school and classroom organisation, resources, and therapy/care. Distinctive provision can be identified for different types of disability and disorder (Farrell, 2008).

Foundational disciplines underpin aspects of contemporary special education, contributing to the understanding and practice of special education and to provision for different types of disability/disorder. Psychotherapeutic underpinnings have particular relevance for pupils with disorders of conduct for example. These disciplines may have relevance for several types of disability/disorder. Among important foundational areas are: legal/typological; terminological; social; medical; neuropsychological; psychotherapeutic; behavioural/observational; developmental; psycholinguistic; technological; and pedagogical (Farrell, 2009, *passim*). Disciplines and perspectives underpinning special education can inform provision and understanding. For example, the discipline of medicine informs classifications and procedures for seizures and epilepsy; implications of traumatic brain injury, and the possible use of medication for attention deficit hyperactivity disorder. Developmental perspectives relating to typically developing infants inform provision for older pupils with profound cognitive impairment.

Methods that aid the learning and development of pupils with disability and disorder include, for example, tactile methods for children who are blind and behavioral methods for children with conduct disorder.

New promising methods are observed, described and analysed to establish which aspects are important and effective. Reasons why the approach works are identified so findings can be extended from particular examples. Hypotheses may be tested and evaluated leading to accounts of evidence-based practice. Methodology therefore ranges from observation and description used for critical reflection to hypotheses and theory. While justifiable methods and evidence-based practice can contribute to this aspiration, families and professionals still have to decide on the suitability of an intervention for a particular child after considering various options.

Ideally evidence involves peer review and the validation interventions through research designs using random samples and control and experimental groups (Simpson, 2005, pp. 141–142, paraphrased). Other methods such as single subject design validation or correlational methods may be appropriate in different circumstances (Ibid. p. 142). Parents and professionals will want to know about the efficacy and anticipated outcomes of a particular practice. They will need to know whether anticipated outcomes are in line with student needs; the potential risks; and the most effective means of evaluation (Ibid. p. 143, paraphrased). Evidence-based practice can inform decisions but these are also influenced by professional judgement and the views of the child and family.

The content knowledge of special education therefore includes understanding of the different types of disability and disorder; their nature, causes, identification and assessment, and associated provision. Provision embraces curriculum, pedagogy, organisation, resources and therapy. It also includes knowledge of disciplines contributing to special education such as sociology, medicine, child development, and behavioural psychology.

The skills base of special education is very wide and includes an ability to work closely with a wide range of professionals such as teachers, therapists, physicians, technicians, social workers, and so on. This may involve joint decision-making, assessment and practice. Particular skills may be developed that relate especially to working with children with a particular disability or disorder. Those working with children with autistic spectrum disorder may be trained and skilled in approaches such as TEACCH. A teacher educating children with profound cognitive impairment may have special skills in interpreting and applying the content of a developmental curriculum and using small steps assessments.

References

Farrell, M. (2001) *Standards and Special Educational Needs*, London, Continuum.

Farrell, M. (2005) *Key Issues in Special Education: Raising Pupils' Achievement and Attainment*, New York and London, Routledge.

Farrell, M. (2008) *Educating Special Children: An Introduction to Provision for Pupils with Disabilities and Disorders*, New York and London, Routledge.

Farrell, M. (2009) *Key Foundations of Special Education: An Introduction*, New York and Chichester, Wiley.

Simpson, R. L. (2005) 'Evidence-based practices and students with ASD', *Focus on Autism and Other Developmental Disabilities* 20, 3, 140–149.

Further reading

Guiliani, G. and Pierangelo, R. (2006) *The Big Book of Special Education Resources*, Thousand Oaks, CA, Corwin Press.

Kauffman, J. M. and Hallahan, D. P. (2005) *Special Education: What It Is and Why We Need It*, Boston, MA, Pearson/Allyn and Bacon.

Reynolds, C. R. and Fletcher-Janzen, E. (Eds) (2004) (2nd edition) *Concise Encyclopaedia of Special Education: A Reference for the Education of Handicapped and Other Exceptional Children and Adults*, Hoboken, NY, Wiley.

Addresses

Council for Exceptional Children
www.cec.sped.org
Based in the USA, this professional organisation aims to improve the outcomes for individuals with disabilities and disorders and those with gifts and talents.

European Agency for Special Needs Education
www.european-agency.org
An organisation whose website provides information on systems and contacts in different European countries.

National Dissemination Center for Children with Disabilities
www.nichcy.org
Regarding individuals with disabilities from birth to age 22 years, the center provides information on disabilities; programmes and services; research-based information on effective practices; and information on aspects of education law and special education law.

Office of Special Education and Rehabilitation services
www.ed.gov/about/offices/list/osers/
Seeks to improve results and outcomes for people with disabilities of all ages and supports programmes serving individuals with disabilities.

The National Association for Special Educational Needs
www.nasen.org.uk
The association aims to promote the development of children and young people with 'special educational needs' and supports those who work with them.

Special educational need

In the United Kingdom, in terms of the Education Act 1996, section 312, children have a 'special educational need' if they have a learning difficulty which calls for special educational provision to be made for them. Children have a learning difficulty if they:

(a) have a significantly greater difficulty in learning than the majority of children of the same age;
(b) have a disability which either prevents of hinders them from making use of educational facilities of a kind generally provided for children of the same age in schools within the area of the local education authority;
(c) are under the compulsory school age and fall within the definition at paragraph (a) and (b) above or would do so if special educational provision were not made for them.

It will be seen from the legal definition that a child may have a 'disability' that does not constitute a 'learning difficulty' because the disability is not such that it prevents or hinders the child from using the educational facilities of the kind 'generally provided' under the Act. Similarly, a child may have a 'difficulty in learning' that does not constitute a 'learning difficulty' because it is not significantly greater than the majority of children of the same age. Even when a 'disability' or a 'difficulty in learning' does constitute a 'learning difficulty' the learning difficulty may still not be considered a 'special educational need' unless the learning difficulty calls for 'special educational provision' to be made. This special educational provision is that which is additional to or different from that generally provided or education in a special school.

A 'special educational need' exists when the child has a learning difficulty requiring special provision. The reason why the child has a learning difficulty relates back to the consequences of a disability or a difficulty in learning. These are elaborated in other government documents (Department for Education and Skills, 2001, 2005) and are similar to the list of disabilities and disorders used in legislation in the United States of America.

The 'learning difficulty' requires ('needs') special educational provision. It looks at first as though the definition is resources-related rather than having much to do with the child. But the provision required: curriculum, pedagogy, resources, therapy, care and organisation, relate to the supposed needs of the child and these may be specific to the disability or disorder.

References

Department of Education and Skills (2001) *Special Educational Needs Code of Practice*, London, DfES.

Department of Education and Skills (2005) (2nd edition) *Data Collection by Special Educational Need*, London, DfES.

Addresses

The National Association for Special Educational Needs
www.nasen.org.uk
The association aims to promote the development of children and young people with 'special educational needs' and supports those who work with them.

Special educational needs coordinator

In England, a special educational needs coordinator (SENCO) is a teacher having responsibilities for coordinating special education under a 'Code of Practice' (Department for Education and Skills, 2001). The head teacher or deputy headteacher may be the SENCO in a small school. A team of teachers may coordinate special education in a large school and may be known as the special educational needs coordination team or the learning support team. In early education settings, the SENCO is responsible for:

- Ensuring liaison with parents and professionals regarding children with special educational needs
- Advising and supporting other practitioners in the setting
- Ensuring that appropriate Individual Education Plans are in place, and
- Ensuring that relevant background information about children with special educational needs is collected, recorded and updated.

In a mainstream secondary school, the duties of the SENCO may include:

- Overseeing the day-to-day operation of the school's special educational needs policy
- Liasing with and advising teacher colleagues
- Coordinating provision for children with special educational needs
- Overseeing records on all pupils with special educational needs
- Liaising with the parents of children with special educational needs
- Contributing to staff in-service training
- Liaising with external agencies such as educational psychology services, health services, social services and voluntary bodies
- Managing learning support assistants (teaching aides working with pupils with special educational needs).

In mainstream secondary schools, the duties of the SENCO are the same as in a primary school except for the last two responsibilities listed above. In a secondary school the liaison with external agencies would also include liaising with a Connexions personal assistant (who helps the pupil in the transition from school to work or further education). As well as managing learning support assistants, in secondary schools, the SENCO would also manage a team of teachers.

(See also, *Qualifications, standards and training for teachers*)

Reference

Department for Education and Skills (2001) *Special Educational Needs Code of Practice*, London, DfES.

Further reading

Jones, F., Jones, K. and Szwed, C. (2001) *The SENCO as Teacher and Manager: A Guide for Practitioners and Trainers*, London, David Fulton Publishers.

Special school

The nature of special schools

Special schools educate pupils with disabilities and disorders together. They may provide for a particular group, for example, Chelfham Mill School in the United Kingdom, educates boys aged 7 to 16 who experience emotional and behavioural difficulties. It provides a range of therapies including play therapy and psychotherapy as well as working within an overall behavioural framework using a token economy system. Special schools may educate pupils with several types of disability and disorder. For example, Manuel Duato Special School, Lima, Peru, run by the Columbian Missionary Society educates pupils with learning difficulties and hearing difficulties. Its pupils range from preschool age to the age of 20 years. For older students, workshops offering vocational education include carpentry, cookery, gardening and handicraft as well as self-development programmes. Some special schools provide for a very wide range of disabilities and disorders, perhaps in several different classes and areas of the school, and are sometimes known as generic special schools. A special school might share a campus with mainstream schools. This enables pupils to meet together at social times and share some classes together, and in best practice the progress and development of special children is evaluated to determine whether such arrangements are benefiting the pupil (Farrell, 2008, pp. 10–13).

Differences in availability of special schools

Data from the Organisation for Economic Co-operation and Development (2005) allows the examination of the location of education of students who fall in a category of 'disability' (other categories were 'learning disability' or 'social disadvantage'). Location is understood as 'regular classes', 'special classes' or 'special schools'. The students were those who receive additional resources over the period of their compulsory education. Countries considered were Spain, England, Mexico, the United States of America, Turkey, France, the Netherlands, Slovak Republic, Japan, Germany, Hungary, Czech Republic and Korea. Regions were Flanders in Belgium and New Brunswick in Canada. In different countries the proportion of students educated in special schools varied considerably. In New Brunswick parents and pupils had no access to special schools. In the United States of America and Spain the proportion of students in special schools was very small. Very large proportions of students were in special schools in Flanders, Czech Republic, Germany, Slovak Republic and the Netherlands. In other countries, the proportions were somewhere in between. (Proportions in special classes also varied considerably with France, Korea, the United States of America and Japan having the highest proportional use.)

References

Farrell, M. (2008) *The Special School's Handbook: Key Issues for All*, London, David Fulton Publishers and the National Association of Special Educational Needs.
Organisation for Economic Co-operation and Development (2005) *Equity in Education: Students with Disabilities, Learning Difficulties and Disadvantages*, Paris, OECD.

Further reading

Farrell, M. (2006) *Celebrating the Special School*, London, David Fulton Publishers.

Addresses

National Association of Independent and Non-maintained Special Schools
www.nasschools.org.uk
A non-profit making organisation representing special schools in England.

Rescare
www.rescare.org.uk
A UK-based organisation with an international membership of parents and others supporting special schools.

Speech and language impairments

Speech comprises the physical utterances an individual makes, while language includes aspects such as grammar. Language may involve verbal communication and non-verbal communication and symbols. It enables a person to make sense of experiences and to communicate. A central role is played in education by language because education centres on communication. Also, problems with language use are important factors in the poor school performance of disadvantaged children. Delayed development in speech and (or) language is one of the commonest reasons for the parents of children requesting the help of physicians before the child starts school (Norbury, Tomblin and Bishop, 2008). Language development involves various aspects. The development of receptive language (e.g. listening and reading) interacts with the development of expressive language (e.g. speaking and writing). The study of the development of phonology (the ability to recognise and produce sound contrasts), vocabulary and grammatical structure indicate that these features develop in a sequence and at typical average ages. However, there are sometimes wide variations in the age ranges at which such features normally develop. The impairment of normal language functioning affects an individual's cognitive, emotional and social skills. Causal factors relating to language impairment may be predominantly biological or environmental.

Among biological causes are hearing impairment, neurological impairments and coordination difficulties. Hearing impairment hinders the reception of speech, which leads to difficulties with speech expression. Certain neurological impairments can lead to communication difficulties even if the necessary mechanisms (auditory, visual and speech) are intact. Coordination problems can lead to writing difficulties.

Environmental causes of language impairment include an environment in which language does not play an important part; or those with whom the child is in regular contact may use language inadequately. It is also detrimental if the child is not encouraged to use and comprehend gradually more complex language.

To assess language development, to determine any difficulties and to resolve them, it is necessary to have a model of language structure. Language disorders can be grouped according to the mode of transmission, that is, speech, print or gesture (including sign language). An example of a speech disorder is stuttering/stammering. A disorder involving print is reading difficulties. Developmental coordination disorder (dyspraxia) is an example of a disorder involving gesture. It involves difficulty in carrying out a pattern of movements despite the individual understanding what is required and being physically able to comply. An aspect of dyspraxia, verbal dyspraxia, concerns deficits in speech coordination in which sounds can be made but not under conscious control to form words.

Another way of grouping language impairment is in terms of expressive or receptive language activity. Receptive language includes reading and hearing and an example of receptive disorder is hearing impairment. Expressive language includes speaking and writing and an example is articulation difficulties. Difficulties with articulation may be associated with cerebral palsy, physical impairments to the palate, and indeed, hearing impairment. Articulation disorders may be substitutions (wead for read), distortions (a lisp), omissions (ca for cat), or additions (carn for car).

A further classification of language disorders is 'organic' and 'functional'. Organic disorders have an explicit medical cause. Aphasia is an absence or loss of language skills caused by damage to, or an abnormality of, the cerebral cortex. Expressive aphasia involves the loss of the ability to form ideas into words. Receptive aphasia is an inability to understand language. Functional disorders have no clear medical pathology and include conditions such as dyslexia/reading disorder.

Another distinction is between language disorder and language deviance. Delay refers to a normal language pattern, which is slow in developing. Deviance is an abnormal language feature, which occurs with development, which is otherwise normal.

The detailed assessment of language impairment may include the contribution of a speech pathologist/therapist, or a psychologist or perhaps a neurologist. A programme may be developed by a speech pathologist working with a teacher. The programme may be delivered by the teacher and by others including the speech pathologist. Depending on the impairment, provision may include individual sessions of structured language teaching and continuing assessments of progress.

Given the distinction between speech and language, a distinction can also be made between 'speech difficulties' and 'language difficulties', making it possible to have speech difficulties but no language difficulties and vice versa. However, speech and language develop together and speech and language difficulties often coexist. Also there is a social and psychological context for communication.

While the prevalence of speech and language difficulties is not easy to determine because the concept of difficulty is relative, about 10 per cent of the school population is estimated to experience speech and language difficulties. Articulation difficulties account for about half of all speech and language difficulties.

Speech and language therapy is an important provision for pupils with speech and language impairments as part of an overall strategy involving related classroom work. In the classroom, a pupil with receptive language difficulties may be helped by various strategies. The teacher may need to simplify or repeat instructions. She may need to demonstrate what is required while accompanying this with the appropriate language. The social dimension of language is encouraged in the classroom and teachers seek to extend the pupil's language into new curriculum areas. As such, a social and educational dimension is not always available to a speech pathologist who may see children individually. It is important that the perspectives of teacher and speech and language pathologist are understood and shared, for example through joint professional working.

Reference

Norbury, C, F., Tomblin, J. B. and Bishop, D. V. M. (2008) *Understanding Developmental Language Disorders*, New York and London, Routledge.

Further reading

McMinn, J. (2006) *Supporting Children with Speech and Language Impairment and Associated Difficulties*, London, Continuum.

Mody, M. and Silliman, E. R. (2008) *Brain, Behaviour, and Learning in Language and Reading Disorders*, New York and London, Guilford Press.

Ripley, K., Barratt, J. and Fleming, P. (2001) *Inclusion for Children with Speech and Language Impairments: Accessing the Curriculum and Promoting Personal and Social Development*, London, David Fulton Publishers.

Addresses

AFASIC-Overcoming Speech Impairments
  www.afasic.org
  Works for improved services for children and young people with speech and language difficulties and provides information and advice for parents and professionals.

I-CAN
  www.ican.org.uk
  A national educational charity based in London, for children with speech and language difficulties.

Speech-language pathology/speech-language pathologist

In the United States of America and in Canada, the term speech-language pathology (e.g. Worthington and Ross, 2005) refers to the study and treatment of certain disorders. These comprise disorders or deficits affecting an individual's speech, language, voice and swallowing, and mental processing and their treatment. It seeks to enable individuals to communicate as well as possible and to achieve independence. Therapy may be provided for adults or children and involves assessing and treating communication problems. Different countries have different terms for the discipline. In the United Kingdom, it is 'speech and language therapy'; in Australia it is 'speech pathology'. Interventions include the provision of practice or exercises, the provision of and support with communication aids such as symbols or manual signing and teaching functional communication.

A practitioner is known as a speech-language pathologist in the United States of America, a speech therapist in the United Kingdom, and as a speech pathologist in Australia. She may qualify through a degree or diploma course. In the United States of America practice is regulated under the laws of particular states. The minimum standards required for certified speech-language pathology membership of the American Speech-Language Hearing Association involved a degree in speech-language pathology, a clinical fellowship year, and passing a further examination.

A speech-language pathologist may work in private practice, in a clinic, in hospital or in a school. In educational settings, it is widely recognised that it is essential for a school speech pathologist and a teacher to work closely together and understand each other's roles. The therapist may work directly with a child or may work in a consultancy role with a teacher and parents who share responsibility for delivering activities designed to improve the child's communication. The speech pathologist works as a member of a multi-professional team where her expertise can be shared with colleagues.

Reference

Worthington, C. K. and Ross, F. P. (2005) *Treatment Resource Manual for Speech-Language Pathology*, Florence, KY, Delmar Publishers.

Further reading

Blosser, J. L. and Neidecker, E. A. (2002) (4th edition) *School Programs in Speech-Language Pathology: Organisation and Service Delivery*, Boston, MA, Allyn and Bacon.
Kersner, M. and Wright, J. (2001) *Speech and Language Therapy: The Decision Making Process when Working with Children*, London, David Fulton Publishers.

Addresses

American Speech-Language Hearing Association
www.asha.org
The professional, scientific and credentialing association for audiologists, speech-language pathologists, and speech, language and hearing scientists in the USA.

The Royal College of Speech and Language Therapists
www.rcslt.org
The professional body for speech and language therapists in the UK maintaining high standards of ethical conduct, clinical practice and education of therapists.

Statement of special educational needs

In England, a statement of special educational needs, usually just called a 'statement', is a document prepared by a local authority. It is made when the local authority decides that special educational provision necessary to meet the child's needs cannot reasonably be provided within resources normally available to mainstream schools in the area.

It follows a statutory assessment of the child's special educational needs which may be requested by the child's parents, the school or setting where the child is educated, or another agency such as the health services or social services.

If the local authority are requested to carry out such a statutory assessment and decide not to, they must write to the child's parents who have a right of appeal to a tribunal. If the local authority carry out an assessment but decide not to issue a statement, they must inform parents who again have a right of appeal.

A statement specifies the child's special educational needs, the proposed provision; the place where the child will be educated; his non-educational needs and the non-educational provision. Parents can appeal against certain aspects of the statement, for example against the description of the child's special educational need, or against the school that is named.

The local authority must review the statement annually or more frequently if necessary. The review meeting, usually held at the child's school, considers the child's progress towards the targets set by the school after the statement was made, and agrees targets for the following year. Guidance on the requirement for statutory assessment, statement and other matters is set out in a code of practice (Department for Education and Skills, 2001, *passim*).

References

Department of Education and Skills (2001) *Special Educational Needs Code of Practice*, London, DfES.

Stuttering/stammering

Stuttering/stammering involves a disturbance of 'normal fluency and time patterning of speech' inappropriate for the individual's age. Typically, it involves sounds or syllables being repeated or stretched out. It interferes with academic or occupational achievement or social communication. A child or young person who stammers may have particular difficulties communicating with peers. Prevalence is about 1 per cent in children and around 0.8 per cent in adolescents (American Psychiatric Association, 2000, p. 67). There are fewer girls affected with the male:female ratio being around 3 to 1. In about 98 per cent of instances, stuttering begins before the age of 10 years.

The exact causes of stuttering are not fully known. Brain functions that relate to the production of speech may be implicated. Evidence points to there being many factors implicated and there is strong evidence of a genetic factor (p. 68).

Teachers and other can help by not rushing or finishing sentences for children who stammer. A child who already stutters may be more likely to do so if excited, stressed, is speaking to someone they do not know well or if they are hurrying to speak. It follows that other things being equal, fluency can be improved if some of these factors can be reduced or managed. This is not to suggest for example that a child should not learn to speak with less familiar people, but confidence can be built in situations that are less demanding. A speech-language pathologist will make an assessment of difficulties and provide advice and support on suitable programmes. The school will need to liaise closely with the speech-language pathologist and the home. Practical approaches for helping with dysfluency are discussed in a therapy manual by Stewart and Turnbull (2007).

References

American Psychiatric Association (2000) *Diagnostic and Statistical Manual of Mental Disorders, Fourth Edition, Text Revision*, Arlington, VA, APA.
Stewart and Turnbull (2007) *Working with Dysfluent Children: Practical Approaches to Assessment and Therapy*, Milton Keynes, UK, Speechmark Publishing.

Addresses

British Stammering Association
www.stammering.org
A British organisation for children and adults who stammer.

National Stuttering Association
www.nsastutter.org/index.php
A self-help support organisation based in the USA.

Symbols

Symbols are a form of graphical communication and may be used for reading, writing and other forms of communication. A well-known example is Blissymbolics, developed by Canadian Charles Bliss. It comprises a series of signs or symbols originally designed to aid international communication. However, it has been adapted as a visual-graphic system to help individuals with severe language difficulties to communicate. Users with physical disabilities and speech impairment can indicate a symbol, perhaps by pointing.

People with moderate to severe cognitive impairment may also use such systems. Each symbols signifies a concept, and symbols can be combined to represent complex ideas. A symbol board display is necessary. If two people using Blissymbolics wish to communicate, they require access to both boards.

Software allows individuals who are at early stages of writing to process simple words and symbols. Users can see the meaning of words as they write because the relevant symbols appear as they write or choose words, for example, from a grid. A commercial example is Symwriter, which uses Widget literacy symbols and pictures.

The Picture Exchange Communication system (www.pecs.org.uk) uses pictures to encourage communication for children and adults with autism or other communication difficulties to initiate communication. For example, the child is taught to hand a picture to the teacher to request something such as a drink and the teacher immediately responds. From these beginnings, the system can be developed for complex communication.

(See also, *Augmentative and alternative communication*)

Further reading

Detheridge, T. and Detheridge, M. (2002) (2nd edition) *Literacy Through Symbols: Improving Access for Children and Adults*, London, David Fulton Publishers.

Syndromes

Syndrome is a term used in both medicine and clinical psychology to refer to a collection of features occurring together. These may be signs, which are features noted by the physician, symptoms, which are reported by the individual concerned, or other characteristics. For example, a description of the characteristics that came to be known as Down syndrome was first given in 1866 by the physician Langdon Down. Strictly, the term syndrome refers to the characteristics and is superseded when the causes of a condition become known. However, the term may persist even when the causes of a condition are identified as they have been with Down syndrome (Candy, Davies and Ross, 2001, pp. 241–243).

Classifying features as a syndrome allows some predictions to be made about likely outcomes. Information about syndromes might include their alternative names, incidence, defining characteristics, prognosis and implications for education and care.

Syndromes are often named after the person who first described the characteristics. Asperger syndrome is named after Hans Asperger who, working in Vienna, published an account of the disorder he called 'autism' in 1944. Coincidentally, Leo Kanner, in Baltimore, published an account of the condition in 1943 leading to it also being called Kanner syndrome. Tourette syndrome gets it name from Giles de la Tourette, the French neurologist, who described it in 1885.

Other syndromes derive their names from persistent or noticeable features associated with them. Among the characteristics of Menkes Kinky Hair syndrome is that of normal hair becoming sparse and twisting. Cat eye syndrome is associated with the self-explanatory characteristic giving it its name.

Yet other syndromes get their names from a feature descriptive of some typical behaviour. Pathological Demand Avoidance syndrome is recognised by, among other conduct, resistance to and avoidance of the regular demands of daily life through the individual adopting strategies such as distracting adults, violence, excuses, and appearing to become incapacitated.

The name of some syndromes indicates the cause. Foetal Dilatin syndrome is so called because of the effects on the foetus of the anticonvulsant drug Phenytoin (Dilatin) taken by the mother. This leads to features such as growth deficiency, heart defects and cognitive impairment. Fragile X syndrome is brought about by the breaking off of the bottom tip of an X chromosome.

In diagnosing, it is important to remember that a minor abnormality occurring on its own does not constitute a syndrome. For example, skin tags in front of the ear when taken with a range of other features may indicate Goldenhar syndrome. These other features include one side of the face being underdeveloped, abnormalities of the vertebrae, possibly hearing loss, eye lesions, limb abnormalities, and heart and lung defects. However, skin tags of themselves could have many other causes and on their own, would not indicate Goldenhar syndrome.

A particular abnormality can occur in several syndromes. Microencephaly, an abnormally small cranium, is an aspect of Smith–Lemli–Opitz syndrome, Williams syndrome and others. A squint is one of a range of characteristics of several syndromes such as Freema–Sheldon syndrome or Cri du Chat syndrome.

Every feature defining the syndrome is not always present in every individual who is diagnosed as having the condition. In some syndromes, the likelihood in general of a feature being present is specified. In Congenital Syphilis syndrome, deafness and seizures occur in some cases but not all. In Coffin–Lowry syndrome, moderate to severe cognitive impairment is present in all affected males but only in a small proportion of affected females. Also, the number and severity of characteristics may differ across different individuals with the same syndrome. In Maroteaux–Lamy Pyknodysostosis syndrome, mild cognitive impairment may occur, or as in most instances, there will be no discernable effect on cognition.

Gilbert (2000) selects 100 syndromes using the criteria that they result in lifelong mental and physical difficulties and that help can be provided to improve the quality of life of those with the syndrome. These are a sample of the thousands of syndromes and inherited disorders that have been so far identified.

Among the main issues for educators concerning syndromes is to focus on the educational implications that may be similar for numerous syndromes. For example, many syndromes are associated with severe cognitive impairment and the educational provision is similar. Others are associated with profound cognitive impairment and again educational, including curricular, implications are similar. At the same time, the teacher will respond to the individual implications of the syndrome and of the individual child. The teacher is likely to begin with assumptions based on her knowledge of typical features and educational implications of a syndrome based on broad knowledge of the syndrome and then modify these in the light of the particular characteristics of the child and the way he learns.

References

Candy, D., Davies, G. and Ross, E. (2001) *Clinical Paediatrics and Child Health*, Edinburgh, Harcourt/W. B. Saunders.
Gilbert, P. (2000) *A to Z of Syndromes and Inherited Disorders*, London, Stanley Thornes.

Address

Contact-a-Family
  www.cafamily.org.uk
  A charity providing support and advice to parents whatever the medical condition their child experiences, and which also has a directory of rare and specific disorders.

There are hundreds of Internet sites that concern specific syndromes.

Systems approach

A systems perspective reflects, 'a view of behaviour which takes account of the context in which it occurs' (Dowling and Osborne, 1994, p. 3). A systems perspective of provision for special children implies examining the school and family contexts of pupil's 'problem' behaviour to avoid prejudging that difficulties such as disorders of conduct lie predominantly in the child. A specialist worker, perhaps a family therapist, may be involved where there are perceived problems with a child. Or a family-school liaison worker might draw on a systems approach. One strategy developed and applied a framework for intervention for schools, addressing behaviour problems at different levels (Ali *et al.*, 1997). It initially concentrated on a behaviour environment plan aimed at school and classroom factors, only later turning if necessary to an additional individual behaviour plan. A central principle was that,

'... problems with behaviour in education settings are usually a product of complex interaction between the individual, school, family, community and wider society' (Daniels and Williams, 2000, p. 222).

Functional Family Therapy (Alexander *et al.*, 2000) is a systems approach, drawing also on learning theory and cognitive theory. In therapy it helps build up explanations about the interactional function of the behaviour of all family members. It helps clients understand how their behaviour regulates family relationships, enabling family members to modify their expectations, attitudes, beliefs and emotions, and empowering them to feel more capable of bringing about changes. Behaviours, including problematic elements, are considered to fulfil particular outcomes. Functional Family Therapy has been used in the treatment of delinquents (Alexander *et al.*, 1988), viewing an adolescent's difficult behaviour is serving a function such as regulating the distance between family members. Consequently intervention not only tackles the adolescent's behavioural problems and cognitive dysfunction, but also aims to change patterns of family interaction and communication to encourage adaptive family functioning.

A systems view of a child's family and school can inform approaches to children who appear to experience psychosocial disorders. The school is regarded as a system in which it is possible to envisage a child having a problem but where the problem may also be understood in relation to the school as a whole. In this interactional and holistic view, behaviour is seen as existing within a particular context where, through a sort of circular causality, sequences of interactions contribute to the continuation of a 'problem'. This makes it more pertinent to ask *how* a problem arises than *why* (Dowling and Osborne, 1994, p. 5). A 'joint systems approach' seeks to understand the child's family and the school as systems and explores ways of taking into account interrelationships between them (Ibid. *passim*). A joint systems approach aims to facilitate communication between school, staff and family members. It tries to clarify differences in perceptions of the problem by focusing on how rather than why it occurs. It seeks to negotiate commonly agreed goals, and begins to explore specific steps towards change (Ibid. p. 15).

References

Ali, D. et al (1997) *Behavior in Schools: A Framework for Intervention*, Birmingham, Birmingham Education Department, UK.

Alexander, J. F., Waldron, H. B., Newberry, A. M. and Liddle, N. (1988) 'Family approaches to treating delinquents' in Nunnally, E. W., Chilman, C. S. and Cox, F. M. (Eds) *Mental Illness, Delinquency, Addictions and Neglect*, Newbury Park, CA, Sage, 128–146.

Alexander, J. F., Pugh, C., Parsons, B. and Sexton, T. L. (Eds) (2000) *Functional Family Therapy*, Golden, CO, Venture.

Daniels, A. and Williams, H. (2000) 'Reducing the need for exclusions and statements for behaviour: The Framework for Intervention Part 1', *Educational Psychology in Practice* 15, 4 January.

Dowling, E. and Osborne, E. (Eds) (1994) (2nd edition) *The Family and the School: A Joint Systems Approach to Problems with Children*, London, Routledge.

Further reading

Gurman, A. S. and Messer, S. B. (Eds) (2003) (2nd edition) *Essential Psychotherapies: Theory and Practice*, New York, Guilford Press, 441–442.

T

Teaching aide

A teaching aide may have a different title in different countries and indeed in different schools. Classroom aide, classroom assistant, and teaching assistant are some of the variations. The teaching aide may not work exclusively with children with disabilities/disorders, but as with a regular teacher, she will need an understanding to special education. Where the teaching aide does work with special children, this may be with individuals or small groups.

The teacher and the teaching aide work closely together and, where possible, share planning for activities. At the very least, time should be allocated so that the teacher can convey the intentions of the lesson and the teaching aide's particular responsibilities within it. It is important that the required outcomes of learning for pupils are clear to the teaching aide and not just the activities she is being asked to lead. The teaching aide may be asked to assess the progress of pupils on a task and record the outcomes so that these can inform subsequent planning. The teacher may need to be careful that she does not lose the skills required in educating special children because their support is always assumed to be the job of the teaching aide. Important skills for the teaching aide include promoting the safety and security of pupils, classroom skills, behaviour management, resource management and liaising with parents (Kamen, 2003).

(See also, *Qualifications, standards and training for teachers*)

Reference

Kamen, T. (2003) *Teaching Assistant's Handbook*, London, Hodder and Stoughton.

Further reading

Balshaw, M. and Farrell, P. (2002) *Teaching Assistants: Practical Strategies for Effective Classroom Support*, London, David Fulton Publishers.

Address

National Association of School Teaching Assistants
www.nasta.co.uk
An independent UK-based professional association.

Technology/technician

The nature and uses of technology

Technology includes a wide range of resources and aids including computer technology that enhance or enable learning or increase autonomy. The Internet and other forms of electronic communication, includes the use of palmtop and laptop computers, interactive whiteboards, and digital cameras.

Educators have to consider aspects of technology to make sure it is serving its purpose. One of these is the properties, or 'qualities', of technology. For example, technology can allow provisional attempts to be made at tasks (Hardy, 2000, pp. 14–17). In word processing, work can be more confidently drafted knowing it can be modified until the pupil is content with the outcome. Similarly, designs can involve several attempts, which can be adjusted and compared before the pupil decides on the best result. Also, technology can be reviewed in relation to elements of the curriculum. The school may ensure there are exciting interactive CD-ROMs for all curriculum subjects and areas. Or the school may examine each curriculum subject and see if a suitable range of technology is available within it. This might include ensuring in science that there are measuring scales with a magnified closed circuit television display for pupils with visual impairment. With regard to access provided by technology, 'physical' and 'cognitive' have been identified (Day, 1995). For example, physical access concerns using technology to try to enable a pupil with physical difficulties to participate.

Technology in relation to special education

In the United States of America, the *Individuals with Disabilities Education Act 1990* (Public Law 101–476) states that students with disabilities should have access to assistive technology equipment and related services. In the reauthorisation of the Individuals with Disabilities Education Act (IDEA) it is expected that assistive technology is considered when developing every pupil's individual education plan.

But it may be easier to recognise opportunities to use technology to aid learning in certain circumstances than in others. It has been argued that educators may continue to expect achievement in reading from a child who fails to progress over a long period, '... using the same visual, perceptual and cognitive functions as everyone else, despite a plethora of data that points to an impairment in those organic systems' (Edyburn, 2005, pp. 21–22). Where, as with traumatic brain injury, there is a specific incident that creates difficulties, it is clearer when to intervene.

Regarding the 'interface' between child and technology, where a child has a prosthetic appliance, the fitting, comfort and easy use of the appliance are self-evidently important. Similarly, but perhaps less obviously, where a piece of technology is intended to improve the communication of a child with profound cognitive impairment, the child must be able to understand it and learn the necessary skills to use the device so its use quickly becomes part of his repertoire.

Also important is the access of pupils to ICT at home and elsewhere. This may be aided by the increasing use of portable equipment with wireless connections enabling pupils to have access to information from home and in the community.

Technology and types of disability/disorder

Where a pupil has cognitive impairment, a switch-activated reinforcer may help him make choices as an aspect of communication. The educator may prompt the pupil to use switch activation or/and discrimination between different choices. For learners with profound cognitive impairment, multiple micro switches can enhance different responses. For a pupil with traumatic brain injury, resources may include adaptive equipment such as a wheelchair, perhaps used temporarily, and environmental modifications. Technology may be used to help manual dexterity. Depending on particular circumstances, resources associated with orthopaedic impairment may be used. For a pupil with reading disorder who is unable to independently read his textbooks, the school may provide text to speech software enabling him to listen to information 'read' by the computer. Information about software to help with memory, reading, writing, mathematics and current events is available (e.g. Edyburn, 2005, pp. 23–25). For developmental coordination disorder, aids to more fluent writing include pencil grips and pens that illuminate when writing pressure is excessive or insufficient). Where there are disabilities relating to language comprehension, the teacher might employ visual aids. For some pupils signing boards may be used allowing kinaesthetic and visual memory to aid comprehension. Communication boards and computer technology can contribute.

Further examples of the use of technology are provided elsewhere and include uses for communication difficulties; visual impairment; hearing impairment; health impairments; mathematics disorder; orthopaedic impairment; and disorder of written expression (Farrell, 2009, 'Technological' chapter).

Technician

Technicians working in special education will have a wide knowledge of the capacities of different products and will be able to provide advice to teachers and others about this. They will be able to set up and carry out maintenance schedules to help ensure technology is properly looked after and well used. They may be involved in the training provided within the school to ensure teachers and others staff are confident and competent in the use of technology so that resources are optimally used.

The technician can advise on the cost of various technological items and systems. While costs in relation to technology capability may have fallen, outlay is still substantial. As Hasselbring and Williams Glaser (2000) state of technology 'the barriers of inadequate training and cost must first be overcome before more widespread use can become a reality'.

References

Day, J. (1995) (2nd edition) *Access Technology: Making the Right Choice*, Coventry, UK, National Council for Educational Technology.

Edyburn, D. (2005) 'Introduction' in Edyburn, D., Higgins, K. and Boone, R. (Eds) *Handbook of Special Education Technology Research and Practice*, Whitefish Bay, WI, Knowledge by Design Incorporated.

Farrell, M. (2009) *Foundations of Special Education: An Introduction*, New York and London, Wiley.

Hasselbring, T. S. and Williams Glasser, C. H. (2000) 'Use of computer technology to help students with special needs' (www.furtureofchildren.org).

Hardy, C. (2000) *Information and Communications Technology for All*, London, David Fulton Publishers.

Further reading

Abbott, C. (2002) (Ed.) *Special Educational Needs and the Internet: Issues in Inclusive Education*, London, RoutledgeFalmer.

Addresses

CAST Universal Design for Living

www.cast.org

A research and development organisation aiming to expand learning opportunities for individuals, especially those with disabilities, through universal design for learning.

The National Early Childhood Technical Assistance Centre, University of North Carolina, USA

www.nectac.org/topics/atech/bibliography.asp

This site includes a 'Selected Bibliography of Articles and Books on Assistive Technology'.

Total communication

Total communication includes all modes of language, gestures devised by the child, the language of signs, speech, speech reading, finger spelling, and reading and writing. The choice of methods is based on a child's particular requirements. For example, in the British context there are four broad options in total communication. As well as spoken English without signing, these are:

- British Sign Language
- Sign supported English, and
- Signed English.

British Sign Language, states the subject first, then verbs, adverbs and adjectives. Meaning is conveyed not just by manual shapes but also by the position of the hands in relation to the body of the signer and by other spatial means. Most signs do not stem directly from English words and cannot always be translated in a one-to-one way. Technical terms and proper names are conveyed by finger spelling.

Sign supported English uses signs derived from British Sign Language to support the use of natural English. One justification is that if the communicator signed every aspect of spoken English, this could be overwhelming for the child receiving the communication.

Signed English is a representation with signs of all aspects of spoken English. The vocabulary, plurals, tenses, gender and other features of natural English are all represented, with the intention of facilitating good English.

Further reading

Turkington, C. and Sussman, A. E. (2001) (2nd edition) *Encyclopaedia of Deafness and Hearing Disorders*, New York, Facts on File.

Tourette syndrome

Giles de la Tourette first diagnosed the syndrome that is named after him in 1885. An inherited neurological condition, more common in males, it is transmitted by an autosomnal dominant gene. In childhood, the condition is associated with repetitive tics and grimaces. As the condition progresses, involuntary noises may be emitted, and in about half the cases episodes of using obscene language appear. The syndrome may co-occur with other conditions including attention deficit hyperactivity disorder and obsessive-compulsive disorder (Woods, 2007). Antipsychotic drugs are sometimes used in treatment.

Among educational implications is the management of the reaction of peers, their possible rejection of the person with Tourette syndrome and the management of the disruption the condition can cause to learning.

Reference

Woods, D. W. (Ed.) (2007) *Treating Tourette Syndrome and Tic Disorders: A Guide for Practitioners*, New York and London, Guilford Press.

Further reading

Carroll, A. and Robertson, M. (2000) *Tourette Syndrome: A Practical Guide for Teachers*, London, David Fulton Publishers.

Addresses

Tourette Syndrome Association
www.tsa-usa.org
Aims to identify the causes of the condition, find a cure for it and control its effects, and offers resources and referrals.

Tourette Syndrome (UK) Association
www.tourettesyndrome.co.uk
The association provides a helpline, membership forums, family networking, publications and advice.

Transition

Transition is important in several senses in special education. It is important that a child is supported when starting school or changing from one school to another because he is moving home or because he is transferring to a different age phase. This can be helped if schools have clear records of progress and the child's requirements, which they transfer promptly to the new setting.

Preparing for transition from school to work or further study is supported in England by transition planning. This is part of certain annual reviews of the progress of a pupil with a 'statement' of special educational need. The first annual review after the young person's fourteenth birthday and any later reviews until he leaves school should contain a transition plan. This draws together information from various sources such as the education services, health services, and social services helping structure the individual's transition to adult life. Issues a transition plan should address are set out in a code of practice (Department for Education and Skills, 2001, paragraphs 3.16–3.17 and 10.17–10.18).

Transition is particularly difficult for pupils with particular disabilities/disorders. A child with autism may find changes of activity difficult and these may be signalled by communicating clearly what is about to happen and by using clear timetables at the beginning of the school day to convey to the child the plan of the day.

Reference

Department for Education and Skills (2001) *Special Educational Needs Code of Practice*, London, DfES.

Traumatic brain injury

The nature of traumatic brain injury

In the United States of America, Code of Federal Regulations define traumatic brain injury as:

> an injury to the brain caused by an external force, resulting in total or partial functional disability or psychosocial impairment or both, that adversely affects the child's educational performance. The term applies to open or closed head injuries resulting in impairments in one or more areas, such as: cognition, language, memory, attention, reasoning, abstract thinking, judgement, problem solving, sensory, perceptual and motor abilities, psycho-social behaviour, physical functions, information processing, and speech. The term does not apply to brain injuries that are congenital or degenerative, or brain injuries induced by birth trauma.
>
> (34 CFR, section 300.7 [c] [12])

Types of neurological problems that can result from traumatic brain injury include: post concussion syndrome, headaches, seizures and motor impairments. Attention problems are common. Although old memories may be in place, the use of memory for new learning may be impaired. Traumatic brain injury can affect the visual system and visual perception. Executive functions are often impaired. The more widespread and diffuse the damage sustained to the brain, the greater the likely effect on speech and language (Schoenbrodt, 2001, pp. 192–195). Many head injuries result in damage to the frontal lobes, involved in the oversight of brain functions such as decision-making and emotional expression.

In the United States of America, by the age of 16 years, 4 per cent of boys and 2.5 per cent of girls sustain a traumatic brain injury. Most such injury is mild, but severe traumatic brain injury remains a common acquired disability in childhood. Among the most frequent causes of traumatic brain injury are a traffic accident, fall, or sport injury (DiScala, Osberg and Savage, 1997). The injury may be the result of an intentional act such as attempted suicide, child physical abuse or other violent crime. Assessments of the child's functioning are important in providing information about the brain injury.

Provision

Provision is complex and relates to the particular problems created by the injury but illustrative examples are given below.

Rehabilitation aims to optimise health and functional abilities, beginning in the intensive care unit and involves relearning to do things the child can no longer do; and using abilities to compensate for inabilities. It might involve modifications in the environment and the use of adaptive equipment and assistive devices. The initial team may be very large, and as progress is made the team tends to become smaller, perhaps comprising a physician, teacher, psychologist and social worker.

Although many children after traumatic brain injury retain the memory of what they previously thoroughly learned, the injury may affect the rate at which the child can learn new information, slowing subsequent progress. Therefore, the curriculum may need to be modified by breaking down content into smaller steps while ensuring it is still coherent. Smaller steps for assessment may be necessary to show progress. If a child has had a traumatic brain injury, it is very important to avoid a second injury, as the effects may be cumulative. Therefore, non-contact sports are encouraged instead of contact sports.

The teacher helps the child communicate by working closely with the speech-language pathologist and supporting communication herself. Communications from the teacher need to be clear and understandable to the child and instructions and information may need to be repeated. Clear signals of a change of conversation topic can help the child. Other systems of communication may be used temporarily such as signing and symbols.

Attention can be helped by developing a stable routine for the child and by giving any instructions clearly. The teacher can also give cues to the information being presented and can limit or break down the amount of information. The layout of the classroom should minimise distractions and the child may be taught in small groups. To aid memory, information may be broken down into smaller units and presented repeatedly enabling extra rehearsal. New information is more likely to be remembered if presented in a meaningful context. The school and family will work together to encourage aids to memory like rehearsal, repetition and practice.

Helping the child with visual functioning difficulties is informed by assessments and advice of the ophthalmologist and occupational therapist. The child's positioning for example at a desk and the positioning of work surfaces require care. The classroom environment is more comprehensible if it is uncluttered and kept tidy. Where the child experiences visual perception problems, materials such as texts used for teaching may be simplified, perhaps using larger, darker print.

Turning to executive functions, impulse control can be helped by teaching the child 'self-talk'; breaking complex tasks and instructions into smaller steps; and encouraging the use of notes and lists. Self-monitoring can be encouraged by getting the child to anticipate how he will deal with a task, then after the activity is completed, comparing the results with the predictions. The teacher can help by prompting appropriate behaviour.

Among approaches to managing behaviour and reducing problems are behaviour management strategies, psychotherapy, and environmental modifications and supports. Resources may include adaptive equipment to help function, such as a wheelchair (which may be used temporarily), and environmental modifications. Technology may be used to help manual dexterity.

References

DiScala, C., Osberg, J. and Savage, R. (1997) 'Children hospitalised for traumatic brain injury: Transition to post acute care', *Journal of Head Trauma Rehabilitation* 12, 3, 1–19.

Schoenbrodt, L. (Ed.) (2001) *Children with Traumatic Brain Injury: A Parent's Guide*, Bethesda, MD, Woodbine House.

Further reading

Farrell, M. (2008) 'Traumatic brain injury' in *Educating Special Children: An Introduction to Provision for Children with Disabilities and Disorders*, New York and London, Routledge.

Walker, S. and Wicks, B. (2005) *Educating Children with Acquired Brain Injury*, London, David Fulton Publishers.

Addresses

Brain Injury Association of America
www.biausa.org
A national organisation in the USA serving and representing individuals, families and professionals touched by traumatic brain injury.

British Institute for Brain Injured Children
www.bibic.org.uk
Provides advice, a multidisciplinary assessment service and programmes for children with brain injury.

Underpinning processes in disabilities/disorders

In some disabilities/disorders, there appear to be underpinning processes that are similar. This is reflected in the way 'learning disability' is defined in the United States of America and in some other countries. Under Regulations for Public Law 101–476, the Individuals with Disabilities Act defines a learning disability. It is a, 'disorder in one or more of the basic psychological processes involved in understanding or in using spoken or written language, which may manifest itself in an imperfect ability to listen, think, speak, read, write, spell or do mathematical calculations'. This suggests that such underpinning processes may be evident in, for example, reading disorder and mathematics disorder.

The approach to some disabilities/disorders reflects this understanding that there are both the outcomes of processes (for example reading disorder) and the processes themselves (for example a phonological deficit) that might both be tackled. Reading disorder may be approached by directly working on phonics when reading. It might also be helped by working on improving processes such as a phonological deficit through verbal tasks of blending and segmenting. Other processes implicated for reading disorder include difficulties with visual processing.

The extent to which one can speak of reading difficulty and a visual processing difficulty or a phonological deficit as it were separately or whether they are descriptions or reifications of the same process is debated. For example, Thomas and Loxley (2007, pp. 66–75) suggest that regarding such supposed underpinnings as being in some way different to the overall activity, for example reading, is misleading. Giving an example of an ability to drive they point out that this depends obviously enough on an ability to move one's arms and legs. But they continue, no one would prescribe an arm movement course as part of a programme to improve driving (Ibid. p. 73). Similarly, it would follow that working on improving phonological processing would not be prescribed to help someone to learn to read. To learn to read, you directly tackle reading. This does not seem to recognise that a phonological deficit is suggested to be a difficulty with segmenting and blending sounds before any consideration of reading. Therefore an approach might be justified that helped the child develop these skills so that they could later be linked with responding to marks on paper, that is reading. This is in fact what may be done by speech-language pathologists and others as part of early intervention programmes.

Furthermore, the response to apparent difficulties with underpinning processes is not always working on the process. Sometimes it is compensatory. Some children with reading disorder appear to have an underpinning difficulty with visual processing. This might be indicated in specific assessments of visual processing. One response is to help the child by reducing the necessity to scan from one plane to another. For example, the child may find it difficult to scan from the teacher's writing on a vertical classroom board to the child's horizontally placed paper when the child is copying writing from the board. The teacher may therefore provide the child with a paper copy of what is written on the board to be kept beside the child's writing paper. In this way scanning becomes much easier. The scanning takes place on the same (horizontal) plane rather than moving from the vertical (board) plane to the horizontal (child's desk) plane. Also the distance between the teacher's paper and the child's writing paper is a few centimetres whereas that between the board and the child's paper may be several metres. These adjustments appear to help the child perform the task.

Reference

Thomas, G. and Loxley, A. (2007) (2nd edition) *Deconstructing Special Education and Constructing Inclusion*, Maidenhead, UK, Open University Press/McGraw-Hill Education.

Further reading

Farrell, M. (2008) *Educating Special Children: Provision for Pupils with Disabilities and Disorders*, New York and London, Routledge.

Visual impairment

Visual impairment, blindness and low vision

The expression, 'visual impairment' is often used to indicate a continuum of loss of sight, which includes blindness. Within this understanding, distinctions may be made between 'blindness' which describes a level of sight loss requiring dependence mainly on tactile methods of learning, and 'low vision' where learners use predominantly methods relying on sight. Visual impairment affects social and emotional development, language development, cognitive development, mobility and orientation, which in turn influence the child's functioning and learning potential.

Prevalence rates range widely from 3.0 to 18.1 per 10,000, which may relate to methodological differences and the procedural differences in gathering the information (Mervis and Boyle, 2002). Most children with visual impairment who read and write use print.

Visual impairment can be caused by genetic factors or factors that occur in foetal development, during the birth process, or in childhood. Among types of visual impairment are refractive errors (myopia or short sightedness, hypermetropia or long sightedness and astigmatism) and other types such as cataract, nystagmus and retinitis pigmentosa. Most severe visual problems are identified very early, perhaps by the maternity hospital, health visitor or parents. Some difficulties may not be appreciated until the child starts school. A full assessment of vision includes tests of distance vision; near vision; field of vision; colour perception; and contrast sensitivity; and an assessment of visual functioning (Mason *et al.*, 1997, p. 53). Certain sub-tests of intelligence assessment are considered suitable for use with children who are blind or have low vision and tactile versions of some sub-tests are available. Reading tests have been standardised for use with blind children.

Provision

Tactile representations may be used such as maps, diagrams, graphs, charts, pictures and mathematical constructions. Labels and instructions in Braille may supplement them. Tactile diagrams may use collage or 'swell' paper with raised black lines contrasting to a flat white background. Hands-on experience is essential, for example in mathematics this includes handling money, weighing, measuring, and exploring geometrical shapes.

Listening is important for personal safety, for example by listening for sound signals at pedestrian road crossings. Information is provided by talking books, electronic reading devices and computer programmes using synthesised speech. The teacher should speak clearly, remembering that visual clues from her body language may not be available to the pupil with visual impairment. When speaking directly to the child, the teacher will use the child's name first, so he knows he is being individually addressed. The child will need to be taught how a conversation partner's tone of voice, rhythm of speaking, pauses and other verbal features are important clues in timing conversational exchanges.

Tactile readers are a minority of children with visual impairment. Tactile reading may involve Braille using a 'cell' of six raised dots, combinations of which make up letters, punctuation and contracted words. Another method is Moon, based on a simplified raised line adaptation of the Roman print alphabet that may be used for pupils with visual impairment and additional difficulties who are unable to learn Braille.

Electronic Braille typewriters use a six-key format for input, each key corresponding to a dot in the Braille cell. Output may be through synthetic speech or a renewable tactile display on the machine. Braille text downloaded to a conventional printer can be translated by software into print. Older school students may use conventional computers with adaptive software and synthesised speech as their main way of writing and storing information. Handwriting tends to be difficult for a pupil with low vision because he cannot easily see and self-correct work. Typing skills allow access to the wider benefits of modern technology such as the Internet.

Self-help skills are best taught in context so the pupil is motivated to exercise and develop the skill to achieve a particular goal. Day-to-day items are carefully chosen. A microwave cooker can have tactile controls, labels and instructions. Liquid level indicators may be used. During school lunchtime teachers might tactfully ensure that the child with visual impairment is in a well-lit, less crowded environment close to friends. Orientation and mobility are central and contribute to improving physical fitness, raising self-esteem, socialising, and enabling travel to and from a place of employment.

Extracurricular activities provide opportunities for a child to make contacts and friends in the local community. Organisers need to be conversant with the implications of the particular visual impairments and of the importance of lighting and the need for good contrast on items such as gymnasium equipment (Lieberman, 2002).

Special arrangements may be made for and during educations examinations. The student may use Braille or large print, use a word processor, have a scribe and a reader, or be allocated extra time. Examination papers may be in Braille, large/modified print or on audiotape. Schools may be allowed to open papers early to check content and a specialist teacher may modify the papers while ensuring they test the skills they are intended to.

In the United States of America, a child who meets state criteria for visual impairment becomes eligible to receive the services of a certified teacher of students with visual impairments. Such a teacher may be responsible for carrying out initial assessments and advising on adaptations and modifications and individual education programmes.

References

Lieberman, L. J. (2002) 'Fitness for individuals who are visually impaired or deafblind', *RE View (Rehabilitation and Education for Blindness and Visual Impairment)* 34, 1, 13.

Mason, H. and McCall, S. with Arter, C. McLinden, M. and Stone, J. (Eds) (1997) *Visual Impairment: Access to Education for Children and Young People*, London, David Fulton Publishers.

Mervis, C.A. and Boyle, C. A. (2002) 'Prevalence and selected characteristics of childhood vision impairment', *Developmental Medicine and Child Neurology* 44, 538–541.

Further reading

Koenig, A. J. and Holbrook, M. C. (Eds) (2000) *Foundations of Education Volume 2: Instructional Strategies for Teaching Children and Youth with Visual Impairments*, New York, American Foundation for the Blind Press.

Addresses

American Foundation for the Blind
www.afb.org
A New York-based organisation aiming to broaden access to technology, improve information for professionals, and promote independent living for individuals with vision loss.

Royal National Institute for the Blind
www.rnib.org.uk
Based in London, UK, the institute provides information, support and advice.

Classified list/thematic index of A–Z entries

Basic terms, ideas and values

Special education issues/terms

Access
Aetiology *see* Causal factors
Autonomy and independence
Barriers
Bio-psycho-social model
Brain basics
Care
Causal factors
Cerebral hemispheres and lobes
Classification of disabilities and disorders
Co-occurrence of conditions
Criteria for disabilities and disorders
Development *see* Child development
Diagnostic and Statistical Manual of Mental Disorders
Difficulty
Disability
Discrimination *see* Equality of opportunity
Disorder
Early intervention
Equality of opportunity
Evidence-based practice
Graduated response
Impairment
Inclusion
International Classification of Functioning, Disability and Health for Children and
    Youth
Learning difficulty
Learning disability
Multi-professional working
Needs
Optimal education

Prevalence and incidence
Progress
Pupil 'voice'
Qualifications, standards and training for teachers
Rights
Special children
Special education
Special educational need
Special educational needs coordinator
Specific learning difficulty *see* Learning disability
Statement of special educational needs
Syndrome
Underpinning processes in disabilities/disorders

Disciplines associated with special education

Audiology/audiologist
Child and adolescent mental health
Child and adolescent psychiatry/child and adolescent psychiatrist
Child development
Clinical psychology *see* Psychology/psychologist
Dentistry/dentist
Education/educator
Educational psychology *see* Psychology/psychologist
History of special education
Legal framework
Medicine
Neurology/neurologist
Neuropsychology/neuropsychologist
Ophthalmology/ophthalmologist
Orthoptics/orthoptist
Orthotics *see* Prosthetics and orthotics
Paediatrics/paediatrician
Pedagogy
Philosophy
Physical therapy/physical therapist
Politics
Postmodernism
Prosthetics and orthotics
Psychiatry *see* Child and adolescent psychiatry/child and adolescent psychiatrist
Psycholinguistics
Psychology/psychologist
Psychotherapy/psychotherapist
Research
Social work/social worker
Sociology
Speech-language pathology/speech-language pathologist
Technology/technician

Venues relating to special education, and school organisation

Boarding special school
Home schooling
Hospital schooling
Mainstream school/classroom
Resource room
Special classes
Special school

Roles and responsibilities

Administration/administrator
Administrator *see* Administration/administrator
Advocate *see* Advocacy/advocate
Art therapist *see* Art therapy/art therapist
Assessment of special educational needs *see* Referral and evaluation
Audiologist *see* Audiology/audiologist
Behaviour therapist *see* Behaviour therapy/behaviour therapist
Child and adolescent mental health
Child and adolescent psychiatrist *see* Child and adolescent psychiatry/child and adolescent psychiatrist
Clinical psychologist *see* Psychology/psychologist
Cognitive-behavioural therapist *see* Cognitive-behavioural therapy/cognitive-behavioural therapist
Conductor *see* Conductive education/conductor
Counsellor *see* Counselling/counsellor
Dance movement therapist *see* Dance movement therapy/dance movement therapist
Dentist *see* Dentistry/dentist
Dietician *see* Diet/dietician
Early years action and early years action plus *see* Referral and evaluation
Educator *see* Education/educator
Educational psychologist *see* Psychology/psychologist
Evaluation for special education *see* Referral and evaluation
Health services
Identification and assessment of special educational needs *see* Referral and evaluation
Legal framework
Mentor for pupils
Music therapist *see* Music therapy/music therapist
Neurologist *see* Neurology/neurologist
Occupational therapist *see* Occupational therapy/occupational therapist
Ophthalmologist *see* Ophthalmology/ophthalmologist
Orthoptist *see* Orthoptics/orthoptist
Orthotist *see* Prosthetics and orthotics
Parents

Pedagogy
Paediatrician *see* Paediatrics/paediatrician
Physical therapist *see* Physical therapy/physical therapist
Physiotherapy *see* Physical therapy/physical therapist
Prosthetist *see* Prosthetics and orthotics
Psychiatrist *see* Child and adolescent psychiatry/child and adolescent psychiatrist
Psychotherapist *see* Psychotherapy/psychotherapist
Referral and evaluation
Regional and local organisation
School action and school action plus *see* Graduated response
School psychologist *see* Psychology/psychologist
Social worker *see* Social work/social worker
Special needs officer *see* Administration/administrator
Speech-language pathologist *see* Speech-language pathology/speech-language pathologist'
Speech and language therapist *see* Speech-language pathology/speech-language pathologist
Statement of special educational needs
Teaching *see* Education/educator
Teacher *see* Education/educator
Teaching aide
Technician *see* Technology/technician
Transition

Individual differences among learners with disabilities/disorders

Adaptive behaviour
Age
Anxiety disorders
Asperger's syndrome
Attention deficit hyperactivity disorder
Autism
Birth difficulties
Brain injury *see* Traumatic brain injury
Bullying
Cerebral palsy
Challenging behaviour
Chromosome abnormalities *see* Genetic disorders
Communication difficulties – comprehension
Communication difficulties – grammar
Communication difficulties – pragmatics
Communication difficulties – semantics
Conduct disorder
Deafblindness
Depressive disorders
Developmental coordination disorder

Curriculum and assessment: resources and technology

Curriculum and assessment

Accreditation/examinations
Curriculum
Functional skills *see* Skills
Handwriting
Key skills *see* Skills
Life skills *see* Skills
Literacy *see* Reading disorder, Disorder of written expression, Handwriting
Numeracy *see* Mathematics disorder
Personal and social education *see* Curriculum
Physical education *see* Curriculum
Play and play areas
Psychometric tests and testing
Skills

Resources and technology

Adaptive equipment
Aids to hearing
Braille and Moon
Buildings and design
Computer technology
Funding
Internet: world wide web sites
Journals and other publications
Low vision devices and lighting
Moon *see* Braille and Moon
Multisensory environments
Play areas *see* Play and play areas
Postural and positional supports
Protective appliances and clothing
Symbols
Talking mats *see* Augmentative and alternative communication

Pedagogy and classroom organisation

Anger management training
Applied behaviour analysis
Augmentative and alternative communication
Autonomy and independence
Behaviour chain interruption strategy
Breaks and lessons structure
Classroom organisation and layout
Community-based vocational instruction
Concrete learning and mild cognitive impairment
Conductive education/conductor
Counselling/counsellor
Discrete trial teaching

Early education
Group communication
Individual education programme/plan
Intensive interaction
Observational learning and modelling
Objects of reference
Oral/aural approaches
Pivotal response training
Play and play areas
Portage
Problem-solving skills training
Research
Self-management *see* Autonomy and independence
Sign bilingualism
Sign language/signing
Social skills training
Symbols
Total communication

Therapy and care

Advocacy/advocate
Art therapy/art therapist
Behaviour therapy/behaviour therapist
Biofeedback
Cognitive-behavioural therapy/cognitive-behavioural therapist
Clinical psychology *see* Psychology/psychologist
Counselling/counsellor
Dance movement therapy/dance movement therapist
Dentistry/dentist
Diet/dietician
Drama therapy/drama therapist
Medication
Music therapy/music therapist
Occupational therapy/occupational therapist
Physical therapy/physiotherapist
Play therapy/play therapist
Psychiatry *see* Child and adolescent psychiatry/child and adolescent psychiatrist
Psychodynamic therapy
Psychotherapy/psychotherapist
Speech-language pathology/speech-language pathologist
Social work/social worker
Systems approach

eBooks – at www.eBookstore.tandf.co.uk

A library at your fingertips!

eBooks are electronic versions of printed books. You can store them on your PC/laptop or browse them online.

They have advantages for anyone needing rapid access to a wide variety of published, copyright information.

eBooks can help your research by enabling you to bookmark chapters, annotate text and use instant searches to find specific words or phrases. Several eBook files would fit on even a small laptop or PDA.

NEW: Save money by eSubscribing: cheap, online access to any eBook for as long as you need it.

Annual subscription packages

We now offer special low-cost bulk subscriptions to packages of eBooks in certain subject areas. These are available to libraries or to individuals.

For more information please contact webmaster.ebooks@tandf.co.uk

We're continually developing the eBook concept, so keep up to date by visiting the website.

www.eBookstore.tandf.co.uk